All rights reserved

All rights Reserved. No part of this publication or the information in it may be quoted from or reproduced in any form by means such as printing, scanning, photocopying or otherwise without prior written permission of the copyright holder.

Disclaimer and Terms of Use: Effort has been made to ensure that the information in this book is accurate and complete, however, the author and the publisher do not warrant the accuracy of the information, text and graphics contained within the book due to the rapidly changing nature of science, research, known and unknown facts and internet. The Author and the publisher do not hold any responsibility for errors, omissions or contrary interpretation of the subject matter herein. This book is presented solely for motivational and informational purposes only.

Or:

Copyright 2020 by Nick Dave - All rights reserved.
All rights Reserved. No part of this publication or the information in it may be quoted from or reproduced in any form by means such as printing, scanning, photocopying or otherwise without prior written permission of the copyright holder.
Disclaimer and Terms of Use: Effort has been made to ensure that the information in this book is accurate and complete, however, the author and the publisher do not warrant the accuracy of the information, text and graphics contained within the book due to the rapidly changing nature of science, research, known and unknown facts and internet. The Author and the publisher do not hold any responsibility for errors, omissions or contrary interpretation of the subject matter herein. This book is presented solely for motivational and informational purposes only.

Table of content

Introduction..................................9

Breakfast.....................................12

- Simple British Eggs............................. 12
- Delicious Toast with Strawberry............ 12
- Batata Chips with Cinnamon.................. 13
- Muffin Cups Cheddar Cheese.................. 13
- English Bacon Pancakes........................ 14
- Lovely Cinnamon Biscuits...................... 14
- Enjoyable Cheddar Cheese Omelet......... 14
- Soufflé Muffins.................................... 15
- Cheddar Cheese Eggs........................... 15
- Lovely Bacon Canapes.......................... 15
- Crispy Cheesy Asparagus...................... 16
- Flavorous Breaded Cauliflowers............. 16
- Raspberry Cakes With Honey................ 16
- Baby Kale Barley................................. 17
- Swedish Waffles.................................. 17
- Palatable Cinnamon Toast..................... 17
- Quick And Simple Donuts..................... 18
- Lovely Potato Gratin............................ 18
- English Breakfast Sandwich................... 19
- AirFryer Toast With Cheese.................. 19
- French Omelet Spinach and Cheese........ 19
- Delicious Breakfast Cheesy Topping Potatoes 20
- Avocado And Baked Eggs..................... 20
- Braekfast Vanilla Toasts....................... 20
- Scottish Spinach Frittata...................... 21
- Tasty Cheesy Potatoes With Garlic........ 21
- German Beef & Egg Scramble............... 21
- Sour Cream Zucchini Bake With Garlic... 22
- Scandinavian Trout Omelette................ 22
- Tasty Egg Bowls.................................. 22
- Fabulous Spanish Chorizo Scrambled Eggs 23
- Easy AirFryer Omelet With Beef............ 23
- Cheesy Noodles With Zucchini.............. 23
- Mushroom and Coconut Cream Frittata 24
- Breakfast Chicken Strips...................... 24
- Keto Air Bread................................... 24
- Nourishing Salmon Breakfast................ 25
- New English Breakfast......................... 25
- Easy Asparagus Frittata....................... 25
- Salmon With Eggs............................... 26
- Wonderful Pumpkin Toast.......................26
- Minced Tomato Scrambled Eggs...............26
- Breakfast Spinach Eggss........................27
- Sandwich With Cheese..........................27
- Dance Of Pepper And Eggs....................27
- Tasty Omelette With Sausages................28
- Amazing Breakfast Muffins.....................28
- Italian Eggs With Cheddar.....................28
- Good Egg Bake With Cheese..................29
- Egg Frittata In Western Style.................29
- Yummy Ham Egg Scramble.....................29
- Hearty Breakfast.................................30
- Miracle Spinach Omelette.....................30
- Healthy Cream Scramble.......................30
- Savory Egg Omelet..............................31
- Easy Egg Frittata................................31
- Egg Frittata With Vegetables.................31
- Mushroom Souffle................................32
- Tender Zucchini Gratin.........................32
- Sophisticated Cheese Tart.....................32
- Piquant Parmesan Casserole..................33
- Scrambled Eggs With Cottage Cheese and Spinach...33
- Classical Tomato Breakfast....................33
- Delightful Mushroom Frittata Breakfast34
- Surprising Squash................................34
- Spanish Savory Frittata........................34
- Easy Dill-Lemon Scallops......................35
- Breakfast Spicy Chicken........................35
- Italian Tender Scallops.........................35
- Nourishing Egg Cups............................36
- Lovely Carrots With Fresh Lime..............36
- Healthy Zucchini Squash Mix..................36
- Creamy Cabbage With Bacon.................36
- Beautiful Lemon Artichokes...................37
- Exciting Almond Crunchy Chicken...........37
- Nutty Chicken Thighs...........................37
- Charming Pesto Salmon With Almond.38
- Strong And Smoothy Radish...................38
- Clean and Simple Treats.......................38
- Omelette With Ceddar Cheese And Mushrooms...39
- Magic Cheese Souffle...........................39
- Wonderful Asparagus Frittata................39
- Chilly Cauliflower Rice.........................40

Stuffed Peppers With Feta And Broccoli 40
Coconut Breakfast Muffins 41

Snacks 42

Savory Spicy Chickpeas 42
Roasted Peanuts 42
Exquisite Grilled Cheese Sandwiches 42
Chili Dip 43
Beautiful Tortilla Chips 43
Sweet Corn and Bell Pepper Sandwich with Barbecue Sauce 44
Charming Beet chips 44
Radish Sticks 44
Great Crispy Cauliflower Poppers 45
Cheese Filled Bell Peppers 45
Simple Cod Nuggets 45
Hot Mexican Bean Dip 46
Easy Roasted Pumpkin Seeds 46
AirFryer Buffalo Cauliflower 46
Super AirFryer Chicken Nuggets 47
AirFryer Chickpeas 47
Fantastic Air Fry Corn Tortilla Chips 47
Pizza Margherita 48
Fabulous Cheesy Scallion Sandwich 48
Tasty Potatoes Au Gratin 48
Fabulous Rosemary Russet Potato Chips 49
AirFryer Kale Chips 49
Dreamy Apple Chips 49
Pork Taquitos 50
Glorious Cheesy Crab Dip 50
Cheese Stuffed Mushrooms 50
Enchanting Parmesan Carrot Fries 51
Chicken Stuffed Poblanos 51
Crispy Tofu 51
Gorgeous Hasselback Zucchini 52
Fat Burger Bombs 52
Crispy Keto Pork Bites 52
Cute Air Fried Kale Chips 53
Bacon Jalapeno Poppers 53
Pleasant Crispy Air Fried Broccoli 53
Garlic-Roasted Mushrooms 54
Marvelous Baked Zucchini Fries 54
AirFryer Brussels Sprouts 54
Wonderful AirFryer Garlic Chicken Wings 55
Old Bay Chicken Wings 55
Mushrooms And Garlic Mushrooms 55
Magical AirFryer Tofu Tots 56
Buffalo Cauliflower Wings 56
Air Fry Bacon Preparation 56
Crunchy Bacon Bites 57
Exciting Italian Dip 57
Sweet Potato Tots 57
Magnificent Ranch Kale Chips 58
Curried Sweet Potato Fries 58
Scrumptious Roasted Almonds 58
Pepperoni Chips 59
Yummy Crispy Eggplant 59
Steak Nuggets 59
Scrummy Cheese Bacon Jalapeno Poppers 60
Cabbage Chips 60
Healthy Broccoli Tots 60
Finger-Licking Crispy & Healthy Kale Chips 61
Juicy Meatballs 61
Delish Bacon Jalapeno Poppers 61
BBQ Chicken Wings 62
Healthy Vegetable Kabobs 62
Luscious Shrimp Kabobs 62
Mild & Sweet Shishito Peppers 63
Mouthwatering Broccoli Cheese Nuggets 63
Artichoke Dip 63
Yummy Chicken Dip 64
Seductive Smoked Almonds 64
Parmesan Zucchini Bites 64
Toothsome Broccoli Pop-corn 65
Easy Rosemary Beans 65
Appetizing Cheesy Brussels sprouts 65
Cute Cajun Kale Chips 66
Cheese Dill Mushrooms 66
Healthy Toasted Nuts 66
Easy Radish Chips 67
Parmesan Turnip Slices 67
Enchanting Chili Pepper Kale Chips 67
Cucumber Chips 68
Hearty Rutabaga Fries 68
Kohlrabi Chips 68
Spectacular Daikon Chips 69
Garlic Mushrooms 69
Savory Spicy Dip 69
Onion Dip 70
Simple Carrot Dip 70
Dreamy Sesame Okra 70

Vegetables and Meatless Meals Recipes 71

Crispy Pickles 71
Fabulous Roasted Brussels sprouts 71
Perfect Crispy Tofu 71
Crisp & Tender Brussels sprouts 72
Dreamy Asian Green Beans 72
Roasted Eggplant 72
Glorious Curried Eggplant Slices 73
Healthy Green Beans 73
Great Roasted Broccoli 73
Air Fried Onion & Bell Peppers 74
Wonderful Roasted Peppers 74
Parmesan Broccoli 74
Easy Air Fried Asparagus 75
Gluten-Free Beans 75
Exciting AirFryer Mushrooms 75
Roasted Acorn Squash 76
Soulful Cheesy Ranch Broccoli 76
Cheesy Brussels sprouts 76
Hearty Roasted Carrots 77
Brussels sprouts with Garlic 77
Spectacular Beans with Mushrooms 77
Garlic Thyme Mushrooms 78
Nourishing Roasted Mushrooms 78
Zucchini Fries 78
Easy Taro Fries 79
Scrummy Beetroot Chips 79
Ricotta Mushrooms 79
Appetizing Shallots Almonds Green Beans   80
Tasty Herb Tomatoes 80
Cute Curried Sweet Potato Fries 80
Basil Tomatoes 81
Sweety Pesto Tomatoes 81
Luscious Stuffed Tomatoes 82
Magical Parmesan Asparagus 82
Wonderful Almond Asparagus 83
Sweet & Spicy Parsnips 83
Toothsome Caramelized Baby Carrots . 84
Carrot with Spinach 84
Delish Broccoli with Sweet Potatoes 85
Broccoli with Olives 85
Dreamy Roasted Beans 86
Healthy Pumpkin Porridge 86
Pretty Baby Bok Choy 86
Spring Onion Pancake 87
Super Oat and Chia Porridge 87
AirFryer Asparagus 87

Exciting Almond Flour Battered And Crisped Onion Rings 88
Brussels Sprouts with Balsamic Oil 88
Simple Crunchy Potato Cubes 88
Baby Carrots 89
Charming Carrot Roast With Cumin 89
Maple Roasted Brussels Sprouts 89
Sweet Potato Fries 90
Fabulous Crispy Fried Avocado 90
Cool Beets Dish 90
Perfect Tasty Garlic Potato Fries 91
Roasted Garlic 91
Delicious Kale 91
Tasty Roasted Green Beans 92
Soulful Shishito Peppers 92
Easy Apple Cinnamon Oatmeal 92
Scrummy Baked Polenta with Chili-Cheese   93
Seasoned Potatoes 93
Mouthwatering Thyme Potatoes 94
Parmesan Broccoli 94
Magnificent Buttered Cauliflower 95
Simple Asparagus 95
Enjoyable Vinegar Brussels Sprout 96
Charming Spiced Zucchini 96
Green Beans with Carrots 97
Enchanting Mixed Veggies Combo 97
Garlic Zucchini Pate 98
Pretty Turnip Mash 98

Poultry 99
Buffalo Chicken Wings 99
Soulful Chicken Fajita Rollups 99
Cute Rosemary Turkey Breast with Maple Mustard Glaze 100
Hearty Mexican Chicken Burgers 100
Crispy Southern Fried Chicken 101
Scrummy AirFryer Turkey Breast 101
Chicken Kabobs 101
Yummy Mustard Chicken Tenders 102
Appetizing Fried "Mock KFC" Chicken 102
Cheesy Chicken Fritters 102
Magical Salt and Pepper Chicken Wing Stir-Fry 103
AirFryer Chicken Parmesan 103
Great Jerk Chicken Wings 104
Crispy Panko Crusted Chicken Balls 104

- Gorgeous Bang Bang Chicken with Yogurt Sauce ... 105
- Charming Air-fried Chicken ... 105
- Pretzel Crusted Chicken Chunks ... 106
- Dreamy Rustic Drumsticks with Tamari and Hot Sauce ... 106
- Crispy Chicken Tenders ... 107
- Pretty Turkey Tenders with Baby Potatoes ... 107
- Lovely Chicken Alfredo Bake ... 108
- Flavorful Chicken Drumsticks ... 108
- Healthy Air Fried Chicken ... 109
- Enjoyable Parmesan Garlic Chicken Wings ... 109
- Healthy Chicken Popcorn ... 110
- Beautiful Oregano Whole Chicken ... 110
- Herbed Turkey Breast ... 111
- Wonderful Mustard Turkey ... 111
- Delicious Rotisserie Chicken ... 112
- Perfect Lemon Chicken Potatoes ... 112
- Chicken Kebabs ... 113
- Fabulous Asian Chicken Kebabs ... 113
- Kebab Tavuk Sheesh ... 114
- Delish Chicken Mushroom Kebab ... 114
- Chicken Fajita Skewers ... 115
- Yummy Zucchini Chicken Kebabs ... 115
- Easy Chicken Soy Skewers ... 116
- Enjoyable Basil-Garlic Breaded Chicken Bake ... 116
- Finger-licking Chicken Alfredo Bake .. 117
- Roasted Goose ... 117
- Holyday Roast Goose ... 118
- Almond Flour Coco-Milk Battered Chicken ... 118
- Fantastic Buffalo Chicken Wings ... 118
- Honey and Wine Chicken Breasts ... 119
- Great Lemon-Pepper Chicken Wings .. 119
- Magnificent Crispy Honey Garlic Chicken Wings ... 120
- Mexican Chicken Burgers ... 120
- Yummy BBQ Chicken Recipe from Greece 121
- Caesar Marinated Grilled Chicken ... 121
- Adorable Fried Chicken Livers ... 121
- Crispy Southern Fried Chicken ... 122
- Pretty Garlic Rosemary Roasted Cornish Hen ... 122
- Ginger-Garam Masala Rubbed Chicken 122
- Tasty Chicken Cordon Bleu ... 123
- Perfect Southern Style Fried Chicken . 123
- Chicken Marinated in Coconut Milk with Ginger-Cilantro ... 123
- Tasty Turkey Meatballs in Cranberry Sauce ... 124
- Creamy Chicken Breasts Bake ... 124
- Lovely Chicken Pot Pie ... 124
- Butter-Lemon on Chicken Thighs ... 125
- Magical Garlicky-Dijon Chicken Thighs 125
- Air Fried Turkey with Maple Mustard Glaze ... 125
- Easy and Healthy Chicken Strips ... 126
- Chicken Fajita Roll-Ups ... 126
- Fantastic Mounceszarella Turkey Rolls 126
- Chicken Kabobs ... 127
- Savory Tandoori Chicken ... 127
- Crispy Coconut Chicken ... 127
- Scrummy Bacon-Wrapped Stuffed Chicken ... 128
- Homemade Chicken Nuggets ... 128
- Appetizing Buffalo Chicken Meatballs 128
- Perfect Chicken Wontons ... 129
- Turkey & Cheese Calz1 ... 129
- Toothsome Turkey & Avocado Burrito 130
- Turkey Sausage Patties ... 130
- Tasty Chicken Quesadilla ... 130
- Wonderful Chicken Popcorn ... 131
- Tasty Whole Chicken ... 131
- Fast & Easy Meatballs ... 131
- Lemon Pepper Chicken Wings ... 132
- Enchanting BBQ Chicken Wings ... 132
- Simple & Crispy Chicken Wings ... 132
- Scrummy Chicken Nuggets ... 133
- Italian Seasoned Chicken Tenders ... 133
- American Chicken Wings ... 134
- Pretty Fried Chicken ... 134
- Gorgeous Cornish Hen ... 134
- Herb Seasoned Turkey Breast ... 135
- Delicious Rotisserie Chicken ... 135
- Spicy Asian Chicken Thighs ... 135
- Wonderful Chicken Vegetable Fry ... 136
- Cilantro Lime Chicken ... 136
- Pleasant Chicken with Mushrooms ... 136
- Tasty Meatloaf ... 137

Yummy Meatloaf 137
Chili Garlic Chicken Wings 137
Finger-licking Garlic Chicken 138

Beef 139

Spicy grilled steak 139
Toothsome Greek vegetable skillet 139
Light herbed meatballs 139
Marvelous Sirloin steak 140
Meatloaf 140
Simple Rib Eye Steak 140
Double Cheeseburger 141
AppetizingCrispy Sirloin Steak 141
Buttered Filet Mignon 141
Savory Spiced & Herbed Skirt Steak ... 142
Nourishing Steak With Bell Peppers ... 142
Bacon-Wrapped Filet Mignon 143
Enchanting Beef Short Ribs 143
Corned Beef 143
Lovely Brussel Sprout Beef Chops 144
Dipping Sauce Beef Dumplings 144
Delectable Kansas Farm Beef Chops ... 145
Air Fry Mounceszarella Beef Brisket .. 145
Delightful Zucchini Lean Beef Burger 145
Roasted Pepper Beef Prosciutto 146
Adorable Creamy Beef Belly Rolls 146
Seasoned Bleu Cordon Beef Belly 147
Exquisite Honey Mustard Cheesy Meatballs
.... 147
Simple Beef Burgers 147
Garlic-Mustard Rubbed Roast Beef 148
Magical Garlic-Rosemary Rubbed Beef Rib Roast 148
Ginger Soy Beef Recipe from the Orient 148
Gorgeous Ginger-Orange Beef Strips .. 149
Gravy Smothered Country Fried Steak 149
Lovely Grilled Beef with Grated Daikon Radish
.... 149
Grilled Spicy Carne Asada 150
Savory Grilled Steak on Tomato-Olive Salad
.... 150
Grilled Tri-Tip over Beet Salad 150
Magnificent Meatloaf Sliders 151
Fast & Easy Steak 151
Excellent Cheeseburger 151
Steak Bites with Mushrooms 152
Easy AirFryer Steak 152

Steak Fajitas 152
Great Beef Roast 152
Tasty Cheeseburgers 153
Asian Sirloin Steaks 153
Pretty Soft & Juicy Beef Kabobs 153
Asian Flavors Beef Broccoli 154
Juicy Rib Eye Steak 154
Scrumptious Stuffed Peppers 154
Italian Marvelous Sausage Meatballs .. 155
Seductive Meatballs 155
Soulful Mushrooms Meatballs 155
Glorious Meatloaf 155
Enjoyable Kabab 156
Exciting Beef Satay 156
Scrummy Meatloaf 156
Fantastic Burger 156
Great Garlic Butter Steak 157
Unbelievable Beef Patties 157
Magical Sirloin Steaks 157
Fabulous Steak with Cheese Butter 157
Dreamy Montreal Steak 158
Savory Juicy & Tender Steak 158
Rosemary Beef Roast 158
Adorable Air Fried Steak 158
Enchanting Beef Broccoli 159
Charming Kabab 159
Yummy Broccoli Beef 159
Pretty Spiced Steak 159
Appetizing Burger Patties 160
Wonderful Asian Beef 160

Pork 161

Delectable Pork satay 161
Hearty Crispy mustard pork tenderloin 161
Exquisite Apple pork tenderloin 161
Glorious grilled pork tenderloin 162
Delightful Pork chops 162
Lovely Pork belly 163
Gordeous Teriyaki Pork 163
Admirable Ribs 163
Fantastic Pork Curry 164
Cufe Pork Posole 164
Luscious Sauerkraut Pork 164
Yummy Pork Adobo 165
Fantastic Pork Chops 165
Great Garlicky Pork Roast 165
Dreamy Herbed Pork Burgers 166

Cute Chinese Style Pork Meatballs 166
Savory Ginger, Garlic 'n Pork Dumplings 166
Seductive Grilled Prosciutto-Wrapped Fig 167
Tasty Grilled Sausages with BBQ Sauce 167
Lovely Crisp Pork Chops 167
Sweet Parmesan Pork Chops 168
Simple Pork Chops 168
Quick Pork Chops 168
Magnificent Pork with Mushrooms 169
Quick Bratwurst with Vegetables 169
Enchanting Cheesy & Juicy Pork Chops 169
Delectable Pork Bites 170
Fantastic Pork Tenderloin 170
Pretty Pesto Pork Chops 170
Beautiful Garlic Thyme Pork Chops 171
Easy Pork Strips 171
Sweet BBQ Ribs 171
Soulful Grilled Pork Shoulder 172
Dreamy Coconut Butter Pork Chops ... 172
Fabulous BBQ Chops 172
Glorious Coconut Pork Chops 173
Enjoyable Pork Chops 173
Fabulos Pork Loin 173
Appetizing Mustard Pork Tenderloin . 174
Charming McCornick Pork Chops 174
Delish Mustard Pork Chops 174
Thoothsome Vietnamese Pork Chop .. 175
Tasty Veggie Pork Tenderloin 175
Wonderful Asian Pork 175
Delightful Classic Pork 176
Simple Pork Chops 176
Scrummy Garlic Pork Chops 176
Perfect Cheese Herb Pork Chops 177
Luscious Creole Pork Chops 177
Fantastic Pork 177

Lamb 178

Flavourful Herbed Lamb Chops 178
Savory Lamb Sirloin Steak 178
Charming Garlic Rosemary Lamb Chops 179
Dreamy Lamb Curry 179
Fabulous Herb Seasoned Lamb 179
Delightful Lamb Korma 180
Tasty & Spicy Lamb 180
Adorable Lamb Stew 180
Exquisite Lamb Shanks 181

Marvelous Asian Lamb Curry 181
Soulful Indian Lamb Curry 181
Simple Rogan Josh 182
Delish Cheesy Lamb Chops 182
Thoothsome Garlicky Lamb 182
Spectacular Mustard Lamb Loin Chops 183
Cute Pesto Coated Rack of Lamb 183
Unbelievable Spiced Lamb Steaks 183
Pretty Leg of Lamb 184
Gorgeous Lamb Kebabs 184
Nourishing Lamb with Potatoes 184
Wonderful Garlic-Rosemary Lamb BBQ 185
Appetizing Lamb Patties 185
Enjoyable Lemon Mustard Lamb Chops 185
Lovely Lamb Meatballs 186
Delectable Spicy Lamb Chops 186
Scrumptious Lamb Roast 186
Glorious Dried Herbs Lamb Chops 187
Magical Lemon Herb Lamb Chops 187
Luscious Lamb Rack 187
Savory Cayenne Cumin Lamb 188
Seductive Thyme Garlic Lamb Chops .. 188
Magnificent Cumin Lamb 188

Seafood Recipes 189

Delicious Crab Cakes 189
Tasty Tuna Patties 189
Adorable Salmon 189
Enjoyable White Fish 190
Exquisite Shrimp with Veggie 190
Savory Salmon Patties 190
Fabulous Salmon 191
Fantastic Shrimp Scampi 191
Wonderful Parmesan Walnut Salmon 191
Scrumpitious Cajun Shrimp 192
Delish Miso Fish 192
Admirable Tilapia Fish Fillets 192
Delectable Garlic Mayo Shrimp 192
Charming Spicy Prawns 193
Enchanting Salmon Fillets 193
Scrummy Shrimp 193
Appetizing Catfish 193
Simple Bacon Shrimp 194
Seductive Almond Coconut Shrimp 194
Magnificent Cajun Cheese Shrimp 194
Delightful Creamy Shrimp 195
Luscious Chili Garlic Shrimp 195

- Easy Salmon Patties 195
- Pretty Lemon Garlic Shrimps 196
- Unbelievable Creamy Breaded Shrimp 196
- Fabulous Coconut Crusted Shrimp 196
- Lovely Rice Flour Coated Shrimp 197
- Magical Buttered Scallops 197
- Thoothsome Honey Glazed Salmon 197
- Glorious Sweet & Sour Glazed Salmon 198
- Dreamy Salmon Parcel 198
- Exciting Ranch Tilapia 199
- Nourishing Spicy Catfish 199
- Savory Fish Sticks 200
- Flavorful Parmesan Shrimp 200
- Cute Salmon Fillets 200
- Delicious Lemon Chili Salmon 201
- Amazingly Pesto Salmon 201
- Tasty Lemon Shrimp 201
- Adorable Creamy Crab Dip 202
- Enjoyable Fish Packets 202
- Fantastic Scallops 202
- Delish King Prawns 203
- Admirable Lemon Butter Salmon 203
- Savory Cheese Crust Salmon 203
- Delightful Lemon Crab Patties 204
- Wonderful Basil Parmesan Shrimp 204
- Perfect Cheesy Crab Dip 204
- Charming Thai Shrimp 205
- Great Salmon Quiche 205
- Tasty Salmon Patties 205
- Enjoyable Beer-Battered Fish and Chips 206
- Soulful Tuna Stuffed Potatoes 206
- Delish Prawn Burgers 207
- Glorious Fish & Chips 207
- Dreamy Shrimp & Sausage Paella 208
- Simple Pressure Cooker Shrimp Boil .. 208
- Scrumptious Oven-Blackened Tilapia 209
- Encharting Crab Herb Croquettes 209
- Scrummy Herb Salmon Fillet 209
- Luscious Crunchy Fish Taco 210
- Fabulous Potato Fish Cake 210
- Exquisite Garlic Salmon Patties 210
- Admirable Cod Parcel 211
- Appetizing Salmon with Prawns & Pasta 211
- Hearty Salmon Burgers 212
- Seductive Cod Burgers 212
- Magnificent Chinese Cod 213
- Yummy Salmon with Broccoli 213

Desserts 214

- Peanut Butter Cookies 214
- Chocolate-Covered Maple Bacon 214
- Pumpkin Spice Pecans 214
- Cinnamon Sugar Pork Rinds 215
- Toasted Coconut Flakes 215
- Blackberry Crisp 215
- Churros 216
- Peanut Butter Cookies 216
- Avocado Pudding 216
- Chia Pudding 217
- Bacon Cookies 217
- Sweet and Cinnamon Donut Holles 217
- Chocolate Peanut Butter and Jelly S'mores 218
- Choco-Bana-Chips 218
- Fiesta pastries 218
- Crispy Fruit Tacos 219
- Dark Chocolate Lava Cakes 219
- Perfect Chocolate Soufflé 219
- Homemade Doughnuts 219
- Authentic Raisin Apple Treat 220
- Crumble with Blackberries & Apricots 220
- Healthy Bananas 220
- Almond biscuit 220
- Triangle Toast 221
- Air sinker 221
- Delicious cake 221
- Yummy Pud 222
- Vanilla biscuit 222
- Ginger plums 222
- Greek coconut 222
- Coconut cheese 223
- Fruit Cream 223
- Angel pie 223
- Yummy Dumplings 223
- Soft Donuts 224
- Wontons Sweet Cream 224
- Wonderful French Toast 224
- Lovely Chickpeas 225
- Amazing fried bananas 225
- Scrumptious Oreos 225
- Adorable banana break 226
- Advanced Chips 226
- Banana muffin 227

The Classical Cookies	227
British Fingers	227
Airy clam	228
Unusual Marshmallow	228
Divine apple pie	228
Flavorous sinker	229
Tender Tartlets	229
Selfmade Oreo	230
Jamaica pie	230
Easy apple snack	231
Flavor apples	231
Ricotta Pie	231
Pineapple hunk	231
Pleasant cream	232
Norwegian pint cake	232
Tasty ricotta pie	232
Swiss fondue	232

TO MY MOM AND DAD

TO MY BEAUTIFUL WIFE

TO MY TWO WONDERFUL BOYS

TO ALL INVOLVED IN WRITING THIS WORK

TO EACH AND EVERYONE OF YOU

FOR SUPPORTING, TRUSTING AND TRYING ALL THIS RECIPES

Nick Dave

Introduction

Now We are happy to introduce you to an amazing AirFryer Cookbook with 700 gorgeous recipes!

AirFryer was specially created for busy people, who can't spend a lot of time in the kitchen. With this lid, you can prepare a meal just in minutes and no one can differ it from restaurant dishes!

So, what are you going to find here? Here is a collection of most famous recipes to cook in the AirFryer, which were taken in various cuisines in different countries and be sure each member of your family will enjoy it very much!

There is an opinion that AirFryer is something difficult to use and not something people want to mess with. That is far from the truth. It's super easy to use, saves time, makes cleanup a breeze, and simply will expand your culinary abilities.

One of the distinguishing features of AirFryer is that you can cook with fewer fats and oils (except oil spray you use before cooking a meal in AirFryer). You are creating mouthwatering dishes that are healthy too! Isn't that amazing?

But be warned, if you are stick to your diet all day and constantly watch your weight, not all recipes in this cookbook are for those. However, the greatest number of following recipes could be used despite strict diets and weight control according to the directions of your nutritionist.

Everyone can find lots of delightful recipes from the beginners to the advanced users in such categories as:

- Breakfast;
- Snacks;
- Vegetables and meatless meal recipes;
- Poultry;
- Beef;
- Pork;
- Lamb;
- Seafood recipes;
- Desserts

AirFryer cooking transforms into a magic process that delivers joy and happiness to you and your family!

"Yummy, finger-licking!" – that are the words that the most precisely describe all you can cook with AirFryer and the recipes in this cookbook/

And here we go!

But "What is it AirFryer?" you may ask.

Ok, let's set it clear!

AirFryer – a small countertop convection oven designed to simulate deep frying without submerging the food in oil

Benefits of using it:

- AirFryer is the healthiest way to fry, using little or no added oil to fry your favorite food
- You can make delicious meals up to 4 people every day. Fits 1 bag of frozen French fries and creates just as crispy as deep-fried results.
- The Air fryer is instantly hot and ready to go in seconds, cooking faster than a conventional oven. With no preheat needed, you can save time and start cooking right away.
- Most of the AirFryers have multi-cooking technology: Air fry, bake, grill, roast, reheat, dehydrate, and toast, but it depends on the model you choose
- Cleaning is simple: AirFryer includes dishwasher-safe removable parts and a quick-clean basket to save you time

Now as you can see, AirFryer becomes an essential thing in your kitchen, because cooking with it is very simple and quick!

So enjoy your meals with this cookbook and your AirFryer!

Breakfast

Simple British Eggs

	Prep Time	Time to cook	Serv
	15 min	15 min	4

Direction:
1. Mix the sausage and 1 tbspnn flour in a bowl.
2. Divide the sausage mixture into 4 equal parts. Get 1 hard-boiled egg in the center, then wrap the sausage around the egg, sealing completely. Repeat with remaining sausage parts and hard-boiled eggs.
3. In a small bowl, whisk the egg and water until smooth.
4. Place the remaining flour and bread crumbs into separate bowls large enough to dredge the sausage-wrapped eggs.
5. Dredge the sausage-wrapped eggs in the flour, then in the whisked egg, and finally coat in the bread crumbs.
6. Arrange them in the basket. Put the AirFryer lid on and cook in the preheated AirFryer at 375°F for 20 min.
7. Flip them over when the lid screen indicates 'TURN FOOD' halfway through, or until the sausage is cooked to desired doneness. Remove from the basket and serve on a plate.

Ingredients:
- 1 pound ground breakfast sausage
- 3 tbspns flour
- 4 hard-boiled eggs, peeled
- 1 egg
- 1 tbspnn water
- ¾ cup panko bread crumbs

Calories	Fat	Carbs	Protein	Sugar	Cholesterol
509	16g	8g	24g	16g	543 mg

Delicious Toast with Strawberry

	Prep Time	Time to cook	Serv
	8 min	10 min	4

Direction:
1. On a plate, place the bread slices.
2. Arrange the bread slices (sprayed side down) in the AirFryer basket. Evenly spread the strawberries onto them and sprinkle with sugar.
3. Put the AirFryer lid on and cook in the preheated AirFryer at 375°F for 8 min, or until the tops are covered with a beautiful glaze.
4. Remove from the basket and serve on a plate.

Ingredients:
- 4 slices bread,
- ½-inch thick 1 cup sliced strawberries
- 1 tspn sugar
- Cooking spray

Calories	Fat	Carbs	Protein	Sugar	Cholesterol
375	22g	2g	14g	5g	182 mg

Batata Chips with Cinnamon

Prep Time	Time to cook	Serv
7 min	8 min	7

Direction:
1. In a bowl, toss the potato slices in olive oil.
2. Sprinkle with the cinnamon and mix well.
3. Lay the potato slices in the AirFryer basket.
4. You may need to work in batches to avoid overcrowding.
5. Put the AirFryer lid on and cook in the preheated AirFryer at 375ºF for 4 min. Shake the basket when the lid screen indicates 'TURN FOOD' Cook for an additional 4 min or until fork-tender.
6. Remove from the basket and serve on a large dish lined with paper towels.

Ingredients:
- 1 small sweet potato, cut into 3/8-inch slices
- 2 tbspns olive oil
- Ground cinnamon

Calories	Fat	Carbs	Protein	Sugar	Cholesterol
385	18g	5g	20g	3g	658 mg

Muffin Cups Cheddar Cheese

Prep Time	Time to cook	Serv
11 min	10 min	10

Direction:
1. On a clean work surface, slice the pork sausage into 2-ounce portions. Shape each portion into a ball and gently flatten it with your palm.
2. Lay the patties in the AirFryer basket and cook in the preheated AirFryer at 375ºF for 6 min. Flip the patties over when the lid screen indicates 'TURN FOOD' during Time to cook.
3. Remove the patties from the basket to a large dish lined with paper towels. Crumble them into small pieces with a fork. Set aside.
4. Line a muffin pan with ten paper liners. Lightly spray the muffin cups with cooking spray. Divide crumbled sausage equally among the ten muffin cups and sprinkle the tops with the cheese.
5. Arrange the muffin pan in the AirFryer basket.
6. Put the AirFryer lid on and cook in the preheated AirFryer at 375ºF for 8 min, until the tops are golden and a toothpick inserted in the middle comes out clean. Remove from the basket and let cool for 5 min before serving.

Ingredients:
- ¼ pound all-natural ground pork sausage
- 3 eggs
- ¾ cup milk
- 4 ounces sharp Cheddar cheese, grated
- 1 muffin pan
- Cooking spray

Calories	Fat	Carbs	Protein	Sugar	Cholesterol
497	25 g	1 g	28 g	5 g	823 mg

English Bacon Pancakes

Prep Time	Time to cook	Serv
5 min	10 min	4

Direction:
1. On a clean work surface, cut each English muffin in half.
2. To assemble a sandwich, layer 2 slices of bacon and 1 cheese slice on the bottom of each muffin and put the other half of the bread on top. Repeat with remaining biscuits, bacon, and cheese slices.
3. Arrange the sandwiches in the AirFryer basket and spritz with cooking spray. You may need to work in batches to avoid overcrowding.
4. Put the AirFryer lid on and cook in the preheated AirFryer at 375°F for 8 min. Flip the sandwiches when it shows 'TURN FOOD' on the AirFryer lid screen during Time to cook. Let them cool for 3 min before serving.

Ingredients:
- 4 English muffins
- Eight slices Canadian bacon
- 4 slices cheese
- Cooking spray

Calories	Fat	Protein	Fiber	Cholesterol
322	15g	24g	4g	58 mg

Lovely Cinnamon Biscuits

Prep Time	Time to cook	Serv
5 min	10 min	4

Direction:
1. On your cutting board, divide each biscuit into quarters.
2. In a mixing bowl, add the brown and white sugar, nutmeg, and cinnamon. Stir. Pour the melted butter into a medium bowl. Dip each biscuit in the melted butter, then in the sugar mixture to coat thoroughly.
3. Arrange the coated biscuits in a 6×6×2-inch baking pan and place the container into the AirFryer basket.
4. Put the AirFryer lid on and bake in batches in the preheated AirFryer at 350°F for 6 to 9 min until set. Transfer to a serving dish and cool for 5 min before serving.

Ingredients:
- 1 can (8-ounce) refrigerated biscuits
- 3 tbspns brown sugar
- ¼ cup white sugar
- ½ tspn cinnamon
- ⅛ tspn nutmeg
- 3 tbspns unsalted butter, melted

Calories	Fat	Protein	Fiber	Cholesterol
1228	42.64g	49.97g	1.2g	433 mg

Enjoyable Cheddar Cheese Omelet

Prep Time	Time to cook	Serv
5 min	10 min	2

Directions
1. Whisk the eggs along with the pepper and soy sauce.
2. 350 degrees preheat the AirFryer.
3. Heat the olive oil and add the egg mixture and the onion.
4. Cook for 8 to 10 min.
5. Top with the grated cheddar cheese.

Ingredients
- 2 eggs
- 2 tbspn. Grated cheddar cheese
- 1 tbspn. Soy sauce
- 1/2 onion, sliced
- 1/4 tbspn. Pepper
- 1 tbspn. Olive oil

Calories	Fat	Carbs	Protein	Fiber
347	23.2g	6 g	13.6g	1.2g

Soufflé Muffins

Prep Time	Time to cook	Serv
5 min	5 min	2

Directions:
1. Preheat the AirFryer to 360 f.
2. Beat the eggs Add the heavy cream. Then sprinkle the egg mixture with the salt, paprika, and ground turmeric. Stir it carefully.
3. Pour the egg mixture into 2 ramekins.
4. Put the ramekins within the AirFryer basket and cook the soufflé for five min. When the soufflé is cooked – chill it for 3 min.

Calories	Fat	Carbs	Protein	Fiber
148	12.2 g	8g	8.7 g	0.2g

Ingredients:
- 3 eggs
- 2 tbspn. Heavy cream
- 1 pinch salt
- 1/4 tbspn. Paprika
- 1/4 tbspn. Ground turmeric

Cheddar Cheese Eggs

Prep Time	Time to cook	Serv
5 min	6 min	2

Directions:
1. Preheat the AirFryer to 360 f.
2. Toss the butter in the AirFryer and melt it.
3. Beat the eggs in the melted butter.
4. Sprinkle the eggs with the salt and minced dill.
5. Cook the eggs for 4 min.
6. After this, sprinkle the eggs with the shredded cheese and cook them for 2 min more.
7. Transfer the cooked eggs to the serving plates.

Calories	Fat	Carbs	Protein	Fiber
305	23.4 g	2.1 g	22 g	0.2g

Ingredients:
- 4 eggs
- 1 pinch salt
- 3 ounces. Cheddar cheese, shredded
- 1 tbspn. Dill, minced
- 1/4 tbspn. Butter

Lovely Bacon Canapes

Prep Time	Time to cook	Serv
8 min	10 min	2

Directions:
1. Peel the boiled eggs.
2. Sprinkle the bacon slices with the salt, cayenne pepper, and paprika.
3. Preheat the AirFryer to 360 f.
4. Put the bacon slices in the AirFryer rack and cook for 5 min.
5. After this, chill the bacon.
6. Wrap the peeled eggs in the bacon slices and secure them gently with the toothpicks.   After this, put the wrapped eggs in the AirFryer basket and sprinkle with the canola oil.
7. Cook the bacon eggs for 5 min more.
8. The eggs are cooked – when the surface of the bacon is a little bit crunchy – the meal is prepared.

Calories	Fat	Carbs	Protein	Fiber
342	25.8 g	1.4 g	25.2 g	0.1 g

Ingredients:
- 4 eggs, boiled
- 4 bacon slices
- 1 pinch salt
- 1 pinch cayenne pepper
- 1 pinch paprika
- 1/2 tbspn. Canola oil

Crispy Cheesy Asparagus

Prep Time	Time to cook	Serv
5 min	10 min	4

Directions:
1. Combines the breadcrumbs and Parmesan cheese in a bowl. Season with salt and pepper. Preheat Cuisinart on Air Fry function to 370 F. Line a baking sheet with parchment paper. Dip the asparagus spears into the flour first, then into the eggs, and finally coat with crumbs.
2. Arrange them on the AirFryer Basket, fit in the baking sheet, and cook for about 8 to 10 min. Serve with melted butter, hollandaise sauce, or freshly squeezed lemon.

Ingredients:
- 1 lb asparagus spears
- ¼ cup flour
- 1 cup breadcrumbs
- ½ cup Parmesan cheese, grated
- 2 eggs, beaten
- Salt and black pepper to taste

Calories	Fat	Carbs	Protein	Fiber
244	44 g	3.8 g	19.8 g	1.2 g

Flavorous Breaded Cauliflowers

Prep Time	Time to cook	Serv
10 min	10 min	4

Directions:
1. Whisk the alfredo sauce along with the butter.
2. In a shallow bowl, combine the breadcrumbs with the sea salt.
3. Dip each cauliflower floret into the alfredo mixture first, and then coat in the crumbs. Drop the prepared florets into the AirFryer basket.
4. Fit in the baking tray. Set the temperature of your Cuisinart to 380 F and cook for 15 min on Air Fry function.
5. Shake the florets twice during cooking. Serve.

Ingredients:
- 4 cups cauliflower florets
- 1 tbspn butter, melted ¼ cup alfredo sauce
- 1 cup breadcrumbs
- 1 tbspn sea sa

Calories	Fat	Carbs	Protein	Fiber
344	34 g	1.8 g	9.8 g	0.9g

Raspberry Cakes With Honey

Prep Time	Time to cook	Serv
10 min	10 min	4

Directions:
1. Preheat fryer on Bake function to 375 F. Divide the cream cheese between the dough sheets and spread it evenly. In a small bowl, combine the berries, honey, and vanilla. Spoon the mixture into the pastry sheets. Pinch the ends of the layers to form puff. Place the winds in a lined baking dish. Place the bowl in the toaster oven and cook for 15 min. Serve chilled.

Ingredients:
- 4 pastry dough sheets
- 2 tbspn mashed strawberries
- 2 tbspn mashed raspberries
- ¼ tbspn vanilla extract
- 2 cups cream cheese, softened
- 1 tbspn honey

Calories	Fat	Carbs	Protein	Fiber
234	44 g	2.3 g	23.8 g	0.6 g

Baby Kale Barley

Prep Time	Time to cook	Serv
10 min	18 min	4

Directions:
1. Add oil into the AirFryer and set the container on sauté mode.
2. Add onion and barley and sauté for 3 min.
3. Add broth and salt and stir everything well.
4. Cook on manual high pressure for 15 min and seal pot with a lid.
5. Once done, then allow to extrication pressure naturally then open the lid.
6. Add kale and stir until kale is wilted.
7. Enjoy.

Ingredients:
- 1 cup pearl barley
- 4 ounces baby kale
- 4 cups vegetable broth
- 1/4 cup onion, minced
- 1 tbspn olive oil
- 1/2 tbspn sea salt

Calories	Fat	Carbs	Protein	Fiber
234	44 g	2.3 g	23.8 g	0.6 g

Swedish Waffles

Prep Time	Time to cook	Serv
5 min	8 min	5

Directions:
1. Preheat your AirFryer to 390F.
2. Put all together with the ingredients in a food processor or blender and blend until the mixture turns into a smooth batter.
3. Pour a ½ cup of the batter in a small cast iron tray or ramekin.
4. Place the tray or ramekin in the basket of your preheated AirFryer and set the timer for 6 to 8 min. Repeat the process with the remaining batter.
5. Serve immediately and garnish with your favorite berries or other fruit.

Ingredients:
- 3 whole eggs
- 1 cup whole grounded wheat flour
- Substitutes: oat flour
- 1 cup almond milk
- Pinch of salt
- 2 heaping tbspns unsweetened applesauce

Calories	Fat	Sugar	Protein	Cholesterol
145	2.1 g	8.2 g	2.3 g	3 mg

Palatable Cinnamon Toast

Prep Time: 5 Min
Time to cook: 6 Min
Serv: 2

Directions:
1. Preheat your AirFryer to 320F.
2. Place all ingredients except for the bread in a medium bowl and use a fork to mix them.
3. Make sure everything is well combined, and toe egg is broken up.
4. Dip the bread in the liquid mixture and shake off any extra liquid.

Ingredients:
- 4 slices of bread
- 2 eggs
- ⅔ cup of milk
- 1 tspn of vanilla
- 1 tbspnn of cinnamon

5. Spray an AirFryer safe pan with cooking spray and place the bread in the pan
6. Place the pan in the basket of your preheated AirFryer and set the timer for 6 min. Flip the bread halfway through
7. Serve immediately.

Calories	Fat	Protein	Sugar	Cholesterol
178	7.6 g	8.7 g	10.2 g	9 mg

Quick And Simple Donuts

Prep Time — 9 min
Time to cook — 6 min
Serv — 6

Directions:
1. Sprinkle the basket of your AirFryer with cooking spray and preheat it to 350F. Separate the dough into individual biscuits.
2. Cut a hole within the center of every donut with an effort glass or biscuit cutter.
3. Place half the dough in your preheated AirFryer and then the metal holder.
4. Place the remaining mixture on the metal holder and set the timer for 4 to 5 min.
5. Mix the cinnamon and sugar in a bowl.
6. Use a brush to coat the cooked donuts with the melted butter.
7. Coat the donuts with the cinnamon and sugar mixture.
8. Allow the donuts to cool for a couple of min before serving.

Ingredients:
- 1 can make flaky pre-made biscuit dough
- 1/2 cup white sugar
- 1 tspn cinnamon
- Coconut oil
- Melted butter

Calories	Fat	Protein	Sugar	Cholesterol
175	1.8 g	5.8 g	7.4 g	8 mg

Lovely Potato Gratin

Prep Time — 15 min
Time to cook — 20 min
Serv — 3

Directions:
1. Slice potatoes.
2. Take the large bowl and combine milk and cream. Season to taste with salt, ground pepper, and nutmeg.
3. Cover the potato slices with milk mixture.
4. Preheat the AirFryer to 370°F.
5. Transfer covered potato slices to the quiche pan. Pour the rest of the milk mixture on the top of the potatoes.
6. Evenly cover the potatoes with grated cheese.
7. Place the quiche pan into the AirFryer and cook for 15-20 min until nicely golden.

Ingredients:
- 1 pound potato, pilled
- 2 ounces milk
- 2 ounces cream
- Ground pepper
- Nutmeg to taste
- 2 ounces cheese, grated

Calories	Carbohydrates	Protein	Sodium	Cholesterol
128.9	19 g	2.3 g	230.2 mg	0 mg

English Breakfast Sandwich

Prep Time	Time to cook	Serv
5 min	7 min	1

Directions:
1. Beat 1 egg into an ovenproof cups or bowl.
2. Preheat the AirFryer to 390°F
3. Place the egg in the cup, bacon stripes, and muffin to the fryer and cook for 6-7 min.
4. Get the sandwich together and enjoy it.

Calories	Fat	Protein	Sodium	Cholesterol
651	44.4 g	38 g	1475 mg	572 mg

Ingredients:
- Online egg, beaten
- 2 streaky bacon stripes
- 1 English muffin
- A pinch of salt and pepper

AirFryer Toast With Cheese

Prep Time	Time to cook	Serv
10 min	6 min	2

Directions:
1. First, toast the dough in the toaster. Once toasted spread the butter on bread pieces. Cover with grated cheese. Preheat the AirFryer to 350°F
2. Place covered bread slices into the Fryer and cook for 4-6 min
3. Serve with your favorite sauce or without it.

Calories	Fat	Protein	Sodium	Cholesterol
402	36 g	18.5 g	613 g	613 mg

Ingredients:
- 4 medium-sized Russell potatoes
- 1 tbspnn unsalted butter
- 4 tbspns sour cream
- 1 ounces grated cheese

French Omelet Spinach and Cheese

Prep Time	Time to cook	Serv
5 min	8 min	2

Directions:
1. In the large bowl, whisk the eggs.
2. Place the eggs during a flat oven-safe form.
3. Stir in shredded cheese and spinach, and season with salt.
4. Preheat the AirFryer to 380 F and cook for about 7-8 min, until ready.

Calories	Fat	Carbohydrates	Protein	Sugar
78.1	4.9 g	9 g	15.9 g	18.2 g

Ingredients:
- 2 slices white bread
- 4 ounces cheese, grated
- A little piece of butter

Delicious Breakfast Cheesy Topping Potatoes

Prep Time: 6 min
Time to cook: 20 min
Serv: 4

Directions:
1. Prepare 4 medium-sized potatoes, wash them, and dry with kitchen towels. Stab potatoes with a fork so that they can breathe.
2. Preheat the AirFryer at 370 F. Place potatoes into the Fryer basket and cook for 15 min, until tender and golden.
3. Meanwhile, prepare your filling. In the medium mixing bowl, combine sour cream with grated cheese and chives until it is equally mixed.
4. When the jacket potatoes are cooked, open them up and spread with butter followed by your topping mixture.
5. Enjoy!

Calories	Fat	Carbohydrates	Protein	Sugar
56.4	5.6 g	5 g	16.9 g	16.5 g

Ingredients:
- 4 large eggs
- ½ cup Cheddar cheese, shredded
- 3 tbspns fresh spinach, minced
- Salt to taste
- 1 tbspnn chives, minced
- 2 ounces cheese, grated
- Salt and ground black pepper

Avocado And Baked Eggs

Prep Time: 20 min
Time to cook: 5 min
Serv: 2

Directions:
1. Cut avocado in half length-wise.
2. Remove the pit and widen the hole in each half by scraping out the avocado flesh with the help of the spoon.
3. Place avocado halves in a small ovenproof baking dish cut side up.
4. Beat an egg into each half of avocado.
5. Season with salt and pepper.
6. Cook for about 10-15 min at 370°F into the AirFryer.
7. Top with grape tomato halves and chives. Enjoy!

Calories	Sodium	Carbohydrates	Protein	Cholesterol
371	379.2 mg	24.1 g	12.7 g	194 mg

Ingredients:
- 1 large avocado halved
- 2 eggs
- 4 grape tomato halved
- 2 tspn chives, minced
- A pinch of sea salt and black pepper

Braekfast Vanilla Toasts

Prep Time: 5 min
Time to cook: 5 min
Serv: 4-5

Directions:
1. Place salted butter to a bowl and add sugar, cinnamon, and seasoning.
2. Mix well and spread the mixture over bread slices.
3. Preheat the AirFryer to 380 F and place bread slices to a fryer.
4. Cook for 4-5 min and serve hot!

Calories	Sodium	Carbohydrates	Protein	Cholesterol
375.3	370.4 mg	60.5 g	6.1 g	100.8 mg

Ingredients:
- Ten medium bread slices
- 1 pack salted butter
- 4 tbspns sugar
- 2 tspns ground cinnamon
- ½ tspn vanilla extract

Scottish Spinach Frittata

Prep Time	Time to cook	Serv
5 min	10-12 min	2

Directions:
1. Preheat the AirFryer to 370 F
2. In a baking pan, heat the oil for about a min.
3. Add dicedonions into the pan and cook for 2-3 min.
4. Add spinach and cook for about 3-5 min to about half baked. They may look a bit dry, but it is ok, just keep frying with the oil.
5. In the large bowl, whisk the beaten eggs, season with salt and pepper, and sprinkle with cheese. Pour the mixture into a baking pan.
6. Place the pan in the AirFryer and cook for 6-8 min or until cooked.

Calories	Sodium	Carbohydrates	Protein	Cholesterol
225.2	220.6 mg	7.4 g	16.7 g	379.5 mg

Ingredients:
- 1 small onion, diced
- 1/3 pack (4ounces) spinach
- 3 eggs, beaten
- 3 ounces mounceszarella cheese
- 1 tbspnn olive oil
- Salt and pepper to taste

Tasty Cheesy Potatoes With Garlic

Prep Time	Time to cook	Serv
10 min	40 min	8

Directions:
1. Brush potatoes with garlic butter and season well with salt and pepper. Place cut side down on a greased baking pan.
2. Position the baking pan in Rack Position 2 and select the Bake setting. Set the temperature to 425 F and the time to 30 min.
3. Remove from the oven, flip and top with parsley, mounceszarella and parmesan.
4. Select the Broil setting. Set the temperature to Broil and the time to 2 min. Season well and serve.

Calories	Fat	Carbs	Protein
162	9 g	5 g	5 g

Ingredients:
- ¼ cup garlic butter, melted
- 4 sweet potatoes halved lengthwise
- ¾ cup Mounceszarella cheese, shredded
- ½ cup Parmesan cheese, grated
- 2 tbspns parsley, minced
- Sea salt and black pepper, to taste

German Beef & Egg Scramble

Prep Time	Time to cook	Serv
10 min	20 min	2

Directions:
1. Preheat the AirFryer at 400oF.
2. In a baking dish that fits your AirFryer mix the ground beef, onion, garlic, olive oil, and bell pepper. Season with salt and pepper to taste.
3. Place dish in AirFryer and cook for 10 min.
4. Open the AirFryer, mix and crumble beef well.
5. Put in the beaten eggs and give a good stir.
6. Continue cooking for 25 min at 3300F.

Calories	Fat	Sugar	Protein	Fiber	Sodium
431	25.9 g	2.7 g	42.8 g	0.9 g	260 mg

Ingredients:
- Salt and pepper to taste
- Eight large eggs, beaten
- 3 cloves of garlic, diced
- 1-pound ground beef, 85% lean
- 1 onion, minced
- 1 green bell pepper, seeded and minced

Sour Cream Zucchini Bake With Garlic

Prep Time	Time to cook	Serv
5 min	20 min	3

Directions:
1. Lightly grease a dish that fits in your AirFryer with cooking spray.
2. Place zucchini slices in a single layer in dish.
3. In a bowl whisk well, remaining Ingredients: except for paprika. Spread on top of zucchini slices. Sprinkle paprika.
4. Cover dish with foil.
5. For 10 min, cook on 390oF.
6. Remove foil and cook for 10 min at 330oF.
7. Enjoy.

Ingredients:
- 1/4 cup grated Parmesan cheese
- paprika to taste
- 1 tbspnn dicedgarlic
- 1 large zucchini cut lengthwise then in half
- 1 cup sour cream
- 1 (8 ounces) package cream cheese, softened

Calories	Fat	Sugar	Protein	Fiber	Sodium
385	32.4 g	5.5 g	11.9 g	1.1 g	553 mg

Scandinavian Trout Omelette

Prep Time	Time to cook	Serv
5 min	15 min	4

Directions:
1. Preheat the AirFryer for 5 min.
2. Place all ingredients in a mixing bowl until well-combined.
3. Put into a baking dish that will fit in the AirFryer.
4. Cook for 15 min at 400F.

Ingredients
- Salt and pepper to taste
- Six eggs, beaten
- 2 tbspns olive oil
- 2 tbspns coconut oil
- 2 fillets smoked trout, shredded
- 1 onion, minced

Calories	Sodium	Protein	Sugar	Fat
283	117 mg	17 g	1.4 mg	22.5 g

Tasty Egg Bowls

Prep Time	Time to cook	Serv
2 min	10 min	4

Directions:
1. Preheat the AirFryer to 350oF.
2. Combine the eggs, butter, and spinach in a mixing bowl. Season with salt and pepper to taste.
3. Grease 4 ramekins with cooking spray and evenly pour the egg mixture into ramekins.
4. Sprinkle with bacon bits.
5. Place the ramekins in the AirFryer. If needed, cook in batches.
6. Cook for 10 min.

Ingredients
- Salt and pepper to taste
- 4 eggs, beaten
- 3 tbspns butter
- 1 bacon strip, fried and crumbled
- ¼ cup spinach, minced finely

Calories	Sodium	Protein	Sugar	Fat
148	84 mg	6 g	0.7 mg	13.2 g

Fabulous Spanish Chorizo Scrambled Eggs

Prep Time	Time to cook	Serv
3 min	15 min	2

Directions:
1. Preheat the AirFryer to 350F.
2. Put the ingredients all together in a bowl until well-incorporated.
3. Pour into a greased baking dish that will fit in the AirFryer basket.
4. Place the baking dish in the AirFryer.
5. Close and cook for 15 min.

Calories	Sodium	Protein	Sugar	Fat
235	292 mg	13.1 g	0.3 g	19.6 g

Ingredients
- A dash of Spanish paprika
- A dash of oregano
- 3 large eggs, beaten
- 1 tbspnn olive oil
- ½ zucchini, sliced
- ½ chorizo sausage, sliced

Easy AirFryer Omelet With Beef

Prep Time	Time to cook	Serv
3 min	20 min	4

Directions:
1. Preheat the AirFryer to 400F.
2. Place a dish inside the AirFryer basket, and grease with oil. Add onion and garlic. Cook for 3 min.
3. Add beef and cook for 10 min. Stirring halfway through Time to cook.
4. Combine the left of the ingredients in a mixing bowl.
5. Once the beef is d1 cooking, crumble, and evenly spread on the bottom of the dish. Pour egg mixture on top.
6. Cook for 20 min at 320F.

Calories	Sodium	Carbohydrates	Protein	Sugar	Fat
240	87 mg	4.6 g	19.1 g	1.9 g	15.7 g

Ingredients
- Salt and pepper to taste
- 3 eggs, beaten
- 3 cloves of garlic, diced
- 1 tbspnn olive oil
- 1 onion, minced
- ½ pound ground beef

Cheesy Noodles With Zucchini

Prep Time	Time to cook	Serv
10 min	44 min	3

Directions:
1. Preheat the AirFryer to 350 F.
2. Add spiralized zucchini and salt in a colander and set aside for 10 min.
3. Wash zucchini noodles and pat dry with a paper towel.
4. Heat oil in a pan over medium heat. Add garlic and onion and sauté for 3-4 min.
5. Add zucchini noodles and cook for 4-5 min or until softened.
6. Add zucchini mixture into the AirFryer baking pan. Add egg, thyme, cheeses. Mix well and season.
7. Place pan in the AirFryer and cook for 30-35 min.
8. Enjoy.

Calories	Fat	Sugar	Protein	Cholesterol
435	29 g	5 g	25 g	120 mg

Ingredients:
- 5 eggs
- 1/3 cup coconut oil, melted
- 2 tbspn baking powder
- 3 tbspn erythritol
- 3 tbspn jalapenos, sliced
- 1/4 cup unsweetened coconut milk
- 2/3 cup coconut flour
- 3/4 tbspn sea salt

Mushroom and Coconut Cream Frittata

Prep Time	Time to cook	Serv
5 min	20 min	4

Directions:
1. Preheat the AirFryer to 320F.
2. Combine the eggs, butter, and coconut cream in a mixing bowl.
3. Pour in a baking dish together with the mushrooms and onion powder.
4. Season with salt and pepper to taste.
5. Place in the AirFryer chamber and cook for 20 min.

Ingredients
- Salt and pepper to taste
- Eight eggs, beaten
- 2 tbspns butter
- 1 tspn onion powder
- 1 cup coconut cream
- ½ cup mushrooms, minced

Calories	Sodium	Carbohydrates	Protein	Sugar	Fat
384	175 mg	6.6 g	14.0 g	1.2 g	35 g

Breakfast Chicken Strips

Prep Time	Time to cook	Serv
7 min	12 min	4

Directions:
1. Cut the chicken fillet into strips.
2. Sprinkle the chicken fillets with salt and pepper.
3. Preheat the AirFryer to 365°F.
4. Place the butter in the air basket tray and add the chicken strips.
5. Cook the chicken strips for 6-min.
6. Turn the chicken strips to the other side and cook them for an additional 5-min.
7. After pieces are cooked, sprinkle them with cream and paprika, then transfer them to serving plates. Serve warm.

Ingredients
- 1 tspn paprika
- 1 tbspnn cream
- 1 lb. chicken fillet
- ½ tspn salt
- ½ tspn black pepper

Calories	Fat	Carbs	Protein
245	11.5 g	0.6 g	33 g

Keto Air Bread

Prep Time	Time to cook	Serv
10 min	25 min	19

Directions:
1. Crack the eggs into a bowl then using a hand blender mix them up. Melt the butter at room temperature.
2. Take the melted butter and add it to the egg mixture. Add the salt, baing powder, and almond flour to egg mixture and knead the dough.
3. Cover the prepared dough with a towel for 10-min to rest. Meanwhie, preheat your AirFryer to 360°F. Place the ready money in the AirFryer tin and cook the bread for 10-min. Reduce the heat to 350°F and bake the food for an additional 15-min.
4. Use a toothpick to make sure the dough is cooked. Transfer the bread to a wooden board to allow it to chill. Once the food has chilled, then slice and serve it.

Ingredients
- 1 cup almond flour
- ¼ sea salt
- 1 tspn baking powder
- ¼ cup butter
- 3 eggs

Nourishing Salmon Breakfast

Prep Time	Time to cook	Serv
6 min	15 min	2

Directions:
1. Add salmon and feta to a bowl. Add carrot, red onion, and cucumber and mix well. In an oven-safe tray, make a layer of bread and then pour the salmon mix over it. Cook in your AirFryer at 300°F for 15-min.

Calories	Fat	Carbs	Protein
226	10.2 g	7.3 g	14.6 g

Ingredients:
- 1 lb. salmon, minced
- 2 cups feta, crumbled
- 4 bread slices
- 3 tbspns pickled red onion
- 2 cucumbers, sliced
- 1 carrot, shredded

New English Breakfast

Prep Time	Time to cook	Serv
2 min	10 min	4

Directions:
1. Get a mixing bowl whisk the eggs, add the ham, bacon, and cheese and stir until well combined. Add to a baking pan that is sprayed with cooking spray. Preheat the AirFryer to 300°F and a cook time of 10-min. Place pan into AirFryer then remove when Time to cook is completed and serve warm.

Calories	Fat	Carbs	Protein
223	9.4 g	9.2 g	13.3 g

Ingredients:
- 4 eggs
- 1/3 cup ham, cooked and minced into small pieces
- 1/3 cup bacon, cooked, cut into small pieces
- 1/3 cup cheddar cheese, shredded

Easy Asparagus Frittata

Prep Time	Time to cook	Serv
3 min	8 min	2

Directions:
1. Mix in a large bowl, eggs, cheese, milk, salt, and pepper then blend them. Spray a baking pan with non-stick cooking spray. Pour the egg mixture into the pan and add the asparagus then place a container inside of the baking basket. Set AirFryer to 320°F for 8-min. Serve warm.

Calories	Fat	Carbs	Protein
231	9.2 g	8 g	12.2 g

Ingredients:
- 3 eggs
- Five steamed asparagus tips
- 2 tbspns of warm milk
- 1 tbspnn parmesan cheese, grated
- Salt and pepper to taste
- Non-stick cooking spray

Salmon With Eggs

Prep Time	Time to cook	Serv
2 min	8 min	4

Directions:
1. Preheat your AirFryer to 300°F for a cook time of 10-min. Butter the inside of 4 ramekins. In each ramekin, place spinach on the bottom, 1 egg, 1 tbspnn of milk, salt, and pepper. Put some ramekins in the AirFryer basket and cook for 8-min.

Calories	Fat	Carbs	Protein
213	9.2 g	8.4 g	13.2 g

Ingredients:
- 1 lb. of spinach, minced
- 7 ounces sliced ham
- 4 eggs
- 1 tbspnn olive oil
- 4 tbspns milk
- Salt and pepper to taste

Wonderful Pumpkin Toast

Prep Time	Time to cook	Serv
9 min	20 min	4

Directions:
1. In a large mixing bowl, mix milk, eggs, pumpkin purée, and pie spice. Whisk until the mixture is smooth. In the egg mixture, dip the bread on both sides. Place rack inside of the AirFryer's cooking basket. Place 2 slices of dough onto the tray. Set the temperature to 340°F for 10-min. Serve pumpkin pie toast with butter.

Calories	Fat	Carbs	Protein
212	8.2 g	7 g	11.3 g

Ingredients:
- 2 large, beaten eggs
- 4 slices of cinnamon swirl bread
- ¼ cup milk
- ¼ cup pumpkin purée
- ¼ tspn pumpkin spices
- ¼ cup butter

Minced Tomato Scrambled Eggs

Prep Time	Time to cook	Serv
5 min	10 min	2

Directions:
1. In a bowl, whisk the eggs, salt, and cream until fluffy. Preheat AirFryer to 300°F. Add butter to baking pan and place it into a preheated AirFryer. Once the butter is melted, add the egg mixture to baking pan and tomato then cook for 10-min. Whisk the eggs until fluffy then serve warm.

Calories	Fat	Carbs	Protein
105	8 g	2.3 g	6.4 g

Ingredients:
- 2 eggs
- 1 tomato, minced
- Dash of salt
- 1 tspn butter
- ¼ cup cream

Breakfast Spinach Eggss

Prep Time	Time to cook	Serv
5 min	15 min	2

Directions:
1. Spray the inside of 2 ramekins with cooking spray. Place 2 flat pieces of bread into each ramekin. Add the ham slice pieces into each ramekin. Crack an egg in each ramekin then sprinkle with cheese. Season with salt and pepper. Place the ramekins into AirFryer at 300°F for 15-min. Serve warm.

Ingredients:
- 2 eggs
- 2 tbspns cheddar cheese, grated
- Salt and pepper to taste
- 1 ham slice, cut into 2 pieces
- 4 bread slices, flatten with a rolling pin

Calories	Fat	Carbs	Protein
162	8 g	10 g	11 g

Sandwich With Cheese

Prep Time	Time to cook	Serv
2 min	6 min	1

Directions:
1. Butter your sliced roll on both sides. Place the eggs in an oven-safe dish and whisk. Add seasoning if you wish, such as dill, chives, oregano, and salt. Place the egg dish, roll, and cheese into the AirFryer. Make sure the buttered sides of the roll are facing upwards. Set the AirFryer to 390°F with a cook time of 6-min. Remove the ingredients when cook time is completed by AirFryer. Place the egg and cheese between the pieces of roll and serve warm. You might like to try adding slices of avocado and tomatoes to this breakfast sandwich!

Ingredients:
- 1-2 eggs
- 1-2 slices of cheddar or Swiss cheese
- A bit of butter
- 1 roll sliced in half (your choice), Kaiser bun, English muffin, etc.

Calories	Fat	Carbs	Protein
212	11.2 g	9.3 g	12.4 g

Dance Of Pepper And Eggs

Prep Time	Time to cook	Serv
10 min	13 min	2

Directions:
1. Put the egg on the bowl and crack 2 eggs into each bell pepper half.
2. Season with red pepper flakes, pepper, and salt.
3. Place bell pepper halves into the AirFryer basket and cook at 390 F for 13 min.
4. Enjoy.

Ingredients:
- 4 eggs
- 1 bell pepper, halved and remove seeds
- Pinch of red pepper flakes
- Pepper
- Salt

Calories	Fat	Sugar	Protein	Carbohydrates	Cholesterol
145	8.9 g	3.7 g	11.7 g	5.3 g	327 mg

Tasty Omelette With Sausages

Prep Time	Time to cook	Serv
10 min	8 min	4

Directions:
1. Spray 4 AirFryer safe ramekins with cooking spray and set aside.
2. In a mixing bowl, whisk eggs with coconut milk, cheese, pepper, and salt. Add sausage and Stir.
3. Pour egg mixture into the prepared ramekins.
4. Place ramekins into the AirFryer basket and cook at 320 F for 8 min or until eggs are cooked.
5. Enjoy.

Ingredients:
- Six eggs
- 1 cup cheddar cheese, shredded
- 3/4 cup coconut milk
- Six sausages, cooked and crumbled
- Pepper
- Salt

Calories	Fat	Sugar	Protein	Cholesterol
449	38.1 g	2.2 g	24.2 g	309 mg

Amazing Breakfast Muffins

Prep Time	Time to cook	Serv
10 min	5 min	4

Directions:
1. Get a bowl and whisk eggs with heavy cream, cheese, pepper, and salt.
2. Pour egg mixture into the 4 silic1 muffin molds.
3. Place muffin molds into the AirFryer basket and cook at 350 F for 5 min.
4. Enjoy.

Ingredients:
- 4 eggs
- 1/4 cup cheddar cheese, shredded
- 1/4 cup heavy cream
- Pepper
- Salt

Calories	Fat	Sugar	Protein	Cholesterol
117	9.5 g	0.4 g	7.5 g	181 mg

Italian Eggs With Cheddar

Prep Time	Time to cook	Serv
10 min	5 min	6

Directions:
1. Spray egg bite mold with cooking spray and set aside.
2. In a bowl, whisk eggs with cheese, milk, pepper, and salt.
3. Pour egg mixture into the prepared mold.
4. Place the mold into the AirFryer basket and cook at 330 F for 5 min. Make sure eggs are lightly browned in color on top.
5. Enjoy.

Ingredients:
- 4 eggs
- 1/4 cup cheddar cheese, shredded
- 4 tbspn almond milk
- Pepper
- Salt

Calories	Fat	Sugar	Protein	Cholesterol
69	5.3 g	0.4 g	4.9 g	114 mg

Good Egg Bake With Cheese

Prep Time: 10 min Time to cook: 5 min Serv: 1

Directions:
1. Spray ramekin dish with cooking spray and set aside.
2. In a small bowl, whisk eggs with parmesan cheese, cheddar cheese, heavy cream, pepper, and salt.
3. Pour egg mixture into the prepared ramekin dish.
4. Place ramekin dish into the AirFryer basket and cook at 330 F for 5 min.
5. Enjoy.

Ingredients:
- 2 eggs
- 1 tbspn parmesan cheese, grated
- 2 tbspn cheddar cheese, shredded
- 2 tbspn heavy cream
- Pepper
- Salt

Calories	Fat	Sugar	Protein	Cholesterol
332	27.5 g	0.8 g	19.7 g	393 mg

Egg Frittata In Western Style

Prep Time: 10 min Time to cook: 6 min Serv: 2

Directions:
1. Spray AirFryer safe pan with cooking spray and set aside.
2. In a small bowl, whisk eggs with cheese, half and half, pepper, and salt.
3. Pour egg mixture into the prepared pan.
4. Place pan in the AirFryer basket and cook at 320 F for 6 min.
5. Enjoy.

Ingredients:
- 4 eggs
- 1/3 cup cheddar cheese, shredded
- 1/2 cup half and half
- Pepper
- Salt

Calories	Fat	Sugar	Protein	Cholesterol
281	22 g	0.9 g	17.6 g	370 mg

Yummy Ham Egg Scramble

Prep Time: 10 min Time to cook: 5 min Serv: 4

Directions:
1. With cooking spray, spray 4 ramekins and set aside.
2. In a small bowl, whisk eggs with cheese, heavy cream, ham, pepper, and salt.
3. Pour egg mixture into the prepared ramekins.
4. Place ramekins into the AirFryer basket and cook at 300 F for 5 min.
5. Enjoy.

Ingredients:
- 4 eggs
- 1/2 cup cheddar cheese, shredded
- 4 tbspn heavy cream
- 1/2 cup ham, diced
- Pepper
- Salt

Calories	Fat	Sugar	Protein	Cholesterol
199	16.1 g	0.4 g	12.2 g	209 mg

Hearty Breakfast

Prep Time: 10 min
Time to cook: 9 min
Serv: 2

Directions:
1. Break 1 egg into each avocado half. Season with red pepper flakes, pepper, and salt.
2. Place avocado halves into the AirFryer basket and cook at 400 F for 5 min or until eggs are cooked. Check after 5 min.
3. Enjoy.

Ingredients:
- 2 eggs
- 1 avocado, cut in half and remove the seed
- Pinch of red pepper flakes
- Pepper
- Salt

Calories	Fat	Sugar	Protein	Cholesterol
268	24 g	0.9 g	7.5 g	164 mg

Miracle Spinach Omelette

Prep Time: 10 min
Time to cook: 8 min
Serv: 2

Directions:
1. Spray AirFryer safe pan with cooking spray and set aside.
2. In a bowl, whisk eggs with cheese, spinach, pepper, and salt.
3. Pour egg mixture into the prepared pan.
4. Place pan into the AirFryer basket and cook at 390 F for 8 min.
5. Enjoy.

Ingredients:
- 3 eggs
- 1/2 cup cheddar cheese, shredded
- 2 tbspn spinach, minced
- Pepper
- Salt

Calories	Fat	Sugar	Protein	Cholesterol
209	15.9 g	0.7 g	15.4 g	275 mg

Healthy Cream Scramble

Prep Time: 10 min
Time to cook: 10 min
Serv: 4

Directions:
1. Preheat the color AirFryer to 390 F.
2. With cooking spray, spray 4 ramekins and set aside.
3. In a bowl, whisk eggs with red chili pepper, cream, pepper, and salt.
4. Pour egg mixture into the prepared ramekins.
5. Place ramekins into the AirFryer basket and cook for 10 min.
6. Enjoy.

Ingredients:
- 4 eggs
- 1/4 tbspn red chili pepper
- 4 tbspn cream
- Pepper
- Salt

Calories	Fat	Sugar	Protein	Cholesterol
71	5 g	0.6 g	5.7 g	166 mg

Savory Egg Omelet

Prep Time	Time to cook	Serv
5 min	8 min	1

Directions:
1. Preheat the AirFryer to 350 F.
2. Spray AirFryer pan with cooking spray.
3. In a bowl, whisk eggs with remaining ingredients until well combined.
4. Pour egg mixture into the prepared pan and place pan in the AirFryer basket.
5. Cook frittata for 8 min or until set.
6. Enjoy.

Calories	Fat	Sugar	Protein	Cholesterol
384	23.3 g	4.1 g	34.3 g	521 mg

Ingredients:
- 3 eggs
- 1 cup spinach, minced
- 1 small onion, diced
- 2 tbspn mounceszarella cheese, grated
- Pepper
- Salt

Easy Egg Frittata

Prep Time	Time to cook	Serv
5 min	8 min	2

Directions:
1. In a bowl, whisk eggs with remaining gradients.
2. Spray 2 ramekins with cooking spray.
3. Pour egg mixture into the prepared ramekins and place into the AirFryer basket. Cook soufflé at 390 F for 8 min.
4. Enjoy.

Calories	Fat	Sugar	Protein	Cholesterol
116	10 g	0.4 g	6 g	184 mg

Ingredients:
- 2 eggs
- 1/4 tbspn chili pepper
- 2 tbspn heavy cream
- 1/4 tbspn pepper
- 1 tbspn parsley, minced
- Salt

Egg Frittata With Vegetables

Prep Time	Time to cook	Serv
10 min	20 min	4

Directions:
1. Spray 4 ramekins with cooking spray and set aside.
2. In a bowl, whisk eggs with onion powder, garlic powder, and red pepper.
3. Add mushrooms and broccoli and Stir.
4. Pour egg mixture into the prepared ramekins and place ramekins into the AirFryer basket. Cook at 350 F for 15 min. Make sure souffle is cooked if souffle is not cooked then cook for 5 min more.
5. Enjoy.

Calories	Fat	Sugar	Protein	Cholesterol
91	5.1 g	2.6 g	7.4 g	186 mg

Ingredients:
- 4 large eggs
- 1 tbspn onion powder
- 1 tbspn garlic powder
- 1 tbspn red pepper, crushed
- 1/2 cup broccoli florets, minced
- 1/2 cup mushrooms, minced

Mushroom Souffle

Prep Time	Time to cook	Serv
10 min	13 min	1

Directions:
1. Spray pan with cooking spray and heat over medium heat.
2. Add mushrooms and sauté for 2-3 min. Add spinach and cook for 1-2 min or until wilted.
3. Transfer mushroom spinach mixture into the AirFryer pan.
4. Whisk egg whites in a mixing bowl until frothy. Season with a pinch of salt.
5. Pour egg white mixture into the spinach and mushroom mixture and sprinkle with parmesan cheese.
6. Place pan in AirFryer basket and cook frittata at 350 F for 8 min.
7. Slice and serve.

Ingredients:
- 1 cup egg whites
- 1 cup spinach, minced
- 2 mushrooms, sliced
- 2 tbspn parmesan cheese, grated
- Salt

Calories	Fat	Sugar	Protein	Cholesterol
176	3 g	2.5 g	31 g	8 mg

Tender Zucchini Gratin

Prep Time	Time to cook	Serv
10 min	24 min	4

Directions:
1. Preheat the AirFryer to 370 F.
2. Arrange zucchini slices in the AirFryer baking dish.
3. In a saucepan, heat almond milk over low heat and stir in Dijon mustard, nutritional yeast, and sea salt. Add beaten egg and whisk well.
4. Pour sauce over zucchini slices.
5. Place dish in the AirFryer and cook for 20-24 min.
6. Enjoy.

Ingredients:
- 1 large egg, lightly beaten
- 1 1/4 cup unsweetened almond milk
- 3 medium zucchinis, sliced
- 1 tbspn Dijon mustard
- 1/2 cup nutritional yeast
- 1 tbspn sea salt

Calories	Fat	Sugar	Protein	Cholesterol
120	3.4 g	2 g	13 g	47 mg

Sophisticated Cheese Tart

Prep Time	Time to cook	Serv
10 min	16 min	4

Directions:
1. Preheat the AirFryer to 325 F.
2. In a bowl, whisk together cheese, eggs, whipping cream, pepper, and salt.
3. Spray AirFryer baking dish with cooking spray.
4. Pour egg mixture into the prepared dish and place in the AirFryer basket.
5. Cook for 16 min or until the egg is set.
6. Enjoy.

Ingredients:
- 8 eggs
- 1 1/2 cups heavy whipping cream
- 1 lb cheddar cheese, grated
- Pepper
- Salt

Calories	Fat	Sugar	Protein	Cholesterol
735	63 g	1.3 g	40.2 g	505 mg

Piquant Parmesan Casserole

Prep Time	Time to cook	Serv
10 min	20 min	3

Directions:
1. Preheat the AirFryer to 325 F.
2. In mixing bowl, combine together cream and eggs.
3. Add cheese and tomato sauce and mix well.
4. Spray AirFryer baking dish with cooking spray.
5. Pour mixture into baking dish and place in the AirFryer basket.
6. Cook for 20 min.
7. Enjoy.

Ingredients:
- 5 eggs
- 2 tbspn heavy cream
- 3 tbspn chunky tomato sauce
- 2 tbspn parmesan cheese, grated

Calories	Fat	Sugar	Protein	Cholesterol
185	14 g	1.2 g	13.6 g	290 mg

Scrambled Eggs With Cottage Cheese and Spinach

Prep Time	Time to cook	Serv
10 min	20 min	4

Directions:
1. Preheat the AirFryer to 350 F.
2. Add eggs, milk, half parmesan cheese, and cottage cheese in a bowl and whisk well. Add spinach and Stir.
3. Pour mixture into the AirFryer baking dish.
4. Sprinkle remaining half parmesan cheese on top.
5. Place dish in the AirFryer and cook for 20 min.
6. Enjoy.

Ingredients:
- 3 eggs
- 1/4 cup coconut milk
- 1/4 cup parmesan cheese, grated
- 4 ounces spinach, minced
- 3 ounces cottage cheese

Calories	Fat	Sugar	Protein	Cholesterol
144	8.5 g	1.1 g	14 g	135 mg

Classical Tomato Breakfast

Prep Time	Time to cook	Serv
10 min	24 min	2

Directions:
1. Preheat the AirFryer to 325 F.
2. Cut off the top of a tomato and spoon out the tomato innards.
3. Break the egg in each tomato and place in AirFryer basket and cook for 24 min. Season with parsley, pepper, and salt.
4. Enjoy.

Ingredients:
- 2 eggs
- 2 large fresh tomatoes
- 1 tbspn fresh parsley
- Pepper
- Salt

Calories	Fat	Sugar	Protein	Cholesterol
95	5 g	5.1 g	7 g	164 mg

Delightful Mushroom Frittata Breakfast

Prep Time	Time to cook	Serv
10 min	32 min	4

Directions:
1. Preheat the AirFryer to 325 F.
2. Spray AirFryer baking dish with cooking spray and set aside.
3. Heat another pan over medium heat. Spray pan with cooking spray.
4. Add mushrooms, leeks, and salt in a pan sauté for 6 min.
5. Break eggs in a bowl and whisk well.
6. Transfer sautéed mushroom and leek mixture into the prepared baking dish.
7. Pour egg over mushroom mixture.
8. Place dish in the AirFryer and cook for 32 min.
9. Enjoy.

Ingredients:
- 6 eggs
- 6 ounces mushrooms, sliced
- 1 cup leeks, sliced
- Salt

Calories	Fat	Sugar	Protein	Cholesterol
116	7 g	2.1 g	10 g	245 mg

Surprising Squash

Prep Time	Time to cook	Serv
10 min	25 min	4

Directions:
1. Add all ingredients into the large bowl and toss well.
2. Preheat the AirFryer to 400 F.
3. Add squash mixture into the AirFryer basket and cook for 10 min.
4. Shake basket and cook for another 10 min. Shake once again and cook for 5 min more.

Ingredients:
- 2 lbs yellow squash, cut into half-moons
- 1 tbspn Italian seasoning
- ¼ tbspn pepper
- 1 tbspn olive oil
- ¼ tbspn salt

Calories	Fat	Sugar	Protein	Cholesterol
70	4 g	2 g	2 g	1 mg

Spanish Savory Frittata

Prep Time	Time to cook	Serv
10 min	6 min	2

Directions:
1. Whisk eggs with garlic powder, onion powder, parmesan cheese, pepper, and salt.
2. Pour egg mixture into the AirFryer baking dish.
3. Place dish in the AirFryer and cook at 360 F for 2 min. Stir quickly and cook for 3-4 min more.
4. Stir and serve.

Ingredients:
- 4 eggs
- 1/4 tbspn garlic powder
- 1/4 tbspn onion powder
- 1 tbspn parmesan cheese
- Pepper
- Salt

Calories	Fat	Sugar	Protein	Cholesterol
149	9.1 g	1.1 g	11 g	325 mg

Easy Dill-Lemon Scallops

Prep Time	Time to cook	Serv
10 min	5 min	4

Directions:
1. Add scallops into the bowl and toss with oil, dill, lemon juice, pepper, and salt.
2. Add scallops into the AirFryer basket and cook at 360 F for 5 min.
3. Enjoy.

Calories	Fat	Sugar	Protein	Cholesterol
121	3.2 g	0.1 g	19 g	37 mg

Ingredients:
- 1 lb scallops
- 2 tbspn olive oil
- 1 tbspn dill, minced
- 1 tbspn fresh lemon juice
- Pepper
- Salt

Breakfast Spicy Chicken

Prep Time	Time to cook	Serv
10 min	30 min	4

Directions:
1. Preheat the AirFryer to 350 F.
2. Place chicken thighs into the AirFryer baking dish and season with pepper and salt. Top with salsa.
3. Place in the AirFryer and cook for 30 min.
4. Enjoy.

Calories	Fat	Sugar	Protein	Cholesterol
233	8 g	2 g	33 g	101 mg

Ingredients:
- 1 lb chicken thighs, boneless and skinless
- 1 cup salsa
- Pepper
- Salt

Italian Tender Scallops

Prep Time	Time to cook	Serv
10 min	8 min	2

Directions:
1. Preheat the AirFryer to 400 F.
2. In a small bowl, mix together lemon juice and butter.
3. Brush scallops with lemon juice and butter mixture and place into the AirFryer basket. Cook scallops for 4 min.
4. Turn halfway through.
5. Again, brush scallops with lemon butter mixture and cook for 4 min more. Turn halfway through.
6. Enjoy.

Calories	Fat	Sugar	Protein	Cholesterol
199	14 g	0.2 g	17 g	111 mg

Ingredients:
- 1 lb jumbo scallops
- 1 tbspn fresh lemon juice
- 2 tbspn butter, melted

Nourishing Egg Cups

Prep Time	Time to cook	Serv
10 min	9 min	4

Directions:
1. Spray silicone muffin molds with cooking spray.
2. In a small bowl, whisk the egg with pepper and salt.
3. Preheat the AirFryer to 350 F.
4. Pour eggs into the silicone muffin molds. Divide cheese and bacon into molds.
5. Top each with tomato slice and place in the AirFryer basket.
6. Cook for 9 min.
7. Enjoy.

Ingredients:
- 3 eggs, lightly beaten
- 4 tomato slices
- 4 tbspn cheddar cheese, shredded
- 2 bacon slices, cooked and crumbled
- Pepper
- Salt

Calories	Fat	Sugar	Protein	Cholesterol
67	4 g	0.7 g	5.1 g	125 mg

Lovely Carrots With Fresh Lime

Prep Time	Time to cook	Serv
10 min	20 min	4

Directions:
1. Add carrots into the bowl and toss with remaining ingredients.
2. Transfer carrots into the AirFryer basket and cook at 320 F for 20 min.
3. Enjoy.

Ingredients:
- 1 lb baby carrots, trimmed
- 2 tbspn fresh lime juice
- 1 tbspn herb de Provence
- 2 tbspn olive oil
- Pepper
- Salt

Calories	Fat	Sugar	Protein	Cholesterol
60	2.5 g	5.4 g	0.7 g	0 mg

Healthy Zucchini Squash Mix

Prep Time	Time to cook	Serv
10 min	35 min	4

Directions:
1. Add all ingredients into the large bowl and mix well.
2. Transfer bowl mixture into the AirFryer basket and cook at 400 F for 35 min.
3. Enjoy.

Ingredients:
- 1 lb zucchini, sliced
- 1 tbspn parsley, minced
- 1 yellow squash, halved, deseeded, and minced
- 1 tbspn olive oil
- Pepper
- Salt

Calories	Fat	Sugar	Protein	Cholesterol
49	3 g	2 g	1.5 g	0 mg

Creamy Cabbage With Bacon

Prep Time	Time to cook	Serv
10 min	20 min	4

Directions:
2. Add all ingredients into the AirFryer baking dish and Stir.
3. Place dish in the AirFryer and cook at 400 F for 20 min.
4. Enjoy.

Ingredients:
- 1 cabbage head, shredded
- 1 cup heavy cream
- 4 bacon slices, minced
- 1 onion, minced
- Pepper
- Salt

Calories	Fat	Sugar	Protein	Cholesterol
163	11 g	7 g	3 g	41 mg

Beautiful Lemon Artichokes

Prep Time	Time to cook	Serv
10 min	15 min	4

Directions:
1. Place artichokes into the AirFryer basket. Drizzle with butter and lemon juice and season with pepper and salt.
2. Cook at 380 F for 15 min.
3. Enjoy.

Calories	Fat	Sugar	Protein	Cholesterol
57	3 g	0.8 g	2.2 g	8 mg

Ingredients:
- 2 medium artichokes, trimmed and halved
- 2 tbspn fresh lemon juice
- 1 tbspn butter, melted
- Pepper
- Salt

Exciting Almond Crunchy Chicken

Prep Time	Time to cook	Serv
10 min	25 min	2

Directions:
1. Add almond into the food processor and process until finely ground. Transfer almonds on a plate and set aside.
2. Mix together mustard and mayonnaise and spread over chicken.
3. Coat chicken with almond and place into the AirFryer basket and cook at 350 F for 25 min.
4. Enjoy.

Calories	Fat	Sugar	Protein	Cholesterol
409	22 g	1.5 g	45 g	134 mg

Ingredients:
- 2 chicken breasts, skinless and boneless
- 1 tbspn Dijon mustard
- 2 tbspn mayonnaise
- ¼ cup almonds
- Pepper
- Salt

Nutty Chicken Thighs

Prep Time	Time to cook	Serv
10 min	20 min	4

Directions:
1. Brush chicken with melted butter.
2. Mix together Italian herbs, onion powder, and garlic powder and rub over chicken.
3. Place chicken into the AirFryer basket and cook at 380 F for 20 min.
4. Enjoy.

Calories	Fat	Sugar	Protein	Cholesterol
330	16 g	0.1 g	42 g	145 mg

Ingredients:
- 4 chicken thighs
- ¼ tbspn onion powder
- ½ tbspn garlic powder
- 2 ½ tbspn dried Italian herbs
- 2 tbspn butter, melted

Charming Pesto Salmon With Almond

Prep Time	Time to cook	Serv
10 min	12 min	2

Directions:
1. Mix together pesto and almond.
2. Brush salmon fillets with melted butter and place into the AirFryer baking dish.
3. Top salmon fillets with pesto and almond mixture.
4. Place dish in the AirFryer and cook at 390 F for 12 min.
5. Enjoy.

Ingredients:
- 2 salmon fillets
- 2 tbspn butter, melted
- ¼ cup pesto
- ¼ cup almond, ground

Calories	Fat	Sugar	Protein	Cholesterol
541	41 g	2.5 g	40 g	117 mg

Strong And Smoothy Radish

Prep Time	Time to cook	Serv
10 min	13 min	4

Directions:
1. Slice onion and radishes using a mandolin slicer.
2. Add sliced onion and radishes in a large mixing bowl and toss with olive oil.
3. Transfer onion and radish slices in AirFryer basket and cook at 360 F for 8 min. Shake basket twice.
4. Return onion and radish slices in a mixing bowl and toss with seasonings.
5. Again, cook onion and radish slices in AirFryer basket for 5 min at 400 F. Shake basket halfway through.
6. Enjoy.

Ingredients:
- 1 lb radishes, washed and cut off roots
- 1 tbspn olive oil
- 1/2 tbspn paprika
- 1/2 tbspn onion powder
- 1/2 tbspn garlic powder
- 1 medium onion
- 1/4 tbspn pepper
- 3/4 tbspn sea salt

Calories	Fat	Sugar	Protein	Cholesterol
62	3.7 g	3.5 g	1.2 g	0 mg

Clean and Simple Treats

Prep Time	Time to cook	Serv
10 min	20 min	4

Directions:
1. Spray 4 ramekins with cooking spray and set aside.
2. In a mixing bowl, whisk eggs with cilantro, half and half, vegetables, 1/2 cup cheese, pepper, and salt.
3. Pour egg mixture into the 4 ramekins.
4. Place ramekins in AirFryer basket and cook at 300 F for 12 min.
5. Top with remaining 1/2 cup cheese and cook for 2 min more at 400 F.
6. Enjoy.

Ingredients:
- 4 eggs
- 1 tbspn cilantro, minced
- 4 tbspn half and half
- 1 cup cheddar cheese, shredded
- 1 cup vegetables, diced
- Pepper
- Salt

Calories	Fat	Sugar	Protein	Cholesterol
194	11.5 g	0.5 g	13 g	190 mg

Omelette With Ceddar Cheese And Mushrooms

Prep Time	Time to cook	Serv
10 min	6 min	2

Directions:
1. In a bowl, whisk eggs with cream, vegetables, pepper, and salt.
2. Preheat the AirFryer to 400 F. Pour egg mixture into the AirFryer pan. Place pan in AirFryer basket and cook for 5 min.
3. Add shredded cheese on top of the frittata and cook for 1 min more.
4. Enjoy.

Calories	Fat	Sugar	Protein	Cholesterol
160	10 g	2 g	12 g	255 mg

Ingredients:
- 3 eggs, lightly beaten
- 2 tbspn cheddar cheese, shredded
- 2 tbspn heavy cream
- 2 mushrooms, sliced
- 1/4 small onion, minced
- 1/4 bell pepper, diced
- Pepper
- Salt

Magic Cheese Souffle

Prep Time	Time to cook	Serv
10 min	6 min	8

Directions:
1. Preheat the AirFryer to 325 F.
2. Spray eight ramekins with cooking spray. Set aside.
3. In a bowl, whisk together almond flour, cayenne pepper, pepper, salt, and xanthan gum.
4. Slowly add heavy cream and mix to combine.
5. Whisk in egg yolks, chives, and cheese until well combined.
6. In a large bowl, add egg whites and cream of tartar and beat until stiff peaks form. Fold egg white mixture into the almond flour mixture until combined.
7. Pour mixture into the prepared ramekins. Divide ramekins in batches.
8. Place the first batch of ramekins into the AirFryer basket.
9. Cook soufflé for 20 min.
10. Enjoy.

Calories	Fat	Sugar	Protein	Cholesterol
210	16 g	0.5 g	12 g	185 mg

Ingredients:
- 6 large eggs, separated
- 3/4 cup heavy cream
- 1/4 tbspn cayenne pepper
- 1/2 tbspn xanthan gum
- 1/2 tbspn pepper
- 1/4 tbspn cream of tartar
- 2 tbspn chives, minced
- 2 cups cheddar cheese, shredded
- 1 tbspn salt

Wonderful Asparagus Frittata

Prep Time	Time to cook	Serv
10 min	10 min	4

Directions:
1. Toss mushrooms and asparagus with melted butter and add into the AirFryer basket.
2. Cook mushrooms and asparagus at 350 F for 5 min. Shake basket twic e.
3. Meanwhile, in a bowl, whisk together eggs, half and half, pepper, and salt.
4. Transfer cook mushrooms and asparagus into the AirFryer baking dish.

Ingredients:
- 6 eggs
- 3 mushrooms, sliced
- 10 asparagus, minced
- 2 tbspn butter, melted
- 1 cup mounceszarella cheese, shredded
- 1 tbspn pepper
- 1 tbspn salt

5. Pour egg mixture over mushrooms and asparagus.
6. Place dish in the AirFryer and cook at 350 F for 5 min or until eggs are set.
7. Slice and serve.

Calories	Fat	Sugar	Protein	Cholesterol
211	13 g	1 g	16 g	272 mg

Chilly Cauliflower Rice

Prep Time: 10 min
Time to cook: 22 min
Serv: 2

Directions:
1. Preheat the AirFryer to 370 F.
2. Add cauliflower florets into the food processor and process until it looks like rice.
3. Transfer cauliflower rice into the AirFryer baking pan and drizzle with half oil.
4. Place pan in the AirFryer and cook for 12 min, stir halfway through.
5. Heat remaining oil in a small pan over medium heat.
6. Add zucchini and cook for 5-8 min.
7. Add onion and jalapenos and cook for 5 min.
8. Add spices and Stir. Set aside.
9. Add cauliflower rice in the zucchini mixture and Stir.
10. Enjoy.

Ingredients:
- 1 cauliflower head, cut into florets
- 1/2 tbspn cumin
- 1/2 tbspn chili powder
- 6 onion spring, minced
- 2 jalapenos, minced
- 4 tbspn olive oil
- 1 zucchini, trimmed and cut into cubes
- 1/2 tbspn paprika
- 1/2 tbspn garlic powder
- 1/2 tbspn cayenne pepper
- 1/2 tbspn pepper
- 1/2 tbspn salt

Calories	Fat	Sugar	Protein	Cholesterol
254	28 g	5 g	4.3 g	0 mg

Stuffed Peppers With Feta And Broccoli

Prep Time: 10 min
Time to cook: 40 min
Serv: 2

Directions:
1. Preheat the AirFryer to 325 F.
2. Stuff feta and broccoli into the bell peppers halved.
3. Beat egg in a bowl with seasoning and pour egg mixture into the pepper halved over feta and broccoli.
4. Place bell pepper halved into the AirFryer basket and cook for 35-40 min.
5. Top with grated cheddar cheese and cook until cheese melted.
6. Enjoy.

Ingredients:
- 4 eggs
- 1/2 cup cheddar cheese, grated
- 2 bell peppers, cut in half and remove seeds
- 1/2 tbspn garlic powder
- 1 tbspn dried thyme
- 1/4 cup feta cheese, crumbled
- 1/2 cup broccoli, cooked
- 1/4 tbspn pepper
- 1/2 tbspn salt

Calories	Fat	Sugar	Protein	Cholesterol
340	22 g	8.2 g	22 g	374 mg

Coconut Breakfast Muffins

Prep Time	Time to cook	Serv
10 min	15 min	8

Directions:
1. Preheat the AirFryer to 325 F.
2. In a large bowl, stir together coconut flour, baking powder, erythritol, and sea salt.
3. Stir in eggs, jalapenos, coconut milk, and coconut oil until well combined.
4. Pour batter into the silic1 muffin molds and place into the AirFryer basket.
5. Cook muffins for 15 min.
6. Enjoy.

Calories	Fat	Sugar	Protein	Cholesterol
125	12 g	6 g	3 g	102 mg

Ingredients:
- 1 egg
- 1/2 cup parmesan cheese, grated
- 1/2 cup feta cheese, crumbled
- 1 tbspn thyme
- 1 garlic clove, minced
- 1 onion, minced
- 2 medium zucchinis, trimmed and spiralized
- 2 tbspn olive oil
- 1 cup mounceszarella cheese, grated
- 1/2 tbspn pepper
- 1/2 tbspn salt

Snacks

Savory Spicy Chickpeas

Prep Time	Time to cook	Serv
5 min	10 min	4

Direction:
1. In a bowl, add all the ingredients and toss to coat thoroughly.
2. Press "Power Button" of Air Fry Oven and turn the dial to select the "Air Fry" mode.
3. Press the Time button and again turn the dial to set the Time to cook to 10 min.
4. Now push the Temp button and rotate the dial to set the temperature at 390 degrees F.
5. Press the "Start/Pause" button to start.
6. When the unit beeps to show that it is preheated, open the lid.
7. Arrange the chickpeas in "Air Fry Basket" and insert it in the oven.
8. Serve warm.

Ingredients:
- 1 (15-ounces.) can chickpeas, rinsed and drained
- 1 tbspnn olive oil
- ½ tspn ground cumin
- ½ tspn cayenne pepper
- ½ tspn smoked paprika
- Salt, as required

Calories	Fat	Sugar	Protein	Carbs	Cholesterol
146	4.5 g	0.1 g	6.3 g	18.8 g	0 mg

Roasted Peanuts

Prep Time	Time to cook	Serv
5 min	14 min	6

Direction:
1. Press "Power Button" of Air Fry Oven and turn the dial to select the "Air Fry" mode. Press the Time button and again turn the dial to set the Time to cook to 14 min. Now push the Temp button and rotate the dial to set the temperature at 320 degrees F. Press the "Start/Pause" button to start.
2. When the unit beeps to show that it is preheated, open the lid.
3. Arrange the peanuts in "Air Fry Basket" and insert it in the oven.
4. Toss the peanuts twice.
5. After 9 min of cooking, spray the peanuts with cooking spray.
6. Serve warm.

Ingredients:
- 1½ cups of raw peanuts
- Nonstick cooking spray

Calories	Fat	Sugar	Protein	Carbs	Cholesterol
207	18 g	1.5 g	9.4 g	5.9 g	0 mg

Exquisite Grilled Cheese Sandwiches

Prep Time	Time to cook	Serv
10 min	5 min	2

Directions:
1. Preheat the AirFryer to 355 and grease an AirFryer basket.

Ingredients:
- 4 white bread slices
- ½ cup melted butter softened
- ½ cup sharp cheddar cheese, grated
- 1 tbspnn mayonnaise

2. Spread the mayonnaise and melted butter over 1 side of each bread slice. Sprinkle the cheddar cheese over the buttered side of the 2 slices.
3. Cover with the remaining slices of bread and transfer into the AirFryer basket.
4. Cook for about 5 min and dish out to serve warm.

Calories	Fat	Sugar	Protein	Carbohydrates	Sodium
445	8.1 g	7.8 g	9.7 g	85.5 g	191 mg

Chili Dip

Prep Time Time to cook Serv
10 min 15 min 8

Directions:
1. In a baking pan, place the cream cheese and spread in an even layer.
2. Top with chili evenly, followed by the cheese.
3. Press "Power Button" of Air Fry Oven and turn the dial to select the "Air Bake" mode.
4. Press the Time button and again turn the dial to set the Time to cook to 15 min.
5. Now push the Temp button and rotate the dial to set the temperature at 375 degrees F.
6. Press the "Start/Pause" button to start.
7. When the unit beeps to show that it is preheated, open the lid.
8. Arrange pan over the "Wire Rack" and insert it in the oven.
9. Serve hot.

Ingredients:
- 1 (8-ounces.) package cream cheese, softened
- 1 (16-ounces.) can Hormel chili without beans
- 1 (16-ounces.) package mild cheddar cheese, shredded

Calories	Fat	Sugar	Protein	Carbs	Cholesterol
388	31.3 g	1.1 g	21.1 g	5.6 g	103 mg

Beautiful Tortilla Chips

Prep Time Time to cook Serv
10 min 6 min 6

Directions:
1. Preheat the AirFryer to 390 of and grease an AirFryer basket.
2. Drizzle the tortilla chips with olive oil and season with salt.
3. Half of the tortilla chips arrange in the AirFryer basket and cook for about 3 min, flipping in between.
4. Repeat with the remaining tortilla chips and dish out to serve warm.

Ingredients:
- Eight corn tortillas, cut into triangles
- 1 tbspnn olive oil
- Salt, to taste

Calories	Fat	Sugar	Protein	Carbohydrates	Sodium
90	3.2 g	0.3 g	1.8 g	14.3 g	42 mg

Sweet Corn and Bell Pepper Sandwich with Barbecue Sauce

Prep Time	Time to cook	Serv
15 min	23 min	2

Directions:
1. Preheat the AirFryer to 355 and grease an AirFryer basket.
2. Heat butter in a skillet on medium heat and add corn.
3. Sauté for about 2 min and dish out in a bowl.
4. Add bell pepper and barbecue sauce to the corn.
5. Spread corn mixture on 1 side of 2 bread slices and top with remaining slices.
6. Dish out and serve warm.

Calories	Fat	Sugar	Protein	Carbohydrates	Sodium
286	15.3 g	12.6 g	4.6 g	36.1 g	377 mg

Ingredients:
- 2 tbspns butter softened
- 1 cup sweet corn kernels
- 1 roasted green bell pepper, minced
- 4 bread slices, trimmed and cut horizontally
- ¼ cup barbecue sauce

Charming Beet chips

Prep Time	Time to cook	Serv
10 min	15 min	6

Directions:
1. Preheat the AirFryer to 325 and grease an AirFryer basket.
2. Mix all the ingredients in a bowl until well combined.
3. Arrange the beet slices in the AirFryer basket and cook for about 15 min.
4. Dish out and serve warm.

Calories	Fat	Sugar	Protein	Carbohydrates	Sodium
60	4.8 g	3.7 g	0.9 g	5.3 g	236 mg

Ingredients:
- 4 medium beetroots, peeled and thinly sliced
- ¼ tspn smoked paprika
- ½ tspn salt
- 2 tbspns olive oil

Radish Sticks

Prep Time	Time to cook	Serv
10 min	12 min	2

Directions:
1. Preheat the AirFryer to 390 of and grease an AirFryer basket.
2. Mix radish with all other ingredients in a bowl until well combined.
3. Arrange the radish sticks in the AirFryer basket and cook for about 12 min.
4. Dish out and serve warm.

Calories	Fat	Sugar	Protein	Carbohydrates	Sodium
96	7.3 g	5.8 g	0.4 g	8.7 g	26 mg

Ingredients:
- 1 large radish, peeled and cut into sticks
- 1 tbspnn fresh rosemary, finely minced
- 1 tbspnn olive oil
- 2 tspns sugar
- ¼ tspn cayenne pepper
- Salt and black pepper, as needed

Great Crispy Cauliflower Poppers

Prep Time	Time to cook	Serv
10 min	20 min	4

Directions:
1. Preheat the AirFryer to 320 and grease an AirFryer basket.
2. Mix the egg white, ketchup, and hot sauce in a bowl until well combined.
3. Stir in the cauliflower florets and generously coat with marinade.
4. Place breadcrumbs in a shallow dish and dredge the cauliflower florets in it.
5. Arrange the cauliflower florets in the AirFryer basket and cook for about 20 min, flipping once in between.
6. Dish out and serve warm.

Calories	Fat	Sugar	Protein	Carbohydrates	Sodium
94	0.5 g	5.5 g	4.6 g	19.6 g	457 mg

Ingredients:
- 1 large egg white
- ¾ cup panko breadcrumbs
- 4 cups cauliflower florets
- 3 tbspns ketchup
- 2 tbspns hot sauce

Cheese Filled Bell Peppers

Prep Time	Time to cook	Serv
15 min	12 min	3

Directions:
1. Preheat the AirFryer to 320 and grease an AirFryer basket.
2. Chop the tops of the bell peppers and remove all the seeds.
3. Mix mounceszarella cheese, cream cheese, and red chili flakes in a bowl.
4. Stuff this cheese mixture in the bell peppers and put back the tops.
5. Arrange in the AirFryer basket and cook for about 12 min.
6. Remove from the AirFryer and serve hot.

Calories	Fat	Sugar	Protein	Carbohydrates	Sodium
185	13.9 g	7.7 g	4.7 g	12.8 g	120 mg

Ingredients:
- 1 small green bell pepper
- 1 small red bell pepper
- 1 small yellow bell pepper
- ½ cup mounceszarella cheese
- ½ cup cream cheese
- 3 tspns red chili flakes

Simple Cod Nuggets

Prep Time	Time to cook	Serv
15 min	10 min	4

Directions:
1. Preheat the AirFryer to 390 of and grease an AirFryer basket.
2. Place flour in a shallow dish and whisk the eggs in a second dish.
3. Place breadcrumbs, salt, and olive oil in a third shallow dish.
4. Coat the cod strips evenly in flour and dip in the eggs.
5. Roll into the breadcrumbs evenly and arrange the nuggets in an AirFryer basket.
6. Cook for about 10 min and dish out to serve warm.

Calories	Fat	Sugar	Protein	Carbohydrates	Sodium
404	11.6 g	1.5 g	34.6 g	36.8 g	307 mg

Ingredients:
- 1 cup all-purpose flour
- 2 eggs
- ¾ cup breadcrumbs
- 1-pound cod, cut into 1x2½-inch strips
- A pinch of salt
- 2 tbspns olive oil

Hot Mexican Bean Dip

Prep Time	Time to cook	Serv
5 min	15 min	4

Directions:
1. Add half of the cheese, black beans, sour cream, salsa, and hot pepper sauce to a blender and blend until slightly chunky.
2. Add to a casserole dish. Add remaining cheese on top.
3. Position the oven rach in Rack Position 1 and place the dish on top. Select the Bake setting. Set the temperature to 350 F and the time to 15 min.

Calories	Fat	Carbs	Protein
310	20.8 g	16 g	14 g

Ingredients:
- ½ cup of salsa
- ½ cup sour cream
- 2 cans (15 ounces. each) black beans, well-drained
- 8 ounces. Monterey Jack cheese, shredded
- 1 tspn hot pepper sauce

Easy Roasted Pumpkin Seeds

Prep Time	Time to cook	Serv
5 min	50 min	4

Directions:
1. Cut off the top of the pumpkin and scoop out pulp and seeds from it and add to a colander. Separate the pulp and strings from the seeds. Rinse the seeds and dry them.
2. Add seeds on the baking pan in 1 layer.
3. Position the baking pan in Rack Position 2 and select the Bake setting. Set the temperature to 300 F and the time to 30 min.
4. Toss seeds with salt and oil in a bowl. Bake for 20 more min. Serve.

Calories	Fat	Carbs	Protein
421	21 g	37 g	21 g

Ingredients:
- 1 tbspnn vegetable oil
- 1 medium pumpkin
- Salt, to taste

AirFryer Buffalo Cauliflower

Prep Time	Time to cook	Serv
5 min	50 min	4

Directions:
1. Add butter to a mug and microwave to melt it. Whisk in the buffalo sauce.
2. Dip each floret into the above mixture and coat well. Dredge it in the panko/salt mixture and add to the AirFryer basket.
3. Place the Air Fry basket on top of the baking pan and position it in Rack Position 2. Set the temperature to 350 F and the time to 17 min.
4. Serve with mayo.

Calories	Fat	Carbs	Protein
305	19 g	28 g	7 g

Ingredients:
- 1 cup panko breadcrumbs mixed with 1 tspn salt
- 4 cups cauliflower florets
- ¼ cup butter, melted
- ¼ cup buffalo sauce
- Mayo

Super AirFryer Chicken Nuggets

Prep Time	Time to cook	Serv
5 min	20 min	4

Directions:
1. Trim fat from chicken and slice into 1/2 " thick slices. Cut each into 2 nuggets. Season with salt and pepper. Add melted butter to a bowl and add breadcrumbs and parmesan to a separate bowl.
2. Dip each chicken piece in butter then the breadcrumbs/cheese mixture.
3. Add to the AirFryer basket in a single layer.
4. Place the Air Fry basket on top of the baking pan and position it in Rack Position 2. Set the temperature to 390 F and the time to 4 min.

Ingredients:
- ½ cup breadcrumbs
- ½ cup unsalted butter, melted
- 1 boneless, skinless chicken breast
- 2 tbspns Parmesan, grated
- ¼ tspn salt
- 1/8 tspn black pepper

Calories	Fat	Carbs	Protein
364	15 g	5 g	14 g

AirFryer Chickpeas

Prep Time	Time to cook	Serv
5 min	20 min	4

Directions:
1. Drain and rinse the chickpeas. Toss with spices and olive oil.
2. Add chickpeas to the AirFryer basket.
3. Place the Air Fry basket on top of the baking pan and position it in Rack Position 2.
   Set the temperature to 390 F and the time to 15 min, shake a couple of times.
4. Remove peas from AirFryer and season well. Serve.

Ingredients:
- 1 tbspnn olive oil
- 19 ounces. chickpeas drained and rinsed
- ¼ tspn garlic powder
- ½ tspn paprika
- ¼ tspn onion powder
- 1/8 tspn salt

Calories	Fat	Carbs	Protein
251	6 g	36 g	11 g

Fantastic Air Fry Corn Tortilla Chips

Prep Time	Time to cook	Serv
5 min	5 min	4-6

Directions:
1. Cut the tortillas in triangles and brush with oil. Add the chips into the AirFryer basket.
2. Place the Air Fry basket on top of the baking pan and position it in Rack Position 2. Set the temperature to 400 F and the time to 3 min.
3. Season and serve.

Ingredients:
- 1 tbspnn olive oil
- Eight corn tortillas
- Salt

Calories	Fat	Carbs	Protein
309	9 g	31 g	26 g

Pizza Margherita

Prep Time	Time to cook	Serv
5 min	13 min	4

Directions:
1. Grease a baking pan with olive oil and add pizza dough onto the pan. Stretch the m1y to cover the pan and spray with oil.
2. Position the baking pan in Rack Position 2 and select the Bake setting. Set the temperature to 400 F and the time to 5 min.
3. Remove from the oven and flip. Add sauce to the middle and spread in a thin layer and leave 1" border for the crust. Add parmesan and top with mounceszarella. Grease border with oil.
4. Return the pan to the oven and cook for 8 min. Add basil on top. Serve.

Calories	Fat	Carbs	Protein
192	2 g	28 g	10 g

Ingredients:
- ½ cup pizza sauce
- 12 ounces. pizza dough
- 2 tbspns parmesan, grated
- 3 ounces. mounceszarella, sliced
- ¼ cup basil leaves
- Olive oil

Fabulous Cheesy Scallion Sandwich

Prep Time	Time to cook	Serv
10 min	20 min	1

Directions:
1. Spread a tbspn. of butter on a slice of bread.
2. Place it in the cooking basket with the buttered side facing down.
3. Add scallions and cheddar cheese on top. Spread the rest of the butter in the other slice of bread.
4. Place it on top of the sandwich and sprinkle with Parmesan cheese.
5. Cook for 10 min at 356 degrees.

Calories	Fat	Carbs	Protein
511	39.4 g	12.9 g	27.6 g

Ingredients:
- 2 slices of bread
- 1 tbspn. grated parmesan cheese
- ¾ cup grated cheddar cheese
- 2 tbspn. butter
- 2 thinly sliced scallions

Tasty Potatoes Au Gratin

Prep Time	Time to cook	Serv
10 min	26 min	6

Directions:
1. Slice the peeled potatoes thinly.
2. Mix the milk and cream in a bowl. Season with nutmeg, salt, and pepper. Add the potato slices and toss until coated.
3. Arrange the coated potato slices in a baking dish.
4. Pour the seasoning mixture on top.
5. Put the baking dish inside the cooking basket.
6. Cook for 25 min at 390 degrees.

Calories	Fat	Carbs	Protein
429	7.29 g	81.05 g	12.82 g

Ingredients:
- 1 tbspn. of black pepper
- Seven peeled russet potatoes
- ½ cup cream
- ½ cup grated semi-mature cheese
- ½ tbspn. of nutmeg
- ½ cup milk

Fabulous Rosemary Russet Potato Chips

Prep Time | Time to cook | Serv
10 min | 1 hour | 4

Directions:
1. Rinse the potatoes and scrub to clean. Peel and cut them in a lengthwise manner similar to thin chips.
2. Put them in a bowl and soak in water for 30 min.
3. Pat the potato chips with paper towels to dry.
4. Toss the chips in a bowl with olive oil. Transfer them to the cooking basket.
5. Cook for 30 min at 330 F. Shake several times during the cooking process. Toss the cooked chips in a bowl with salt and rosemary while warm.

Ingredients:
- 4 russet potatoes
- ½ tbspn. salt
- 1 tbspn. olive oil
- 2 tbspn. minced rosemary

Calories	Fat	Carbs	Protein
322	3.69 g	66 g	7.5 g

AirFryer Kale Chips

Prep Time | Time to cook | Serv
1 min | 8 min | 4

Directions:
1. Preheat AirFryer to a temperature of 370°F (190°C).
2. Place kale leaves into fryer basket evenly and drizzle cooking oil.
3. Sprinkle some salt and let cook for 8 min.
4. Serve!

Ingredients:
- Salt
- 1-lb. kale leaves
- 1 tbspn. cooking oil

Calories	Fat	Carbs	Protein
66	2.18 g	9.92 g	4.85 g

Dreamy Apple Chips

Prep Time | Time to cook | Serv
2 min | 8 min | 4

Directions:
1. In a bowl, add chips with vinegar and sugar, toss to combine.
2. Preheat AirFryer to a temperature of 400°F (200°C).
3. Place chips into fryer basket, drizzle with a ½ tbspn. of olive oil, and cook for 8 min.
4. Serve!

Ingredients:
- 4 large sliced apples
- ¼ tbspn. apple cider vinegar
- ½ tbspn. olive oil
- 2 tbspn. sugar

Calories	Fat	Carbohydrates	Protein
126	0.95 g	32.08 g	0.58 g

Pork Taquitos

Prep Time	Time to cook	Serv
10 min	10 min	4

Directions:
1. AirFryer preheats you to 380 degrees F.
2. Stir the lime juice over the shredded pork tenderloins.
3. Soften the tortillas in your AirFryer by microwaving it for 10 seconds.
4. For each tortilla, add 3-ounces of the shredded pork and ¼ cup of the mounceszarella cheese.
5. Lightly roll up the tortillas.
6. Then spray a nonstick cooking spray over the tortillas and place it inside your AirFryer.
7. Cook it for 10 min or until it gets a golden brown color, as you flip after 5 min, then Enjoy.

Ingredients:
- Small whole-wheat tortillas, 10.
- Shredded mounceszarella cheese, 2 ½ cup
- Cooked and shredded pork tenderloin, 30 ounces.
- Lime juice, 1 lime

Calories	Fat	Carbs	Protein
210	29 g	15 g	7 g

Glorious Cheesy Crab Dip

Prep Time	Time to cook	Serv
10 min	12 min	8

Directions:
1. Spray AirFryer safe dish with cooking spray and set aside.
2. In a mixing bowl, mix crabmeat, Italian seasoning, cheddar cheese, mayonnaise, sour cream, and cream cheese.
3. Pour crabmeat mixture into the prepared dish.
4. Place dish into the AirFryer basket and cook at 320 F for 12 min.
5. Enjoy.

Ingredients:
- 8 ounces lump crabmeat
- 1 tbspn Italian seasoning
- 1/2 cup cheddar cheese, shredded
- 1/4 cup mayonnaise
- 1/4 cup sour cream
- 4 ounces cream cheese

Calories	Fat	Sugar	Protein	Carbohydrates	Cholesterol
156	12.3 g	0.7 g	8.9 g	2.7 g	58 mg

Cheese Stuffed Mushrooms

Prep Time	Time to cook	Serv
10 min	5 min	3

Directions:
1. Mix cream cheese in a small bowl, chives, butter, bacon, pepper, and salt.
2. Stuff cream cheese mixture into the mushrooms.
3. Place mushrooms into the AirFryer basket and cook at 350 F for 5 min.
4. Enjoy.

Ingredients:
- 12 baby mushrooms
- 1 tbspn chives, diced
- 4 ounces cream cheese
- 2 tbspn butter, melted
- 4 bacon slices, cooked and crumbled
- Pepper
- Salt

Calories	Fat	Sugar	Protein	Carbohydrates	Cholesterol
397	32.2 g	4.9 g	21.1 g	10.6 g	90 mg

Enchanting Parmesan Carrot Fries

Prep Time	Time to cook	Serv
10 min	15 min	4

Directions:
1. In a mixing bowl, toss carrot fries, parmesan cheese, garlic, oil, pepper, and salt.
2. Add carrot fries into the AirFryer basket and cook at 350 F for 15 min. Turn chips halfway through.
3. Enjoy.

Calories	Fat	Sugar	Protein	Carbohydrates	Cholesterol
126	8.5 g	4.5 g	3.3 g	10.7 g	5 mg

Ingredients:
- Six carrots, peeled and cut into fries shapes
- 2 tbspn parmesan cheese, grated
- 2 tbspn garlic, diced
- 2 tbspn olive oil
- Pepper
- Salt

Chicken Stuffed Poblanos

Prep Time	Time to cook	Serv
10 min	15 min	6

Directions:
1. In a small bowl, mix chicken, spinach artichoke dip, and half cheddar cheese.
2. Stuff chicken mixture into the poblano peppers.
3. Place stuffed poblano peppers into the AirFryer basket. Sprinkle remaining cheese on top of peppers.
4. Cook at 350 F for 12-15 min.
5. Enjoy.

Calories	Fat	Sugar	Protein	Carbohydrates	Cholesterol
91	5.6 g	1.5 g	7.1 g	3 g	24 mg

Ingredients:
- 3 poblano peppers, cut in half & remove seeds
- 2 ounces cheddar cheese, grated
- 1 1/2 cup spinach artichoke dip
- 1 cup chicken breast, cooked and minced

Crispy Tofu

Prep Time	Time to cook	Serv
10 min	15 min	4

Directions:
1. In a mixing bowl, mix tofu, sesame oil, vinegar, and soy sauce. Marinate for 15 min.
2. Spray AirFryer basket with cooking spray.
3. Remove tofu from marinade and place into the AirFryer basket and cook at 400 F for 15 min. Turn tofu after 10 min.
4. Enjoy.

Calories	Fat	Sugar	Protein	Carbohydrates	Cholesterol
120	7.7 g	0.7 g	11.7 g	2.9 g	0 mg

Ingredients:
- 16 ounces extra-firm tofu, and cut into cubes
- 1 tbspn sesame oil
- 1 tbspn rice vinegar
- 2 tbspn soy sauce

Gorgeous Hasselback Zucchini

Prep Time	Time to cook	Serv
10 min	20 min	3

Directions:
1. The AirFryer should preheat at 3500F for 5 min.
2. Line up chopsticks on both facets of the zucchini and slice thinly till you hit the stick. Brush the zucchinis with olive.
3. Place the zucchini in the AirFryer. Bake for 20 min at 350F.
4. Meanwhile, combine the coconut cream and lemon juice in a mixing bowl. Season with salt and pepper to taste.
5. Once the zucchini is cooked, scoop the coconut cream mixture and drizzle on top. Sprinkle with bacon bits.
6. Enjoy!

Ingredients:
- 3 medium zucchini
- 3 tbspns olive oil
- 4 tbspns coconut cream
- 1 tbspnn lemon juice
- Salt and pepper to taste
- 3 slices bacon, fried and crumbled

Calories	Fat	Sugar	Protein	Carbohydrates
245	22.3 g	4 g	6.7 g	6.7 g

Fat Burger Bombs

Prep Time	Time to cook	Serv
2 hour	20 min	6

Directions:
1. In a mixing bowl, integrate all ingredients besides for the olive oil.
2. Use your hands to form small balls with the mixture. Place in a baking sheet and allow it to set in the fridge for at least 2 hours.
3. Preheat the AirFryer at 350F for 5 min.
4. Brush the meatballs with olive oil on all sides.
5. Place in the AirFryer basket.
6. Cook for 20 min at 350F.
7. Halfway through the Time to cook, shake the fryer basket for a more even cooking.
8. Enjoy!

Ingredients:
- 12 slices uncured bacon, minced
- 1 cup almond flour
- 2 eggs, beaten
- ½ pound ground beef
- Salt and pepper to taste
- 3 tbspns olive oil

Calories	Fat	Sugar	Protein	Carbohydrates
402	32.3 g	0.9 g	24 g	4.5 g

Crispy Keto Pork Bites

Prep Time	Time to cook	Serv
2 hour	25 min	3

Directions:
1. Place all comp1nts in a mixing bowl and marinate within the fridge for 2 hours.
2. Preheat the AirFryer at 350F for 5 min.
3. Place the pork strips in the AirFryer and bake for 25 min at 350F.
4. Enjoy!

Ingredients:
- ½-pound pork belly, sliced to thin strips
- 1 tbspnn butter
- 1 medium onion, diced
- 4 tbspns coconut cream
- Salt and pepper to taste

Calories	Fat	Sugar	Protein	Carbohydrates
307	24.3 g	1.7 g	18 g	3.7 g

Cute Air Fried Kale Chips

Prep Time	Time to cook	Serv
5 min	10 min	2

Directions:
1. Preheat the AirFryer at 350F for 5 min.
2. In a bowl, combine all ingredients until the kale leaves are coated with the other parts.
3. Place in a fryer basket and cook for 10 min at 3500F until crispy.
4. Enjoy!

Calories	Fat	Sugar	Protein	Carbohydrates
220	18 g	2.8 g	5.5 g	13.5 g

Ingredients:
- 1 bunch kale, minced into large pieces
- 2 tbspns olive oil
- 2 tbspns almond flour
- 1 tspn garlic powder
- Salt and pepper to taste

Bacon Jalapeno Poppers

Prep Time	Time to cook	Serv
15 min	15 min	8

Directions:
1. Preheat the AirFryer at 350F for 5 min.
2. In a blending bowl, mix the cream cheese, cheddar cheese, salt, and paprika collectively till nicely combined.
3. Scoop a tspn onto each half of jalapeno peppers.
4. Use a thin strip of bacon and wrap it around the cheese-filled jalapeno half. Wear gloves when doing this step because jalapeno is very spicy.
5. Place inside the AirFryer basket and prepare dinner for 15 min at 350F.
6. Enjoy!

Calories	Fat	Sugar	Protein	Carbohydrates
132	10.1 g	1.8 g	8 g	3 g

Ingredients:
- 4-ounce cream cheese
- ¼ cup cheddar cheese, shredded
- Salt to taste
- 1 tspn paprika
- 16 fresh jalapenos, sliced lengthwise and seeds removed
- 16 strips of uncured bacon, cut into half

Pleasant Crispy Air Fried Broccoli

Prep Time	Time to cook	Serv
5 min	15 min	6

Directions:
1. Preheat the AirFryer at 350F for 5 min.
2. In a bowl, combine all ingredients until the broccoli florets are coated with the other parts.
3. Place in a fryer basket and cook at 350F for 15 min until crispy.
4. Enjoy!

Calories	Fat	Sugar	Protein	Carbohydrates
32	1.8 g	0.6 g	1.3 g	3.5 g

Ingredients:
- ½-pound broccoli, cut into florets
- 2 tbspns coconut milk
- ¼ tspn turmeric powder
- 1 tbspnn almond flour
- Salt and pepper to taste
- 1 tspn Garam Masala

Garlic-Roasted Mushrooms

Prep Time	Time to cook	Serv
5 min	25 min	4

Directions:
1. Preheat the AirFryer at 350F for 5 min.
2. Place all ingredients in a baking dish that will fit in the AirFryer.
3. Mix to combine. Place the baking dish in the AirFryer.
4. Cook for 25 min at 350F.
5. Enjoy!

Ingredients:
- 2 pounds mushrooms
- 3 tbspns heart-healthy oil
- ½ tspn dicedgarlic
- Salt and pepper to taste
- 2 tspns herbs de Provence

Calories	Fat	Sugar	Protein	Carbohydrates
158	11.8 g	5.3 g	5 g	12.3 g

Marvelous Baked Zucchini Fries

Prep Time	Time to cook	Serv
5 min	15 min	6

Directions:
1. Preheat the AirFryer at 425F for 5 min.
2. In a mixing bowl, combine the garlic powder and almond flour. Season with salt and pepper to taste.
3. Soak the zucchini in the beaten eggs and then dredge in the almond flour mixture. Place inside the AirFryer basket and prepare dinner for 15 min at 450F.
4. Enjoy!

Ingredients:
- 3 medium zucchinis, sliced into fry sticks
- 2 large egg whites, beaten
- ½ cup almond flour
- ¼ tspn garlic powder
- Salt and pepper to taste

Calories	Fat	Sugar	Protein	Carbohydrates
77	5 g	2.3 g	4.5 g	5.2 g

AirFryer Brussels Sprouts

Prep Time	Time to cook	Serv
5 min	15 min	4

Directions:
1. Preheat the AirFryer at 350F for 5 min.
2. Mix all substances in a bowl until the Brussels sprouts are adequately coated.
3. Place in the AirFryer basket.
4. Cook for 15 min at 350F.
5. Enjoy!

Ingredients:
- 2 cups Brussels sprouts, halved
- 2 tbspns olive oil
- 1 tbspnn balsamic vinegar
- ¼ tspn salt

Calories	Fat	Sugar	Protein	Carbohydrates
91	7.3 g	2 g	2 g	6.3 g

Wonderful AirFryer Garlic Chicken Wings

　　　　Prep Time　　　Time to cook　　Serv
　　　　5 min　　　　　25 min　　　　　4

Directions:
1. Preheat the AirFryer at 400F for 5 min.
2. In a mixing bowl, combine the chicken wings, almond flour, stevia powder, and garlic. Season with salt and pepper to taste.
3. Place in the AirFryer basket and cook for 25 min at 400F.
4. Halfway through the Time to cook, make sure that you give the fryer basket a shake.
5. Once cooked, place in a bowl and drizzle with melted butter. Toss to coat.
6. Enjoy!

Calories	Fat	Sugar	Protein	Carbohydrates
558	46 g	0.9 g	28.5 g	14.5 g

Ingredients:
- 16 pieces of chicken wings
- ¾ cup almond flour
- 2 tbspns stevia powder
- 4 tbspns dicedgarlic
- Salt and pepper to taste
- ¼ cup butter, melted

Old Bay Chicken Wings

　　　　Prep Time　　　Time to cook　　Serv
　　　　5 min　　　　　25 min　　　　　4

Directions:
1. Preheat the AirFryer at 350F for 5 min.
2. In a mixing bowl, integrate all ingredients except for the butter.
3. Place in the AirFryer basket.
4. Cook for 25 min at 350F.
5. Halfway through the Time to cook, shake the fryer basket for even cooking.
6. Once cooked, drizzle with melted butter.
7. Enjoy!

Calories	Fat	Sugar	Protein	Carbohydrates
7	58.8 g	1 g	28.8 g	5 g

Ingredients:
- 16 pieces of chicken wings
- ¾ cup almond flour
- 1 tbspnn old bay spices
- 1 tspn lemon juice, freshly squeezed
- Salt and pepper to taste
- ½ cup butter

Mushrooms And Garlic Mushrooms

　　　　Prep Time　　　Time to cook　　Serv
　　　　2 hour　　　　　20 min　　　　　4

Directions:
1. Place all ingredients in a dish and mix until well combined.
2. Marinate for 2 hours in the fridge.
3. Preheat the AirFryer at 350F for 5 min.
4. Place the mushrooms in a heatproof dish that will fit in the AirFryer.
5. Cook for 20 min at 350F.
6. Enjoy!

Calories	Fat	Sugar	Protein	Carbohydrates
84	5.6 g	4.1 g	2.5 g	7.8 g

Ingredients:
- 2 pounds mushrooms, sliced
- 3 tbspns olive oil
- 2 cloves of garlic, diced
- ¼ cup coconut aminos

Magical AirFryer Tofu Tots

Prep Time	Time to cook	Serv
30 min	20 min	6

Directions:
1. Whisk together oil, paprika, and salt in a large bowl. Add tofu pieces and leave to marinate for 30 min.
2. Dust tofu with cornstarch.
3. Arrange tofu pieces in the frying basket and cook for 20 min at 370F, shaking to flip halfway through the Time to cook.

Ingredients:
- 400 grams Firm Tofu, cut into bite-sized cubes
- ¼ cup Sunflower Oil
- 1 tbspn Paprika
- ½ tbspn Salt
- 1 tbspn Cornstarch

Calories	Fat	Carbs	Protein
183	15 g	4 g	10 g

Buffalo Cauliflower Wings

Prep Time	Time to cook	Serv
10 min	14 min	4

Directions:
1. Spray AirFryer basket with cooking spray.
2. In a bowl, mix together buffalo sauce, butter, pepper, and salt.
3. Add cauliflower florets into the AirFryer basket and cook at 400 F for 7 min.
4. Transfer cauliflower florets into the buffalo sauce mixture and toss well.
5. Again, add cauliflower florets into the AirFryer basket and cook for 7 min more at 400 F.
6. Enjoy.

Ingredients:
- 1 cauliflower head, cut into florets
- 1 tbspn butter, melted
- 1/2 cup buffalo sauce
- Pepper
- Salt

Calories	Fat	Sugar	Protein	Carbohydrates	Cholesterol
44	3 g	1.6 g	1.3 g	3.8 g	8 mg

Air Fry Bacon Preparation

Prep Time	Time to cook	Serv
5 min	10 min	11

Directions:
1. Place half bacon slices in AirFryer basket.
2. Cook at 400 F for 10 min.
3. Cook remaining half bacon slices using same steps.
4. Enjoy.

Ingredients:
- 11 bacon slices

Calories	Fat	Sugar	Protein	Carbohydrates	Cholesterol
103	7.9 g	0 g	7 g	0.3 g	21 mg

Crunchy Bacon Bites

Prep Time	Time to cook	Serv
5 min	10 min	4

Directions:
1. Add bacon pieces in a bowl.
2. Add hot sauce and toss well.
3. Add crushed pork rinds and toss until bacon pieces are well coated.
4. Transfer bacon pieces in AirFryer basket and cook at 350 F for 10 min.
5. Enjoy.

Calories	Fat	Sugar	Protein	Carbohydrates	Cholesterol
112	9.7 g	0.2 g	5.2 g	0.3 g	3 mg

Ingredients:
- 4 bacon strips, cut into small pieces
- 1/2 cup pork rinds, crushed
- 1/4 cup hot sauce

Exciting Italian Dip

Prep Time	Time to cook	Serv
10 min	12 min	8

Directions:
1. Add parmesan cheese and cream cheese into the food processor and process until smooth.
2. Transfer cheese mixture into the AirFryer pan and spread evenly.
3. Pour basil pesto on top of cheese layer.
4. Sprinkle roasted pepper on top of basil pesto layer.
5. Sprinkle mounceszarella cheese on top of pepper layer and place dish in AirFryer basket.
6. Cook dip at 250 F for 12 min.
7. Enjoy.

Calories	Fat	Sugar	Protein	Carbohydrates	Cholesterol
115	10.7 g	0.6 g	3.6 g	1.6 g	34 mg

Ingredients:
- 8 ounces cream cheese, softened
- 1 cup mounceszarella cheese, shredded
- 1/2 cup roasted red peppers
- 1/3 cup basil pesto
- 1/4 cup parmesan cheese, grated

Sweet Potato Tots

Prep Time	Time to cook	Serv
10 min	31 min	24

Directions:
1. Add water in large pot and bring to boil. Add sweet potatoes in pot and boil for 15 min. Drain well.
2. Grated boil sweet potatoes into a large bowl using a grated.
3. Add cajun seasoning and salt in grated sweet potatoes and mix until well combined.
4. Spray AirFryer basket with cooking spray.
5. Make small tot of sweet potato mixture and place in AirFryer basket.
6. Cook at 400 F for 8 min. Turn tots to another side and cook for 8 min more.

Calories	Fat	Sugar	Protein	Carbohydrates	Cholesterol
15	0 g	0.6 g	0.2 g	3.5 g	0 mg

Ingredients:
- 2 sweet potatoes, peeled
- 1/2 tbspn cajun seasoning
- Salt

Magnificent Ranch Kale Chips

Prep Time	Time to cook	Serv
5 min	5 min	4

Directions:
1. Add all ingredients into the large mixing bowl and toss well.
2. Spray AirFryer basket with cooking spray.
3. Add kale in AirFryer basket and cook for 4-5 min at 370 F. Shake halfway through.
4. Enjoy.

Ingredients:
- 4 cups kale, stemmed
- 1 tbspn nutritional yeast flakes
- 2 tbspn ranch seasoning
- 2 tbspn olive oil
- 1/4 tbspn salt

Calories	Fat	Sugar	Protein	Carbohydrates	Cholesterol
102	7 g	0 g	3 g	8 g	0 mg

Curried Sweet Potato Fries

Prep Time	Time to cook	Serv
10 min	20 min	3

Directions:
1. Add all ingredients into the large mixing bowl and toss well.
2. Spray AirFryer basket with cooking spray.
3. Transfer sweet potato fries in the AirFryer basket.
4. Cook for 20 min at 370 F. Shake halfway through.
5. Enjoy.

Ingredients:
- 2 small sweet potatoes, peel and cut into fries shape
- 1/4 tbspn coriander
- 1/2 tbspn curry powder
- 2 tbspn olive oil
- 1/4 tbspn sea salt

Calories	Fat	Sugar	Protein	Carbohydrates	Cholesterol
118	9 g	2 g	1 g	9 g	0 mg

Scrumptious Roasted Almonds

Prep Time	Time to cook	Serv
5 min	8 min	8

Directions:
1. Add pepper, paprika, garlic powder, and soy sauce in a bowl and Stir.
2. Add almonds and stir to coat.
3. Spray AirFryer basket with cooking spray.
4. Add almonds in AirFryer basket and cook for 6-8 min at 320 F. Shake basket after every 2 min.
5. Enjoy.

Ingredients:
- 2 cups almonds
- 1/4 tbspn pepper
- 1 tbspn paprika
- 1 tbspn garlic powder
- 1 tbspn soy sauce

Calories	Fat	Sugar	Protein	Carbohydrates	Cholesterol
143	11.9 g	1.3 g	5.4 g	6.2 g	0 mg

Pepperoni Chips

Prep Time	Time to cook	Serv
2 min	8 min	6

Directions:
1. Place 1 batch of pepperoni slices in the AirFryer basket.
2. Cook for 8 min at 360 F.
3. Cook remaining pepperoni slices using same steps.
4. Enjoy.

Calories	Fat	Sugar	Protein	Carbohydrates	Cholesterol
51	1 g	1.3 g	0 g	2 g	0 mg

Ingredients:
- 6 ounces pepperoni slices

Yummy Crispy Eggplant

Prep Time	Time to cook	Serv
5 min	20 min	4

Directions:
1. Add all ingredients into the large mixing bowl and toss well.
2. Transfer eggplant mixture into the AirFryer basket.
3. Cook at 375 F for 20 min. Shake basket halfway through.
4. Enjoy.
5.

Calories	Fat	Sugar	Protein	Carbohydrates	Cholesterol
99	7.5 g	4.5 g	1.5 g	8.7 g	0 mg

Ingredients:
- 1 eggplant, cut into 1-inch pieces
- 1/2 tbspn Italian seasoning
- 1 tbspn paprika
- 1/2 tbspn red pepper
- 1 tbspn garlic powder
- 2 tbspn olive oil

Steak Nuggets

Prep Time	Time to cook	Serv
10 min	15 min	4

Directions:
1. Add egg in a small bowl.
2. In a shallow bowl, mix together pork rind, cheese, and salt.
3. Dip each steak chunk in egg then coat with pork rind mixture and place on a plate. Place in refrigerator for 30 min.
4. Spray AirFryer basket with cooking spray.
5. Preheat the AirFryer to 400 F.
6. Place steak nuggets in AirFryer basket and cook for 15-18 min or until cooked. Shake after every 4 min.
7. Enjoy.

Calories	Fat	Sugar	Protein	Carbohydrates	Cholesterol
609	38 g	0.4 g	63 g	2 g	195 mg

Ingredients:
- 1 lb beef steak, cut into chunks
- 1 large egg, lightly beaten
- 1/2 cup pork rind, crushed
- 1/2 cup parmesan cheese, grated
- 1/2 tbspn salt

Scrummy Cheese Bacon Jalapeno Poppers

Prep Time: 10 min
Time to cook: 5 min
Serv: 5

Directions:
1. In a bowl, combine together bacon, cream cheese, and cheddar cheese.
2. Stuff each jalapeno half with bacon cheese mixture.
3. Spray AirFryer basket with cooking spray.
4. Place stuffed jalapeno halved in AirFryer basket and cook at 370 F for 5 min.
5. Enjoy.

Ingredients:
- 10 fresh jalapeno peppers, cut in half and remove seeds
- 2 bacon slices, cooked and crumbled
- 1/4 cup cheddar cheese, shredded
- 6 ounces cream cheese, softened

Calories	Fat	Sugar	Protein	Carbohydrates	Cholesterol
195	17.3 g	1 g	7.2 g	3.2 g	52 mg

Cabbage Chips

Prep Time: 10 min
Time to cook: 30 min
Serv: 6

Directions:
1. Preheat the AirFryer to 250 F.
2. Add all ingredients into the large mixing bowl and toss well.
3. Spray AirFryer basket with cooking spray.
4. Divide cabbage in batches.
5. Add 1 cabbage chips batch in AirFryer basket and cook for 25-30 min at 250 F or until chips are crispy and lightly golden brown.
6. Enjoy.

Ingredients:
- 1 large cabbage head, tear cabbage leaves into pieces
- 2 tbspn olive oil
- 1/4 cup parmesan cheese, grated
- Pepper
- Salt

Calories	Fat	Sugar	Protein	Carbohydrates	Cholesterol
96	5.1 g	6.7 g	3 g	12.1 g	1 mg

Healthy Broccoli Tots

Prep Time: 10 min
Time to cook: 25 min
Serv: 4

Directions:
1. Add broccoli into the microwave-safe bowl and microwave for 3 min.
2. Transfer steamed broccoli into the food processor and process until it looks like rice. Transfer broccoli to a large mixing bowl.
3. Add remaining ingredients into the bowl and mix until well combined.
4. Spray AirFryer basket with cooking spray.
5. Make small tots from broccoli mixture and place into the AirFryer basket.
6. Cook broccoli tots for 12 min at 375 F.
7. Enjoy.

Ingredients:
- 1 lb broccoli, minced
- 1/2 cup almond flour
- 1/4 cup ground flaxseed
- 1/2 tbspn garlic powder
- 1 tbspn salt

Calories	Fat	Sugar	Protein	Carbohydrates	Cholesterol
161	9.2 g	2.1 g	7.5 g	12.8 g	0 mg

Finger-Licking Crispy & Healthy Kale Chips

Prep Time   Time to cook   Serv
5 min   5 min   2

Directions:
1. Preheat the AirFryer to 370 F.
2. Add all ingredients into the large bowl and toss well.
3. Transfer kale mixture into the AirFryer basket and cook for 3 min.
4. Shake basket well and cook for 2 min more.
5. Enjoy.

Ingredients:
- 1 bunch of kale, remove stem and cut into pieces
- 1/2 tbspn garlic powder
- 1 tbspn olive oil
- 1/2 tbspn salt

Calories	Fat	Sugar	Protein	Carbohydrates	Cholesterol
37	1 g	1 g	3 g	6 g	0 mg

Juicy Meatballs

Prep Time   Time to cook   Serv
10 min   14 min   5

Directions:
1. Spray AirFryer basket with cooking spray.
2. Preheat the AirFryer to 390 F.
3. Add all ingredients into the bowl and mix until well combined.
4. Make balls from meat mixture and place into the AirFryer basket.
5. Cook meatballs for 14 min. Shake basket 3-4 times while cooking.
6. Enjoy.

Ingredients:
- 1 lb ground beef
- 1 tbspn garlic powder
- 1 egg, lightly beaten
- 1/2 onion, diced
- 1/4 tbspn pepper
- 1 tbspn salt

Calories	Fat	Sugar	Protein	Carbohydrates	Cholesterol
259	18 g	0.5 g	17 g	3 g	95 mg

Delish Bacon Jalapeno Poppers

Prep Time   Time to cook   Serv
10 min   8 min   10

Directions:
1. Preheat the AirFryer to 370 F.
2. Stuff cream cheese into each jalapeno half.
3. Wrap each jalapeno half with half bacon strip and place in the AirFryer basket.
4. Cook for 6-8 min.
5. Enjoy.

Ingredients:
- 10 jalapeno peppers, cut in half and remove seeds
- 1/3 cup cream cheese, softened
- 5 bacon strips, cut in half

Calories	Fat	Sugar	Protein	Carbohydrates	Cholesterol
83	7.4 g	0.5 g	2.8 g	1.3 g	9 mg

BBQ Chicken Wings

Prep Time	Time to cook	Serv
10 min	15 min	4

Directions:
1. Preheat the AirFryer to 400 F.
2. Season chicken wings with garlic powder and pepper and place into the AirFryer basket.
3. Cook chicken wings for 15 min. Shake basket 3-4 times while cooking.
4. Transfer cooked chicken wings in a large mixing bowl. Pour BBQ sauce over chicken wings and toss to coat.
5. Enjoy.

Ingredients:
- 1 lb chicken wings
- 1/2 cup BBQ sauce, sugar-free
- 1/4 tbspn garlic powder
- Pepper

Calories	Fat	Sugar	Protein	Carbohydrates	Cholesterol
263	8.5 g	8 g	32 g	11.5 g	100 mg

Healthy Vegetable Kabobs

Prep Time	Time to cook	Serv
10 min	10 min	4

Directions:
1. Cut all vegetables into 1-inch pieces.
2. Thread vegetables onto the soaked wooden skewers and season with pepper and salt.
3. Place skewers into the AirFryer basket and cook for 10 min at 390 F. Turn halfway through.
4. Enjoy.

Ingredients:
- 1/2 onion
- 1 zucchini
- 1 eggplant
- 2 bell peppers
- Pepper
- Salt

Calories	Fat	Sugar	Protein	Carbohydrates	Cholesterol
61	0.5 g	8 g	2 g	14 g	0 mg

Luscious Shrimp Kabobs

Prep Time	Time to cook	Serv
10 min	8 min	2

Directions:
1. Preheat the AirFryer to 350 F.
2. Add shrimp, lime juice, garlic, pepper, and salt into the bowl and toss well.
3. Thread shrimp onto the soaked wooden skewers and place into the AirFryer basket.
4. Cook for 8 min. Turn halfway through.
5. Enjoy.

Ingredients:
- 1 cup shrimp
- 1 lime juice
- 1 garlic clove, diced
- 1/4 tbspn pepper
- 1/8 tbspn salt

Calories	Fat	Sugar	Protein	Carbohydrates	Cholesterol
75	1 g	0.5 g	13 g	4 g	160 mg

Mild & Sweet Shishito Peppers

Prep Time | Time to cook | Serv
5 min | 5 min | 2

Directions:
1. Add shishito peppers into the bowl and toss with olive oil.
2. Add shishito peppers into the AirFryer basket and cook at 390 F for 5 min. Shake halfway through.
3. Season shishito peppers with salt.
4. Enjoy.

Calories	Fat	Sugar	Protein	Carbohydrates	Cholesterol
20	1 g	2 g	1 g	5 g	0 mg

Ingredients:
- 20 shishito Peppers
- 1 tbspn olive oil
- Salt

Mouthwatering Broccoli Cheese Nuggets

Prep Time | Time to cook | Serv
10 min | 15 min | 4

Directions:
1. Preheat the AirFryer to 325 F.
2. Spray AirFryer basket with cooking spray.
3. Add cooked broccoli into the bowl and using masher mash broccoli into the small pieces.
4. Add remaining ingredients to the bowl and mix well to combine.
5. Make small nuggets from broccoli mixture and place into the AirFryer basket.
6. Cook broccoli nuggets for 15 min.
7. Turn halfway through.
8. Enjoy.

Calories	Fat	Sugar	Protein	Carbohydrates	Cholesterol
175	13 g	1 g	12 g	5 g	30 mg

Ingredients:
- 1/4 cup almond flour
- 2 cups broccoli florets, cooked until soft
- 1 cup cheddar cheese, shredded
- 2 egg whites
- 1/8 tbspn salt

Artichoke Dip

Prep Time | Time to cook | Serv
10 min | 24 min | 6

Directions:
1. Preheat the AirFryer to 325 F.
2. Add all ingredients into the blender and blend until smooth.
3. Pour artichoke mixture into AirFryer baking dish and place into the AirFryer basket.
4. Cook dip for 24 min.
5. Serve with vegetables and enjoy.

Calories	Fat	Sugar	Protein	Carbohydrates	Cholesterol
190	13 g	2.5 g	7.5 g	13 g	25 mg

Ingredients:
- 15 ounces artichoke hearts, drained
- 1 tbspn Worcestershire sauce
- 3 cups arugula, minced
- 1 cup cheddar cheese, shredded
- 1 tbspn onion, diced
- 1/2 cup mayonnaise

Yummy Chicken Dip

Prep Time	Time to cook	Serv
10 min	20 min	6

Directions:
1. Preheat the AirFryer to 325 F.
2. Add all ingredients in a large bowl and mix until well combined.
3. Transfer mixture in AirFryer baking dish and place in the AirFryer.
4. Cook chicken dip for 20 min.
5. Enjoy.

Calories	Fat	Sugar	Protein	Carbohydrates	Cholesterol
245	17 g	0.2 g	16 g	1.5 g	85 mg

Ingredients:
- 2 cups chicken, cooked and shredded
- 3/4 cup sour cream
- 1/4 tbspn onion powder
- 8 ounces cream cheese, softened
- 3 tbspn hot sauce
- 1/4 tbspn garlic powder

Seductive Smoked Almonds

Prep Time	Time to cook	Serv
5 min	6 min	6

Directions:
1. Add almond into the bowl and remaining ingredients and toss to coat.
2. Transfer almonds into the AirFryer basket and cook at 320 F for 6 min. Shake halfway through.
3. Enjoy.

Calories	Fat	Sugar	Protein	Carbohydrates	Cholesterol
107	9.6 g	0.7 g	3.4 g	3.7 g	0 mg

Ingredients:
- 1 cup almonds
- 1/4 tbspn cumin
- 1 tbspn chili powder
- 1/4 tbspn smoked paprika
- 2 tbspn olive oil

Parmesan Zucchini Bites

Prep Time	Time to cook	Serv
10 min	10 min	6

Directions:
1. Add all ingredients into the bowl and mix until well combined.
2. Spray AirFryer basket with cooking spray.
3. Make small balls from zucchini mixture and place into the AirFryer basket and cook at 400 F for 10 min.
4. Enjoy.

Calories	Fat	Sugar	Protein	Carbohydrates	Cholesterol
88	6.2 g	3.2 g	3.7 g	6.6 g	29 mg

Ingredients:
- 1 egg, lightly beaten
- 4 zucchinis, grated and squeeze out all liquid
- 1 cup shredded coconut
- 1 tbspn Italian seasoning
- 1/2 cup parmesan cheese, grated

Toothsome Broccoli Pop-corn

Prep Time	Time to cook	Serv
10 min	6 min	4

Directions:
1. In a bowl whisk egg yolk with melted butter, pepper, and salt. Add coconut flour and stir to combine.
2. Preheat the AirFryer to 400 F.
3. Spray AirFryer basket with cooking spray.
4. Coat each broccoli floret with egg mixture and place into the AirFryer basket and cook for 6 min.
5. Enjoy.

Ingredients:
- 2 cups broccoli florets
- 2 cups coconut flour
- 1/4 cup butter, melted
- 4 eggs yolks
- Pepper
- Salt

Calories	Fat	Sugar	Protein	Carbohydrates	Cholesterol
147	12 g	2 g	2 g	7 g	31 mg

Easy Rosemary Beans

Prep Time	Time to cook	Serv
10 min	5 min	2

Directions:
1. Preheat the AirFryer to 390 F.
2. Add all ingredients into the bowl and toss well.
3. Transfer green beans into the AirFryer basket and cook for 5 min.
4. Enjoy.

Ingredients:
- 1 cup green beans, minced
- 2 garlic cloves, diced
- 2 tbspn rosemary, minced
- 1 tbspn butter, melted
- 1/2 tbspn salt

Calories	Fat	Sugar	Protein	Carbohydrates	Cholesterol
83	6.4 g	0.8 g	1.4 g	7 g	15 mg

Appetizing Cheesy Brussels sprouts

Prep Time	Time to cook	Serv
10 min	5 min	2

Directions:
1. Toss Brussels sprouts with oil and season with salt.
2. Preheat the AirFryer to 375 F.
3. Transfer Brussels sprouts into the AirFryer basket and top with shredded cheese.
4. Cook for 5 min.
5. Enjoy.

Ingredients:
- 1 cup Brussels sprouts, halved
- 1/4 cup mounceszarella cheese, shredded
- 1 tbspn olive oil
- 1/4 tbspn salt

Calories	Fat	Sugar	Protein	Carbohydrates	Cholesterol
89	7.8 g	1 g	2.5 g	4.1 g	2 mg

Cute Cajun Kale Chips

Prep Time	Time to cook	Serv
10 min	4 min	4

Directions:
1. Add all ingredients into the large bowl and toss well.
2. Transfer kale into the AirFryer basket and cook at 195 F for 4-5 min.
3. Enjoy.

Calories	Fat	Sugar	Protein	Carbohydrates	Cholesterol
106	7.1 g	1.7 g	2.2 g	8.3 g	0 mg

Ingredients:
- 3 kale heads, cut into pieces
- 2 tbspn Worcestershire sauce
- 2 tbspn sesame oil
- 1 1/2 tbspn Cajun spice mix
- Pepper
- Salt

Cheese Dill Mushrooms

Prep Time	Time to cook	Serv
10 min	5 min	6

Directions:
1. Chop mushrooms stem finely and place into the bowl.
2. Add parsley, dill, cheese, butter, and salt into the bowl and mix until well combined. Preheat the AirFryer to 400 F.
3. Stuff bowl mixture into the mushroom caps and place into the AirFryer basket.
4. Cook mushrooms for 5 min.
5. Enjoy.

Calories	Fat	Sugar	Protein	Carbohydrates	Cholesterol
141	11.5 g	0.9 g	8.5 g	1.9 g	35 mg

Ingredients:
- 9 ounces mushrooms, cut stems
- 1 tbspn dried parsley
- 1 tbspn dried dill
- 6 ounces cheddar cheese, shredded
- 1 tbspn butter
- 1/2 tbspn salt

Healthy Toasted Nuts

Prep Time	Time to cook	Serv
10 min	9 min	4

Directions:
1. Preheat the AirFryer to 320 F.
2. Add all nuts into the AirFryer basket and cook for 8 min. Shake halfway through.
3. Drizzle nuts with olive oil and season with salt and toss well.
4. Cook nuts for 1 min more.
5. Enjoy.

Calories	Fat	Sugar	Protein	Carbohydrates	Cholesterol
240	24.9 g	1.1 g	8.5 g	4.1 g	0 mg

Ingredients:
- 1/2 cup macadamia nuts
- 1/2 cup pecans
- 1 tbspn olive oil
- 1/4 cup walnuts
- 1/4 cup hazelnuts
- 1 tbspn salt

Easy Radish Chips

Prep Time: 10 min
Time to cook: 15 min
Serv: 12

Directions:
1. Preheat the AirFryer to 375 F.
2. Add all ingredients into the large bowl and toss well.
3. Add radish slices into the AirFryer basket and cook for 15 min. Shake basket 2-3 times while cooking.
4. Enjoy.

Ingredients:
- 1 lb radish, wash and slice into chips
- 2 tbspn olive oil
- 1/4 tbspn pepper
- 1 tbspn salt

Calories	Fat	Sugar	Protein	Carbohydrates	Cholesterol
26	2.4 g	0.7 g	0.3 g	1.3 g	0 mg

Parmesan Turnip Slices

Prep Time: 10 min
Time to cook: 10 min
Serv: 8

Directions:
1. Preheat the AirFryer to 360 F.
2. Add all ingredients into the mixing bowl and toss to coat.
3. Transfer turnip slices into the AirFryer basket and cook for 10 min.
4. Enjoy.

Ingredients:
- 1 lb turnip, peel and cut into slices
- 1 tbspn olive oil
- 3 ounces parmesan cheese, shredded
- 1 tbspn garlic powder
- 1 tbspn salt

Calories	Fat	Sugar	Protein	Carbohydrates	Cholesterol
66	4.1 g	2.2 g	4 g	4.3 g	8 mg

Enchanting Chili Pepper Kale Chips

Prep Time: 10 min
Time to cook: 8 min
Serv: 14

Directions:
1. Preheat the AirFryer to 370 F.
2. Add kale pieces into the AirFryer basket. Drizzle kale with oil.
3. Sprinkle chili pepper and salt over the kale and toss well.
4. Cook kale for 5 min. Shake well and cook for 3 min more.
5. Enjoy.

Ingredients:
- 1 lb kale, wash, dry and cut into pieces
- 2 tbspn olive oil
- 1 tbspn chili pepper
- 1 tbspn salt

Calories	Fat	Sugar	Protein	Carbohydrates	Cholesterol
22	0.7 g	0 g	1 g	3.4 g	0 mg

Cucumber Chips

Prep Time	Time to cook	Serv
10 min	11 min	12

Directions:
1. Wash cucumber and slice thinly using a mandolin slicer.
2. Preheat the AirFryer to 370 F.
3. Add cucumber slices into the AirFryer basket and sprinkle with garlic powder, paprika, and salt.
4. Toss well and cook for 11 min. Shake halfway through.
5. Enjoy.

Ingredients:
- 1 lb cucumber
- 1/2 tbspn garlic powder
- 1 tbspn paprika
- 1 tbspn salt

Calories	Fat	Sugar	Protein	Carbohydrates	Cholesterol
8	0.1 g	0.7 g	0.4 g	1.8 g	0 mg

Hearty Rutabaga Fries

Prep Time	Time to cook	Serv
10 min	18 min	8

Directions:
1. Add all ingredients into the large mixing bowl and toss to coat.
2. Preheat the AirFryer to 365 F.
3. Transfer rutabaga fries into the AirFryer basket and cook for 18 min. Shake 2-3 times.
4. Enjoy.

Ingredients:
- 1 lb rutabaga, cut into fries shape
- 2 tbspn olive oil
- 1 tbspn garlic powder
- 1/2 tbspn chili pepper
- 1/2 tbspn salt

Calories	Fat	Sugar	Protein	Carbohydrates	Cholesterol
32	1.3 g	3.3 g	0.8 g	4.9 g	0 mg

Kohlrabi Chips

Prep Time	Time to cook	Serv
10 min	20 min	10

Directions:
1. Preheat the AirFryer to 320 F.
2. Add all ingredients into the bowl and toss to coat.
3. Transfer kohlrabi into the AirFryer basket and cook for 20 min.
4. Toss halfway through.
5. Enjoy.

Ingredients:
- 1 lb kohlrabi, peel and slice thinly
- 1 tbspn paprika
- 1 tbspn olive oil
- 1 tbspn salt

Calories	Fat	Sugar	Protein	Carbohydrates	Cholesterol
13	1.4 g	0 g	0 g	0.1 g	0 mg

Spectacular Daikon Chips

Prep Time	Time to cook	Serv
10 min	16 min	6

Directions:
1. Preheat the AirFryer to 375 F.
2. Add all ingredients into the bowl and toss to coat.
3. Transfer sliced the daikon into the AirFryer basket and cook for 16 min.
4. Toss halfway through.
5. Enjoy.

Ingredients:
- 15 ounces Daikon, slice into chips
- 1 tbspn olive oil
- 1 tbspn chili powder
- 1/2 tbspn pepper
- 1 tbspn salt

Calories	Fat	Sugar	Protein	Carbohydrates	Cholesterol
36	2.4 g	1.5 g	1.5 g	3.2 g	0 mg

Garlic Mushrooms

Prep Time	Time to cook	Serv
10 min	20 min	8

Directions:
1. Add all ingredients into the large mixing bowl and mix well. Place in refrigerator for 2 hours. Preheat the AirFryer to 350 F.
2. Add Transfer marinated mushrooms into the AirFryer basket and cook for 20 min. Toss halfway through.
3. Enjoy.

Ingredients:
- 2 lbs mushrooms, sliced
- 1/4 cup coconut amino
- 2 garlic cloves, diced
- 3 tbspn olive oil

Calories	Fat	Sugar	Protein	Carbohydrates	Cholesterol
78	5.6 g	2 g	3.6 g	5.5 g	0 mg

Savory Spicy Dip

Prep Time	Time to cook	Serv
5 min	5 min	6

Directions:
1. Add all ingredients into the AirFryer baking dish and Stir.
2. Place dish in the AirFryer and cook at 380 F for 5 min.
3. Transfer pepper mixture into the blender and blend until smooth.
4. Enjoy.

Ingredients:
- 12 ounces hot peppers, minced
- 1 1/2 cups apple cider vinegar
- Pepper
- Salt

Calories	Fat	Sugar	Protein	Carbohydrates	Cholesterol
35	0.3 g	3.3 g	1.1 g	5.6 g	0 mg

Onion Dip

Prep Time	Time to cook	Serv
10 min	25 min	8

Directions:
1. Melt butter in a pan over medium heat.
2. Add onion and baking soda and sauté for 5 min.
3. Transfer onion mixture into the AirFryer baking dish.
4. Place in the AirFryer and cook at 370 F for 25 min.
5. Enjoy.

Calories	Fat	Sugar	Protein	Carbohydrates	Cholesterol
122	8.8 g	4.8 g	1.3 g	10.6 g	23 mg

Ingredients:
- 2 lbs onion, minced
- 1/2 tbspn baking soda
- 6 tbspn butter, softened
- Pepper
- Salt

Simple Carrot Dip

Prep Time	Time to cook	Serv
10 min	15 min	6

Directions:
1. Add all ingredients into the AirFryer baking dish and stir until well combined.
2. Place dish in the AirFryer and cook at 380 F for 15 min.
3. Transfer cook carrot mixture into the blender and blend until smooth.
4. Enjoy.

Calories	Fat	Sugar	Protein	Carbohydrates	Cholesterol
83	7.7 g	1.8 g	0.4 g	3.7 g	20 mg

Ingredients:
- 2 cups carrots, grated
- 1/4 tbspn cayenne pepper
- 4 tbspn butter, melted
- 1 tbspn chives, minced
- Pepper
- Salt

Dreamy Sesame Okra

Prep Time	Time to cook	Serv
10 min	4 min	4

Directions:
1. In a bowl, whisk together egg, pepper, and salt.
2. Add okra into the whisked egg. Sprinkle with sesame seeds.
3. Preheat the AirFryer to 400 F.
4. Stir okra well. Spray AirFryer basket with cooking spray.
5. Place okra pieces into the AirFryer basket and cook for 4 min.
6. Enjoy.

Calories	Fat	Sugar	Protein	Carbohydrates	Cholesterol
82	5 g	1.2 g	3 g	6.2 g	41 mg

Ingredients:
- 11 ounces okra, wash and chop
- 1 egg, lightly beaten
- 1 tbspn sesame seeds
- 1 tbspn sesame oil
- 1/4 tbspn pepper
- 1/2 tbspn salt

Vegetables and Meatless Meals Recipes

Crispy Pickles

    Prep Time   Time to cook   Serv
    10 min   6 min   4

Directions:
1. Take 3 bowls. Mix together pork rinds and cheese in the first bowl.
2. In a second bowl, add the egg.
3. In the last bowl add the almond flour.
4. Coat each pickle slice with almond flour then dip in egg and finally coat with pork and cheese mixture.
5. Spray AirFryer basket with cooking spray.
6. Place coated pickles in the AirFryer basket.
7. Cook pickles for 6 min at 370 F.
8. Enjoy.

Ingredients:
- 16 dill pickles, sliced
- 1 egg, lightly beaten
- 1/2 cup almond flour
- 3 tbspn parmesan cheese, grated
- 1/2 cup pork rind, crushed

Calories	Fat	Sugar	Protein	Carbohydrates	Cholesterol
245	17 g	2 g	17 g	4 g	41 mg

Fabulous Roasted Brussels sprouts

    Prep Time   Time to cook   Serv
    10 min   8 min   4

Directions:
1. Add all ingredients into the large bowl and toss well.
2. Pour Brussels sprout mixture into the AirFryer basket.
3. Cook Brussels sprouts at 390 F for 8 min.
4. Enjoy.

Ingredients:
- 1 lb Brussels sprouts, cleaned and trimmed
- 1 tbspn garlic powder
- 1 tbspn dried parsley
- 2 tbspn olive oil
- 1/2 tbspn dried thyme
- 1/4 tbspn salt

Calories	Fat	Sugar	Protein	Carbohydrates	Cholesterol
72	2.7 g	2.6 g	4 g	10.9 g	0 mg

Perfect Crispy Tofu

    Prep Time   Time to cook   Serv
    10 min   20 min   4

Directions:
1. In a bowl, toss tofu with oil, vinegar, and soy sauce and let sit for 15 min.
2. Toss marinated tofu with arrowroot flour.
3. Spray AirFryer basket with cooking spray.
4. Add tofu in AirFryer basket and cook for 20 min at 370 F. Shake basket halfway through.
5. Enjoy.

Ingredients:
- 1 block firm tofu, pressed and cut into 1-inch cubes
- 1 tbspn arrowroot flour
- 2 tbspn sesame oil
- 1 tbspn vinegar
- 2 tbspn soy sauce

Calories	Fat	Sugar	Protein	Carbohydrates	Cholesterol
42	0.5 g	0.3 g	12.4 g	1.3 g	0 mg

Crisp & Tender Brussels sprouts

Prep Time	Time to cook	Serv
10 min	10 min	2

Directions:
1. Add all ingredients into the large bowl and toss well.
2. Spray AirFryer basket with cooking spray.
3. Transfer Brussels sprouts mixture into the AirFryer basket.
4. Cook Brussels sprouts at 400 F for 10 min.
5. Shake basket halfway through.
6. Enjoy.

Calories	Fat	Sugar	Protein	Carbohydrates	Cholesterol
100	7.3 g	1.9 g	3 g	8.1 g	0 mg

Ingredients:
- 2 cups Brussels sprouts, sliced
- 1 tbspn balsamic vinegar
- 1 tbspn olive oil
- 1/4 tbspn sea salt

Dreamy Asian Green Beans

Prep Time	Time to cook	Serv
5 min	10 min	2

Directions:
1. Add all ingredients into the large mixing bowl and toss well.
2. Spray AirFryer basket with cooking spray.
3. Transfer green beans in AirFryer basket and cook at 400 F for 10 min.
4. Toss halfway through.
5. Enjoy.

Calories	Fat	Sugar	Protein	Carbohydrates	Cholesterol
58	2 g	3 g	3 g	8 g	0 mg

Ingredients:
- 8 ounces green beans, trimmed and cut in half
- 1 tbspn sesame oil
- 1 tbspn tamari

Roasted Eggplant

Prep Time	Time to cook	Serv
10 min	12 min	2

Directions:
1. Spray AirFryer basket with cooking spray.
2. Add all ingredients into the mixing bowl and toss well.
3. Transfer eggplant mixture into the AirFryer basket and cook at 390 F for 6 min. Toss well and cook for 6 min more.
4. Enjoy.

Calories	Fat	Sugar	Protein	Carbohydrates	Cholesterol
120	7.5 g	7.1 g	2.4 g	14.2 g	0 mg

Ingredients:
- 1 eggplant, washed and cubed
- 1/2 tbspn garlic powder
- 1/4 tbspn marjoram
- 1/4 tbspn oregano
- 1 tbspn olive oil

Glorious Curried Eggplant Slices

Prep Time	Time to cook	Serv
10 min	10 min	2

Directions:
1. Preheat the AirFryer to 300 F.
2. Add all ingredients into the large mixing bowl and toss to coat.
3. Transfer eggplant slices into the AirFryer basket.
4. Cook eggplant slices for 10 min or until lightly brown. Shake basket halfway through.
5. Enjoy.

Calories	Fat	Sugar	Protein	Carbohydrates	Cholesterol
122	7.5 g	6.9 g	2.4 g	14.4 g	0 mg

Ingredients:
- 1 large eggplant, cut into
- 1/2-inch thick slices
- 1 garlic clove, diced
- 1 tbspn olive oil
- 1/2 tbspn curry powder
- 1/8 tbspn turmeric
- Salt

Healthy Green Beans

Prep Time	Time to cook	Serv
5 min	6 min	4

Directions:
1. Spray AirFryer basket with cooking spray.
2. Preheat the AirFryer to 400 F.
3. Add green beans in AirFryer basket and season with pepper and salt.
4. Cook green beans for 6 min. Turn halfway through.
5. Enjoy.

Calories	Fat	Sugar	Protein	Carbohydrates	Cholesterol
35	0.1 g	1.6 g	2.1 g	8.1 g	0 mg

Ingredients:
- 1 lb green beans, trimmed
- Pepper
- Salt

Great Roasted Broccoli

Prep Time	Time to cook	Serv
10 min	7 min	4

Directions:
1. Add broccoli, oil, pepper, and salt in a bowl and toss well.
2. Add 1/4 cup of water into the bottom of AirFryer (under the basket).
3. Transfer broccoli into the AirFryer basket and cook for 7 min at 400 F.
4. Enjoy.

Calories	Fat	Sugar	Protein	Carbohydrates	Cholesterol
61	3.8 g	1.6 g	2.6 g	6.1 g	0 mg

Ingredients:
- 4 cups broccoli florets
- 1/4 cup water
- 1 tbspn olive oil
- 1/4 tbspn pepper
- 1/8 tbspn kosher salt

Air Fried Onion & Bell Peppers

Prep Time: 10 min | Time to cook: 25 min | Serv: 3

Directions:
1. Add all ingredients into the large mixing bowl and toss well.
2. Preheat the AirFryer to 320 F.
3. Transfer bell pepper and onion mixture into the AirFryer basket and cook for 15 min.
4. Toss well and cook for 10 min more.
5. Enjoy.

Ingredients:
- 6 bell pepper, sliced
- 1 tbspn Italian seasoning
- 1 tbspn olive oil
- 1 onion, sliced

Calories	Fat	Sugar	Protein	Carbohydrates	Cholesterol
129	6.1 g	10 g	3 g	14 g	3 mg

Wonderful Roasted Peppers

Prep Time: 5 min | Time to cook: 8 min | Serv: 3

Directions:
1. Spray AirFryer basket with cooking spray.
2. Add bell peppers into the AirFryer basket and cook at 360 F for 8 min.
3. Season peppers with pepper and salt.
4. Enjoy.

Ingredients:
- 3 1/2 cups bell peppers, cut into chunks
- Pepper
- Salt

Calories	Fat	Sugar	Protein	Carbohydrates	Cholesterol
33	0 g	4 g	1 g	7 g	0 mg

Parmesan Broccoli

Prep Time: 10 min | Time to cook: 5 min | Serv: 2

Directions:
1. Preheat the AirFryer to 360 F.
2. Add all ingredients into the large bowl and toss well.
3. Transfer broccoli mixture into the AirFryer basket and cook for 4-5 min.
4. Enjoy.

Ingredients:
- 3 cups broccoli florets
- 1/4 cup parmesan cheese, grated
- 2 tbspn olive oil
- 2 garlic cloves, diced

Calories	Fat	Sugar	Protein	Carbohydrates	Cholesterol
182	15.2 g	2.4 g	5.1 g	10.2 g	3 mg

Easy Air Fried Asparagus

Prep Time	Time to cook	Serv
5 min	7 min	2

Directions:
1. Brush asparagus with olive oil and season with pepper and salt.
2. Place asparagus into the AirFryer basket and cook at 400 F for 7 min.
3. Shake halfway through.
4. Enjoy.

Calories	Fat	Sugar	Protein	Carbohydrates	Cholesterol
51	0.9 g	4.3 g	5 g	8.8 g	0 mg

Ingredients:
- 1 lb asparagus
- 1/4 tbspn olive oil
- Pepper
- Salt

Gluten-Free Beans

Prep Time	Time to cook	Serv
5 min	10 min	2

Directions:
1. Add all ingredients into the zip-lock bag and shake well.
2. Place green beans into the AirFryer basket and cook at 400 F for 10 min. Turn halfway through.
3. Enjoy.

Calories	Fat	Sugar	Protein	Carbohydrates	Cholesterol
55	2 g	3 g	3 g	8 g	0 mg

Ingredients:
- 8 ounces green beans, cut ends and cut beans in half
- 1 tbspn sesame oil
- 1 tbspn tamari

Exciting AirFryer Mushrooms

Prep Time	Time to cook	Serv
5 min	8 min	1

Directions:
1. Add all ingredients into the bowl and toss well.
2. Spray AirFryer basket with cooking spray.
3. Transfer mushrooms into the AirFryer basket and cook at 380 F for 8 min. Toss halfway through.
4. Enjoy.

Calories	Fat	Sugar	Protein	Carbohydrates	Cholesterol
62	5 g	2 g	3 g	3 g	0 mg

Ingredients:
- 12 button mushrooms, cleaned
- 1 tbspn olive oil
- 1/4 tbspn garlic salt
- Pepper
- Salt

Roasted Acorn Squash

Prep Time	Time to cook	Serv
10 min	25 min	4

Directions:
1. Preheat the AirFryer to 370 F.
2. Remove seed from squash and cut into 3/4-inch slices.
3. Add squash slices, olive oil, thyme, parmesan cheese, pepper, and salt in a bowl and toss to coat.
4. Add squash slices into the AirFryer basket and cook for 25 min. Turn halfway through.
5. Enjoy.

Ingredients:
- 1 large acorn squash, cut in half lengthwise
- 2 tbspn olive oil
- 1/4 cup parmesan cheese, grated
- 1/4 tbspn pepper
- 8 fresh thyme sprigs

Calories	Fat	Sugar	Protein	Carbohydrates	Cholesterol
250	16.1 g	0 g	13 g	11 g	30 mg

Soulful Cheesy Ranch Broccoli

Prep Time	Time to cook	Serv
10 min	24 min	6

Directions:
1. Add all ingredients into the large bowl and toss well to coat.
2. Spread broccoli mixture into the AirFryer baking dish and place into the AirFryer.
3. Cook at 350 F for 24 min.
4. Stir and serve.

Ingredients:
- 4 cups broccoli florets
- 1/2 cup cheddar cheese, shredded
- 1/4 cup ranch dressing
- 1/4 cup heavy whipping cream
- Pepper
- Salt

Calories	Fat	Sugar	Protein	Carbohydrates	Cholesterol
80	5 g	1.4 g	4 g	4.5 g	17 mg

Cheesy Brussels sprouts

Prep Time	Time to cook	Serv
10 min	8 min	6

Directions:
1. Preheat the AirFryer to 325 F.
2. Melt butter in a pan over medium-high heat. Add Brussels sprouts and water. Stir.
3. Cover and steam for 5 min.
4. Transfer Brussels sprouts into the AirFryer baking dish. Set aside.
5. Add cream cheese into the same pan and melt over medium heat.
6. Add cheese and heavy cream and whisk until smooth.
7. Pour cheese mixture over Brussels sprouts.
8. Place dish into the AirFryer and cook for 8 min.
9. Enjoy.

Ingredients:
- 2 lbs Brussels sprouts, cleaned and halved
- 1 cup heavy cream
- 4 ounces cream cheese
- 1 cup Asiago cheese, shredded
- 2 tbspn water
- 2 tbspn butter

Calories	Fat	Sugar	Protein	Carbohydrates	Cholesterol
314	25 g	3 g	12 g	14 g	78 mg

Hearty Roasted Carrots

Prep Time | Time to cook | Serv
10 min | 25 min | 6

Directions:
1. Preheat the AirFryer to 350 F.
2. In a bowl, mix together oil, carrots, basil, garlic, and salt.
3. Transfer carrots into the AirFryer basket and cook for 20-25 min. Shake basket 2-3 times while cooking.
4. Garnish with parsley and serve.

Ingredients:
- 16 small carrots
- 1 tbspn fresh parsley, minced
- 1 tbspn dried basil
- 6 garlic cloves, diced
- 4 tbspn olive oil
- 1 1/2 tbspn salt

Calories	Fat	Sugar	Protein	Carbohydrates	Cholesterol
140	9.4 g	5 g	1.3 g	14 g	0 mg

Brussels sprouts with Garlic

Prep Time | Time to cook | Serv
10 min | 30 min | 8

Directions:
1. Preheat the AirFryer to 370 F.
2. In a bowl, mix together Brussels sprouts, coconut oil, and garlic.
3. Transfer Brussels sprouts into the AirFryer basket and cooks for 30 min. Shake basket halfway through.
4. Season with pepper and salt.
5. Enjoy.

Ingredients:
- 2 lbs Brussels sprouts, trimmed and quartered
- 2 tbspn coconut oil, melted
- 5 garlic cloves, sliced
- 1/8 tbspn pepper
- 1 tbspn salt

Calories	Fat	Sugar	Protein	Carbohydrates	Cholesterol
80	3.8 g	32.5 g	4 g	11 g	0 mg

Spectacular Beans with Mushrooms

Prep Time | Time to cook | Serv
10 min | 20 min | 4

Directions:
1. Preheat the AirFryer to 370 F.
2. In a bowl, combine together olive oil, pepper, garlic, and salt.
3. Pour olive oil mixture over green beans and mushrooms and stir to coat.
4. Spread green beans and mushroom mixture into the AirFryer basket and cook for 20 min.
5. Enjoy.

Ingredients:
- 2 cups green beans, clean and cut into pieces
- 1/4 cup olive oil
- 2 cups mushrooms, sliced
- 2 tbspn garlic, diced
- 1 tbspn pepper
- 1 tbspn sea salt

Calories	Fat	Sugar	Protein	Carbohydrates	Cholesterol
135	12.8 g	1.4 g	2.3 g	6 g	0 mg

Garlic Thyme Mushrooms

Prep Time	Time to cook	Serv
10 min	23 min	2

Directions:
1. Preheat the AirFryer to 370 F.
2. Spray AirFryer basket with cooking spray.
3. In a bowl, combine together mushrooms, pepper, salt, thyme, and oil.
4. Spread mushrooms into the AirFryer basket and cook for 20 min. Shake basket halfway through.
5. Add garlic and Stir and cook for 2-3 min.
6. Enjoy.

Ingredients:
- 10 ounces mushrooms, quartered
- 1 tbspn thyme, minced
- 2 tbspn olive oil
- 2 garlic cloves, sliced
- 1/4 tbspn pepper
- 1/4 tbspn salt

Calories	Fat	Sugar	Protein	Carbohydrates	Cholesterol
155	14.5 g	2.5 g	5 g	6 g	0 mg

Nourishing Roasted Mushrooms

Prep Time	Time to cook	Serv
10 min	15 min	4

Directions:
1. Add mushrooms in a bowl with remaining ingredients and toss well.
2. Transfer mushrooms into the AirFryer basket and cook at 320 F for 15 min. Toss halfway through.
3. Enjoy.

Ingredients:
- 2 lbs mushrooms, clean and quarters
- 2 tbspn vermouth
- 2 tbspn herb de Provence
- 1/2 tbspn garlic powder
- 1 tbspn butter, melted

Calories	Fat	Sugar	Protein	Carbohydrates	Cholesterol
253	11.5 g	4 g	26.2 g	8.5 g	8 mg

Zucchini Fries

Prep Time	Time to cook	Serv
10 min	15 min	2

Directions
1. Preheat the AirFryer to 390 F.
2. Add all ingredients into the bowl and mix well.
3. Place coated zucchini fries in AirFryer basket and air fry for 15 min.
4. Enjoy.

Ingredients:
- 2 medium zucchini, cut into French fries shape
- 2 tbspn arrowroot powder
- 1 tbspn water
- 1/2 tbspn olive oil
- Salt

Calories	Fat	Sugar	Protein	Carbohydrates	Cholesterol
90	4 g	3.4 g	2.4 g	13 g	0 mg

Easy Taro Fries

Prep Time	Time to cook	Serv
10 min	20 min	2

Directions:
1. Add taro slice in a bowl and toss well with olive oil and salt.
2. Transfer taro slices into the AirFryer basket.
3. Cook at 360 F for 20 min. Toss halfway through.
4. Enjoy.

Calories	Fat	Sugar	Protein	Carbohydrates	Cholesterol
115	7 g	0.2 g	0.8 g	12 g	0 mg

Ingredients:
- 8 small taro, peel and cut into fries shape
- 1 tbspn olive oil
- 1/2 tbspn salt

Scrummy Beetroot Chips

Prep Time	Time to cook	Serv
10 min	15 min	4

Directions:
1. Sprinkle rosemary and salt on the beetroot slices.
2. Preheat the AirFryer to 300 F.
3. Add beetroot slices into the AirFryer basket. Drizzle beetroot slices with olive oil.
4. Cook for 15 min. Shake basket after every 5 min while cooking.
5. Enjoy.

Calories	Fat	Sugar	Protein	Carbohydrates	Cholesterol
31	1 g	4 g	0.5 g	5 g	0 mg

Ingredients:
- 2 medium beetroot, wash, peeled, and sliced thinly
- 1 tbspn olive oil
- 1 sprig rosemary, minced
- Salt

Ricotta Mushrooms

Prep Time	Time to cook	Serv
10 min	12 min	2

Directions:
1. Coat mushrooms with olive oil.
2. Transfer mushrooms into the AirFryer basket and cook at 350 F for 2 min.
3. In a bowl, mix together remaining ingredients.
4. Stuff bowl mixture into the mushrooms and place into the AirFryer basket and cook for 10 min more.
5. Enjoy.

Calories	Fat	Sugar	Protein	Carbohydrates	Cholesterol
69	5.1 g	0.1 g	3.5 g	2.2 g	6 mg

Ingredients:
- 4 large Portobello mushrooms caps
- 1 tbspn olive oil
- 1/4 cup parmesan cheese, grated
- 1/4 tbspn rosemary, minced
- 1 cup spinach, minced
- 1/4 cup ricotta cheese

Appetizing Shallots Almonds Green Beans

Prep Time	Time to cook	Serv
10 min	15 min	2

Directions:
1. Add all ingredients into the large bowl and toss well.
2. Transfer green bean mixture into the AirFryer basket and cook at 400 F for 15 min.
3. Enjoy.

Calories	Fat	Sugar	Protein	Carbohydrates	Cholesterol
125	7 g	2 g	4 g	14 g	0 mg

Ingredients:
- 1/4 cup almonds, toasted
- 1 1/2 lbs green beans, trimmed and steamed
- 2 tbspn olive oil
- 1/2 lb shallots, minced
- Pepper
- Salt

Tasty Herb Tomatoes

Prep Time	Time to cook	Serv
10 min	15 min	4

Directions:
1. Add all ingredients into the bowl and toss well.
2. Transfer tomatoes into the AirFryer basket and cook at 390 F for 15 min.
3. Enjoy.

Calories	Fat	Sugar	Protein	Carbohydrates	Cholesterol
49	3.7 g	2.4 g	0.9 g	4.1 g	0 mg

Ingredients:
- 2 large tomatoes, halved
- 1 tbspn olive oil
- 1/2 tbspn thyme, minced
- 2 garlic cloves, diced
- Pepper
- Salt

Cute Curried Sweet Potato Fries

Prep Time	Time to cook	Serv
10 min	20 min	3

Directions:
1. Add all ingredients into the mixing bowl and toss to coat.
2. Transfer sweet potato fries into the AirFryer basket and cook at 370 F for 20 min.
3. Toss halfway through.
4. Enjoy.

Calories	Fat	Sugar	Protein	Carbohydrates	Cholesterol
118	9 g	2 g	1 g	9 g	0 mg

Ingredients:
- 2 sweet potatoes, peeled and cut into fries shape
- 1/4 tbspn ground coriander
- 1/2 tbspn curry powder
- 2 tbspn olive oil
- Pepper
- Salt

Basil Tomatoes

Prep Time	Time to cook	Serv
10 min	10 min	2

Directions:
1. Drizzle cut sides of the tomato halves with cooking spray evenly.
2. Sprinkle with salt, black pepper, and basil.
3. Press "Power Button" of Air Fry Oven and turn the dial to select the "Air Fry" mode.
4. Press the Time button and again turn the dial to set the Time to cook to 10 min.
5. Now push the Temp button and rotate the dial to set the temperature at 320 degrees F.
6. Press the "Start/Pause" button to start.
7. When the unit beeps to show that it is preheated, open the lid.
8. Arrange the tomatoes in "Air Fry Basket" and insert them in the oven.
9. Serve warm.

Ingredients:
- 3 tomatoes halved
- Olive oil cooking spray
- Salt and ground black pepper, as required
- 1 tbspnn fresh basil, minced

Calories	Fat	Sugar	Protein	Fiber	Cholesterol
34	0.4 g	4.9 g	1.7 g	9 g	0 mg

Sweety Pesto Tomatoes

Prep Time	Time to cook	Serv
15 min	14 min	4

Directions:
1. Spread some pesto on each slice of tomato.
2. Top each tomato slice with a feta slice and onion and drizzle with oil.
3. Press "Power Button" of Air Fry Oven and turn the dial to select the "Air Fry" mode.
4. Press the Time button and again turn the dial to set the Time to cook to 14 min.
5. Now push the Temp button and rotate the dial to set the temperature at 390 degrees F.
6. Press the "Start/Pause" button to start.
7. When the unit beeps to show that it is preheated, open the lid.
8. Arrange the tomatoes in greased "Air Fry Basket" and insert them in the oven.
9. Serve warm.

Ingredients:
- 3 large heirloom tomatoes, cut into ½ inch thick slices.
- 1 cup pesto
- 8 ounces. feta cheese, cut into ½ inch thick slices.
- ½ cup red onions, sliced thinly
- 1 tbspnn olive oil

Calories	Fat	Sugar	Protein	Fiber	Cholesterol
480	41.9 g	10.5 g	15.4 g	3 g	65 mg

Luscious Stuffed Tomatoes

Prep Time	Time to cook	Serv
15 min	15 min	2

Directions:
1. Carefully cut the top of each tomato and scoop out pulp and seeds.
2. In a bowl, mix minced broccoli, cheese, salt, and black pepper.
3. Stuff each tomato with broccoli mixture evenly.
4. Press "Power Button" of Air Fry Oven and turn the dial to select the "Air Fry" mode.
5. Press the Time button and again turn the dial to set the Time to cook to 15 min.
6. Now push the Temp button and rotate the dial to set the temperature at 355 degrees F.
7. Press the "Start/Pause" button to start.
8. When the unit beeps to show that it is preheated, open the lid.
9. Arrange the tomatoes in greased "Air Fry Basket" and insert them in the oven.
10. Serve warm with the garnishing of thyme.

Ingredients:
- 2 large tomatoes
- ½ cup broccoli, minced finely
- ½ cup Cheddar cheese, shredded
- Salt and ground black pepper, as required
- 1 tbspnn unsalted butter, melted
- ½ tspn dried thyme, crushed

Calories	Fat	Sugar	Protein	Fiber	Cholesterol
206	15.6 g	5.3 g	9.4 g	2.9 g	45 mg

Magical Parmesan Asparagus

Prep Time	Time to cook	Serv
10 min	10 min	3

Directions:
1. In a bowl, mix the asparagus, cheese, butter, garlic powder, salt, and black pepper.
2. Press "Power Button" of Air Fry Oven and turn the dial to select the "Air Fry" mode.
3. Press the Time button and again turn the dial to set the Time to cook to 10 min.
4. Now push the Temp button and rotate the dial to set the temperature at 400 degrees F.
5. Press the "Start/Pause" button to start.
6. When the unit beeps to show that it is preheated, open the lid.
7. Arrange the veggie mixture in greased "Air Fry Basket" and insert it in the oven.
8. Serve hot.

Ingredients:
- 1 lb. fresh asparagus, trimmed
- 1 tbspnn Parmesan cheese, grated
- 1 tbspnn butter, melted
- 1 tspn garlic powder
- Salt and ground black pepper, as required

Calories	Fat	Sugar	Protein	Fiber	Cholesterol
73	4.4 g	3.1 g	4.2 g	3.3 g	12 mg

Wonderful Almond Asparagus

Prep Time	Time to cook	Serv
15 min	6 min	3

Directions:
1. In a bowl, mix the asparagus, oil, vinegar, salt, and black pepper.
2. Press "Power Button" of Air Fry Oven and turn the dial to select the "Air Fry" mode.
3. Press the Time button and again turn the dial to set the Time to cook to 6min.
4. Now push the Temp button and rotate the dial to set the temperature at 400 degrees F.
5. Press the "Start/Pause" button to start.
6. When the unit beeps to show that it is preheated, open the lid.
7. Arrange the veggie mixture in greased "Air Fry Basket" and insert it in the oven.
8. Serve hot.

Ingredients:
- 1 lb. asparagus
- 2 tbspns olive oil
- 2 tbspns balsamic vinegar
- Salt and ground black pepper, as required
- 1/3 cup almonds, sliced

Calories	Fat	Sugar	Protein	Fiber	Cholesterol
173	14.8 g	3.3 g	5.6 g	4.5 g	0 mg

Sweet & Spicy Parsnips

Prep Time	Time to cook	Serv
15 min	44 min	5

Directions:
1. Mix the parsnips and butter in a large bowl,
2. Press "Power Button" of Air Fry Oven and turn the dial to select the "Air Fry" mode.
3. Press the Time button and again turn the dial to set the Time to cook to 44 min.
4. Now push the Temp button and rotate the dial to set the temperature at 355 degrees F.
5. Press the "Start/Pause" button to start.
6. When the unit beeps to show that it is preheated, open the lid.
7. Arrange the squash chunks in greased "Air Fry Basket" and insert it in the oven.
8. Mix the remaining ingredients meanwhile, in another large bowl.
9. After 40 min of cooking, press the "Start/Pause" button to pause the unit.
10. Transfer the parsnips chunks into the bowl of honey mixture and toss to coat thoroughly.
11. Again, arrange the parsnip chunks in "Air Fry Basket" and insert it in the oven.
12. Serve hot.

Ingredients:
- 1½ lbs. parsnip, peeled and cut into 1-inch chunks
- 1 tbspnn butter, melted
- 2 tbspns honey
- 1 tbspnn dried parsley flakes, crushed
- ¼ tspn red pepper flakes, crushed
- Salt and ground black pepper, as required

Calories	Fat	Sugar	Protein	Fiber	Cholesterol
149	2.7 g	13.5 g	1.7 g	6.7 g	6 mg

Toothsome Caramelized Baby Carrots

Prep Time	Time to cook	Serv
10 min	15 min	4

Directions:
1. In a bowl, mix the butter, brown sugar, and carrots.
2. Press "Power Button" of Air Fry Oven and turn the dial to select the "Air Fry" mode.
3. Press the Time button and again turn the dial to set the Time to cook to 15 min.
4. Press the "Start/Pause" button to start.
5. When the unit beeps to show that it is preheated, open the lid.
6. Arrange the carrots in greased "Air Fry Basket" and insert it in the oven.
7. Serve warm.

Ingredients:
- ½ cup butter, melted
- ½ cup brown sugar
- 1 lb. bag baby carrots

Calories	Fat	Sugar	Protein	Fiber	Cholesterol
312	23.2 g	23 g	1 g	3.3 g	61 mg

Carrot with Spinach

Prep Time	Time to cook	Serv
15 min	35 min	4

Directions:
1. In a bowl, mix 2 tspns of the butter and carrots.
2. Press "Power Button" of Air Fry Oven and turn the dial to select the "Air Fry" mode.
3. Press the Time button and again turn the dial to set the Time to cook to 35 min.
4. Presently thrust the Temp button and turn the dial to set the temperature at 400 degrees F.
5. Press the "Start/Pause" button to start.
6. When the unit beeps to show that it is preheated, open the lid.
7. Arrange the carrots in greased "Air Fry Basket" and insert it in the oven.
8. Mix remaining butter meanwhile, in a large bowl, zucchini, basil, salt, and black pepper.
9. After 5 min of cooking, place the zucchini mixture into the basket with carrots. Toss the vegetable mixture 2-3 times during the cooking.
10. Serve hot.

Ingredients:
- 4 tspns butter, melted and divided
- ¼ lb. carrots, peeled and sliced
- 1 lb. zucchinis, sliced
- 1 tbspnn fresh basil, minced
- Salt and ground black pepper, as required

Calories	Fat	Sugar	Protein	Fiber	Cholesterol
64	4 g	3.4 g	1.7 g	2 g	10 mg

Delish Broccoli with Sweet Potatoes

Prep Time	Time to cook	Serv
15 min	20 min	4

Directions:
1. Toss to coat thoroughly and Add all the ingredients in a large bowl, and Press "Power Button" of Air Fry Oven and turn the dial to select the "Air Roast" mode.
2. Press the Time button and again turn the dial to set the Time to cook to 20 min. Now push the Temp button and rotate the dial to set the temperature at 415 degrees F.
3. Press the "Start/Pause" button to start.
4. When the unit beeps to show that it is preheated, open the lid.
5. Arrange the carrots in greased "Air Fry Basket" and insert it in the oven.
6. Mix remaining butter meanwhile, in a large bowl, zucchini, basil, salt, and black pepper.
7. After 5 min of cooking, place the zucchini mixture into the basket with carrots.
8. Serve hot.

Ingredients:
- peeled and cut in 1-inch cubes 2 sweet potatoes
- 1 head broccoli, cut in 1-inch florets
- 2 tbspns vegetable oil
- Salt and ground black pepper, as required

Calories	Fat	Sugar	Protein	Fiber	Cholesterol
170	7.1 g	1.5 g	2.9 g	4.7 g	0 mg

Broccoli with Olives

Prep Time	Time to cook	Serv
15 min	15 min	6

Directions:
1. In a pan of the boiling water, add the broccoli and cook for about 3-4 min.
2. Drain the broccoli well.
3. In a bowl, place the broccoli, oil, salt, and black pepper and toss to coat thoroughly.
4. Press "Power Button" of Air Fry Oven and turn the dial to select the "Air Fry" mode.
5. Press the Time button and again turn the dial to set the Time to cook to 15 min.
6. Now push the Temp button and rotate the dial to set the temperature at 355 degrees F.
7. Press the "Start/Pause" button to start.
8. When the unit beeps to show that it is preheated, open the lid.
9. Arrange the broccoli in greased "Air Fry Basket" and insert it in the oven.
10. After 8 min of cooking, toss the broccoli florets.
11. Transfer the broccoli into a large bowl and immediately stir in the olives, lemon zest, and cheese.
12. Serve immediately.

Ingredients:
- 1½ lbs. broccoli head stemmed and cut into 1-inch florets
- 2 tbspns olive oil
- Salt and ground black pepper, as required
- 1/3 cup Kalamata olives, halved and pitted
- 2 tspns fresh lemon zest, grated
- ¼ cup Parmesan cheese, grated

Calories	Fat	Sugar	Protein	Fiber	Cholesterol
100	6.6 g	2 g	4.6 g	3.2 g	3 mg

Dreamy Roasted Beans

Prep Time	Time to cook	Serv
10 min	30 min	6

Directions:
1. In a massive bowl, add all comp1nts and toss them well.
2. Arrange green beans into the AirFryer AirFryer basket and place basket in the pot.
3. Seal the pot with AirFryer lid and select bake mode and cook at 400 f for 25-30 min.
4. Enjoy.

Calories	Fat	Sugar	Protein	Carbohydrates	Cholesterol
99	7.2 g	1.8 g	2.2 g	8.9 g	0 mg

Ingredients:
- 1 lb green beans
- 1/2 tbspn onion powder
- 2 tbspn olive oil
- 3/4 tbspn garlic powder
- 1/2 tbspn pepper
- 1/2 tbspn salt

Healthy Pumpkin Porridge

Prep Time	Time to cook	Serv
10 min	3 min	2

Directions:
1. Add all ingredients into the inner pot of instantaneous pot duo crisp and Stir.
2. Seal the pot with pressure cooking lid and cook on high for 3 min.
3. Once d1, allow to extrication pressure naturally. Remove lid.
4. Stir and serve warm.

Calories	Fat	Sugar	Protein	Carbohydrates	Cholesterol
333	17.2 g	8.9 g	7.5 g	40.8 g	0 mg

Ingredients:
- 1/2 cup pumpkin puree
- 3/4 tbspn pumpkin pie spice
- 1/2 cup almond milk
- 1 1/4 cups water
- 1 tbspn brown sugar
- 1 cup quick oats

Pretty Baby Bok Choy

Prep Time	Time to cook	Serv
10 min	5 min	4

Directions:
1. Switch on the AirFryer, insert the fryer basket, then shut it with the lid, set the frying temperature 350 degrees F, and let it preheat for 5 min.
2. Meanwhile, prepare the bok choy and for this, slice off the bottom, separate the leaves, rinse and drain well.
3. Open the preheated fryer, place bok choy in it, spray generously with olive oil, sprinkle with garlic powder, shake well, close the lid and cook for 6 min until golden brown and toasted, stirring halfway.
4. When d1, the AirFryer will beep, then open the lid and transfer bok choy to a dish.
5. Serve straight away.

Calories	Fat	Carbs	Protein	Fiber
58	2 g	5 g	1 g	1 g

Ingredients:
- 4 bunches of babies bok choy
- 1 tspn garlic powder
- Olive oil spray

Spring Onion Pancake

Prep Time	Time to cook	Serv
10 min	15 min	6

Directions:
1. Pour boiling water into a bowl and mix with almond flour using a spatula. Pour in cold water and knead the pancake mix. Brush oil over the dough and cover with cling wrap and leave to rest for 1 hour. After resting, the m1y should have a smooth, shiny look to it. The gluten in the mixture also makes it more elastic and stretchable. Divide the dough into 4 equal parts. Flatten each piece with hands. Brush oil over the dough and sprinkle with onion and salt. Gently press the onion into the mixture. Roll dough into a barrel shape. Roll to elongate dough. Coil the dough into a spiral and coat it with the last coating of the coil. Leave it on a plate covered with cling wrap for an hour to rest. Gently press the spiral pancake flat. Heat your AirFryer to 365°F for 3-min. Cook the pancake for 15-min and serve warm.

Ingredients:
- 1 cup almond flour
- ¾ cup boiling water
- ¼ cup of cold water
- ½ cup spring onion, minced
- 1 tspn of sea salt
- Olive oil as needed

Calories	Fat	Carbs	Protein
228	11.2 g	10.3 g	13.2 g

Super Oat and Chia Porridge

Prep Time	Time to cook	Serv
5 min	5 min	4

Directions:
1. Preheat your AirFryer to 390°F. Whisk the peanut butter, butter, milk and Stevia in a bowl. Stir in the oats and chia seeds. Put the mixture into an oven-proof dish and place in the AirFryer and cook for 5-min.

Ingedients:
- 2 tbspns peanut butter
- 2 tspns liquid Stevia
- 1 tbspnn butter, melted
- 4 cups of milk
- 2 cups oats
- 1 cup chia seeds

Calories	Fat	Carbs	Protein
228	11.4 g	10.2 g	14.5 g

AirFryer Asparagus

Prep Time	Time to cook	Serv
5 min	8 min	2

Directions:
1. Wash asparagus and then trim off thick, woody ends.
2. Spray asparagus with olive oil spray and sprinkle with yeast.
3. Add the asparagus to the AirFryer rack/basket in a single layer. Set temperature to 360°F, and set time to 8 min. Select START/STOP to begin.

Ingredients:
- Nutritional yeast
- Olive oil non-stick spray
- 1 bunch of asparagus

Calories	Fat	Protein
17	4 g	9 g

Exciting Almond Flour Battered And Crisped Onion Rings

Prep Time	Time to cook	Serv
5 min	15 min	3

Directions
1. Preheat the AirFryer oven for 5 min.
2. In a mixing bowl, mix the almond flour, baking powder, smoked paprika, salt, and pepper.
3. In another bowl, combine the eggs and coconut milk.
4. Soak the onion slices into the egg mixture.
5. Dredge the onion slices in the almond flour mixture.
6. Pour into the Oven rack/basket. Place the temperature to 325°F, and set time to 15 min. Select START/STOP to begin. Shake the fryer basket for even cooking.

Calories	Fat	Protein
217	17.9 g	5.3 g

Ingredients:
- ½ cup almond flour
- ¾ cup of coconut milk
- 1 big white onion, sliced into rings
- 1 egg, beaten
- 1 tbspnn baking powder
- 1 tbspnn smoked paprika

Brussels Sprouts with Balsamic Oil

Prep Time	Time to cook	Serv
5 min	15 min	4

Directions:
1. Preheat the AirFryer oven for 5 min.
2. Put all together ingredients in a bowl until the zucchini fries are well coated.
3. Place in the AirFryer oven basket.
4. Close and cook for 15 min for 350°F.

Calories	Fat	Protein
82	6.8 g	1.5g

Ingredients:
- ¼ tspn salt
- 1 tbspnn balsamic vinegar
- 2 cups Brussels sprouts, halved
- tbspns olive oil

Simple Crunchy Potato Cubes

Prep Time	Time to cook	Serv
10 min	20 min	4

Directions:
1. Cut potatoes into cubes
2. Sprinkle potato cubes with dill, oregano and chili flakes
3. Mix potatoes, pre-heat your AirFryer to 400 degrees F in "AIR FRY" mode
4. Transfer to AirFryer and cook for 15 min
5. Stir while cooking, once they are crunchy
6. Enjoy!

Calories	Fat	Carbs	Protein
119	4 g	20 g	12 g

Ingredients:
- 1 pound potato, peeled
- 1 tbspnn olive oil
- 1 tspn dried dill
- 1 tspn dried oregano
- 1/4 tspn chili flakes

Baby Carrots

Prep Time	Time to cook	Serv
10 min	12 min	4

Directions:
1. Pre-heat your Fryer to 350-degree F in "AIR FRY" mode
2. Take a mixing bowl and add oil, honey, and carrots
3. Give it a gentle stir and make sure that they are coated well
4. Season with some dill, pepper, and salt
5. Transfer the mix to your fryer and cook for 12 min and enjoy!

Ingredients:
- 1-pound baby carrots
- 1 tspn dried dill
- 1 tbspnn olive oil
- 1 tbspnn honey
- Salt and pepper to taste

Calories	Fat	Carbs	Protein
350	28 g	5 g	4 g

Charming Carrot Roast With Cumin

Prep Time	Time to cook	Serv
10 min	10 min	4

Directions:
1. Pre-heat your Fryer to 350-degree F in "AIR FRY" mode
2. Take a mixing bowl and add oil, honey, and carrots
3. Give it a gentle stir and make sure that they are coated well
4. Season with some dill, pepper, and salt
5. Transfer the mix to your fryer and cook for 12 min and enjoy!

Ingredients:
- 21 ounces carrots, peeled
- 1 tbspnn olive oil
- 1 tspn cumin seeds
- Handful fresh coriander

Calories	Fat	Carbs	Protein
210	5 g	20 g	4 g

Maple Roasted Brussels Sprouts

Prep Time	Time to cook	Serv
5 min	10 min	2

Directions:
1. Switch on the AirFryer, insert the fryer basket, then shut it with the lid, set the frying temperature 400 degrees F, and let it preheat for 5 min.
2. Meanwhile, take a large bowl, add Brussel sprouts in it, season with salt, drizzle with vinegar and toss until well coated with maple syrup.
3. Open the preheated fryer, place Brussel sprouts in it, close the lid and cook for 10 min until golden brown and toasted, shaking halfway.
4. When d1, the AirFryer will beep, then open the lid and transfer Brussel sprouts to a dish.
5. Serve straight away.

Ingredients:
- 2 cups Brussels sprouts,
- ¼-inch thick sliced
- 1/4 tspn sea salt
- 1 tbspnn balsamic vinegar
- 1 tbspnn maple syrup

Calories	Fat	Carbs	Protein	Fiber
85.3	3.3 g	13.1 g	2.8 g	2.8 g

Sweet Potato Fries

Prep Time	Time to cook	Serv
10 min	25 min	4

Directions:
1. AirFryer preheat to 400 degrees F for 8 min in "AIR FRY" mode
2. Spray oil in the fryer basket
3. Cut the potatoes in this way so that it makes ¼ inch thick fries
4. Toss with oil, garlic powder, paprika, salt, and black pepper
5. Cook in 2 to 3 batches
6. Do not overcrowd the pan
7. Cook for 8 min
8. Turn halfway
9. Enjoy!

Ingredients:
- 2 medium sweet potatoes, peeled
- 1/4 tspn sweet paprika
- 2 tspn olive oil
- 1/2 tspn garlic powder
- 1/2 tspn kosher salt
- Fresh black pepper, to taste

Calories	Fat	Carbs	Protein
220	5 g	42 g	3 g

Fabulous Crispy Fried Avocado

Prep Time	Time to cook	Serv
10 min	20 min	4

Directions:
1. Take a shallow bowl and add almond meal, salt
2. Pour aquafaba in another bowl, dredge avocado slices in aquafaba and then into the crumbs to get a nice coating
3. Arrange the layer on AirFryer cooking basket, don't overlap
4. Cook for 10 min at 390 degrees F, give the basket a shake and cook for 5 min more in "AIR FRY" mode
5. Enjoy!

Ingredients:
- 1/2 cup almond meal
- 1/2 tspn salt
- 1 Hass avocado, peeled, pitted and sliced
- Aquafaba from 1 bean can (bean liquid)

Calories	Fat	Carbs	Protein
350	14 g	8 g	23 g

Cool Beets Dish

Prep Time	Time to cook	Serv
10 min	10 min	4

Directions:
1. Wash your beets and peel them
2. Cut beets into cubes
3. Take a bowl and mix in the rosemary, pepper, salt, vinegar, and honey
4. Cover beets with the prepared sauce
5. Coat the beets with olive oil
6. Pre-heat your Fryer to 400-degree F in "AIR FRY" mode
7. Transfer beets to AirFryer cooking basket and cook for 10 min
8. Serve with your cheese sauce and enjoy!

Ingredients:
- 4 whole beets
- 1 tbspnn balsamic vinegar
- 1 tbspnn olive oil
- 1 tbspnn honey
- Salt and pepper to taste
- 2 springs rosemary

Calories	Fat	Carbs	Protein
160	4 g	4 g	30 g

Perfect Tasty Garlic Potato Fries

Prep Time	Time to cook	Serv
35 min	30 min	4

Directions:
1. Leave the potatoes for 30 min in water. Take a paper towel and blot dry with it. Use garlic powder to coat the vegetables. Spray with oil. Place it into the AirFryer. The minimum degrees to cook is at 360 degrees F for 25 min
2. Serve with mayo and enjoy!

Calories	Fat	Carbs	Protein
313	41 g	9 g	12 g

Ingredients:
- 28 ounces potatoes cut into strips
- Mayo
- 2 tspns garlic powder
- Water
- Cooking spray

Roasted Garlic

Prep Time	Time to cook	Serv
10 min	25 min	4

Directions:
1. Switch on the AirFryer, insert the fryer basket, then shut it with the lid, set the frying temperature 400 degrees F, and let it preheat for 5 min.
2. Meanwhile, remove excess peel from the garlic head, and then expose the top of garlic by removing ¼-inch off the top.
3. Spray the garlic head with oil generously and then wrap with a foil.
4. Open the preheated fryer, place wrapped garlic head in it, close the lid and cook for 25 min until d1.
5. When d1, the AirFryer will beep, then open the lid, transfer garlic to a dish and let it cool for 5 min.
6. Take off or squeeze the garlic out of its skin and serve with warmed garlic or as desired.

Calories	Fat	Carbs	Protein	Fiber
160	2.5 g	27 g	6 g	3 g

Ingredients:
- 1 medium head of garlic
- Olive oil spray

Delicious Kale

Prep Time	Time to cook	Serv
10 min	5 min	4

Directions:
1. AirFryer preheat your to 390 degrees F
2. Season the kale with olive oil and soy sauce
3. Cook for 3-5 min
4. Enjoy!

Calories	Fat	Carbs	Protein
105	5 g	14 g	5 g

Ingredients:
- 4 cups kale leaves, torn into pieces
- 1 tspn soy sauce
- 1 tbspnn olive oil

Tasty Roasted Green Beans

Prep Time	Time to cook	Serv
5 min	10 min	2

Directions:
1. Switch on the AirFryer, insert the fryer basket, then shut it with the lid, set the frying temperature 400 degrees F, and let it preheat for 5 min.
2. Meanwhile, snap the green beans into half, place them in a large bowl, add oil and soy sauce and toss until well coated.
3. Open the preheated fryer, place green beans in it, spray with olive oil, close the lid and cook for almost 10 min until golden brown and toasted, shaking halfway.
4. When d1, the AirFryer will beep and then open the lid and transfer green beans to a dish.
5. Serve straight away.

Calories	Fat	Carbs	Protein	Fiber
33.2	2.5 g	2.7 g	0.7 g	1.3 g

Ingredients:
- 8 ounces green beans, trimmed
- 1 tspn sesame oil
- 1 tbspnn soy sauce

Soulful Shishito Peppers

Prep Time	Time to cook	Serv
5 min	6 min	4

Directions:
1. Switch on the AirFryer, insert the fryer basket, then shut it with the lid, set the frying temperature 390 degrees F, and let it preheat for 5 min.
2. Open the preheated fryer, place peppers in it, spray well with olive oil, close the lid and cook for 6 min until cooked and lightly charred, shaking halfway.
3. When d1, the AirFryer will beep, open the lid, transfer peppers to a dish, and season with salt.
4. Serve straight away.

Calories	Fat	Carbs	Protein	Fiber
21	1 g	5 g	1 g	2 g

Ingredients:
- 20 Shishito peppers
- 1 tspn salt
- Olive oil spray

Easy Apple Cinnamon Oatmeal

Prep Time	Time to cook	Serv
10 min	3 min	2

Directions:
1. Add water and oats into the fryer of AirFryer duo crisp.
2. Seal the pot with pressure cooking lid and cook on high for 3 min.
3. Once d1, allow to extrication pressure naturally. Remove lid.
4. Just before serving, add apple and cinnamon.
5. Stir and serve.

Calories	Fat	Sugar	Protein	Carbohydrates	Cholesterol
273	3.1 g	23.6 g	6 g	59.2 g	0 mg

Ingredients:
- 1 cup quick oats
- 3 cups of water
- 3/4 tbspn cinnamon
- 2 medium apples, minced

Scrummy Baked Polenta with Chili-Cheese

Prep Time	Time to cook	Serv
10 min	5 min	3

Directions:
1. Place the baking dish accessory in the AirFryer.
2. The polenta should arrange slices in the baking dish.
3. Add the chili powder and cheddar cheese sauce.
4. Cook for 10 min at 390F and close the AirFryer

Ingredients:
- 1 commercial polenta roll, sliced
- 1 cup cheddar cheese sauce
- 1 tbspn chili powder

Calories	Fat	Carbs	Protein
206	4.2 g	25.3 g	3.2 g

Seasoned Potatoes

Prep Time	Time to cook	Serv
10 min	40 min	2

Directions:
1. Mix the spices and salt in a small bowl.
2. With a fork, prick the potatoes.
3. Coat the potatoes with butter and sprinkle with spice mixture.
4. Arrange the potatoes onto a cooking tray.
5. Arrange the drip pan at the bottom of the Instant Vortex Plus AirFryer Oven cooking chamber.
6. Choose "Air Fry" and then adjust the temperature to 400 degrees F.
7. Set the timer for 40 min and press the "Start."
8. When the display shows "Add Food" insert the cooking rack in the center position.
9. When the display shows "Turn Food," do nothing.
10. Remove the tray from Vortex and serve hot. When Time to cook is complete,

Ingredients
- 2 russet potatoes, scrubbed
- ½ tbspn butter, melted
- ½ tspn garlic & herb blend seasoning
- ½ tspn garlic powder
- Salt, to taste

Calories	Fat	Sugar	Protein	Carbs	Cholesterol
176	2.1 g	2.6 g	3.8 g	34.2 g	8 mg

Mouthwatering Thyme Potatoes

Prep Time	Time to cook	Serv
15 min	20 min	3

Directions:
1. In a bowl, add all the ingredients except lemon zest and toss to coat thoroughly.
2. Place the potatoes in the rotisserie basket and attach the lid.
3. Arrange the drip pan at the bottom of the Instant Vortex Plus AirFryer Oven cooking chamber.
4. Select "Air Dry" and then adjust the temperature to 400 degrees F.
5. Set the timer for 20 min and press the "Start."
6. Then, close the door and touch "Rotate."
7. When the display shows "Add Food" arrange the rotisserie basket, on the rotisserie spit.
8. Then, close the door and touch "Rotate."
9. When Time to cook is complete, press the red lever to extrication the rod.
10. Remove from the Vortex and transfer the potatoes into a bowl.
11. Add the lemon zest and toss to coat thoroughly.
12. Serve immediately.

Ingredients:
- 1 pound small red potatoes, cut into 1-inch pieces
- 1 tbspn olive oil
- 2 tspns fresh thyme, minced
- Salt and ground black pepper, as required
- 1 tbspn lemon zest, grated

Calories	Fat	Sugar	Protein	Carbs	Cholesterol
112	3.7 g	1.2 g	2.2 g	18.7 g	0 mg

Parmesan Broccoli

Prep Time	Time to cook	Serv
10 min	6 min	4

Directions:
1. In a bowl, add all the ingredients and toss to coat well.
2. Arrange the broccoli florets onto a cooking tray.
3. Arrange the drip pan at the bottom of the Instant Vortex Plus AirFryer Oven cooking chamber.
4. Select "Air Dry" and then adjust the temperature to 350 degrees F.
5. Set the timer for 6 min and press the "Start."
6. When the display shows "Add Food" insert the cooking tray in the center position.
7. When the display shows "Turn Food," turn the broccoli florets.
8. When Time to cook is complete, remove the tray from Vortex and serve hot.

Ingredients:
- 1 pound small broccoli florets
- 1 tbspn garlic, diced
- 2 tbspns olive oil
- ¼ cup Parmesan cheese, grated

Calories	Fat	Sugar	Protein	Carbs	Cholesterol
143	3.2 g	1.5 g	2.6 g	20 g	0 mg

Magnificent Buttered Cauliflower

Prep Time	Time to cook	Serv
15 min	15 min	6

Ingredients:
- 1 pound cauliflower head, cut into florets
- 1 tbspn butter, melted
- ½ tspn red pepper flakes, crushed
- Salt and ground black pepper, as required

Directions:
1. In a bowl, add all the ingredients and toss to coat well.
2. Place the potatoes in the rotisserie basket and attach the lid.
3. Arrange the drip pan at the bottom of the Instant Vortex Plus AirFryer Oven cooking chamber.
4. Select "Air Dry" and then adjust the temperature to 400 degrees F.
5. Set the timer for 15 min and press the "Start."
6. Then, close the door and touch "Rotate."
7. When the display shows "Add Food" arrange the rotisserie basket, on the rotisserie spit.
8. Then, close the door and touch "Rotate."
9. When Time to cook is complete, press the red lever to extrication the rod.
10. Remove from the Vortex and serve immediately.

Calories	Fat	Sugar	Protein	Carbs	Cholesterol
55	3 g	2.7 g	2.3 g	6.1 g	8 mg

Simple Asparagus

Prep Time	Time to cook	Serv
10 min	10 min	3

Ingredients:
- 1 pound fresh thick asparagus, trimmed
- 1 tbspn olive oil
- Salt and ground black pepper, as required

Directions:
1. In a bowl, add all the ingredients and toss to coat thoroughly.
2. Arrange the asparagus onto a cooking tray.
3. Arrange the drip pan at the bottom of the Instant Vortex Plus AirFryer Oven cooking chamber.
4. Select "Air Dry" and then adjust the temperature to 350 degrees F.
5. Set the timer for 10 min and press the "Start."
6. When the display shows "Add Food" insert the cooking tray in the center position.
7. When the display shows "Turn Food," turn the asparagus.
8. When Time to cook is complete, remove the tray from Vortex and serve hot.

Calories	Fat	Sugar	Protein	Carbs	Cholesterol
70	4.9 g	2.8g	3.3 g	5.9 g	0 mg

Enjoyable Vinegar Brussels Sprout

Prep Time	Time to cook	Serv
15 min	20 min	4

Directions:
1. In a bowl, add all the ingredients and toss to coat well.
2. Place the Brussels Sprouts in the rotisserie basket and attach the lid.
3. Arrange the drip pan at the bottom of the Instant Vortex Plus AirFryer Oven cooking chamber.
4. Select "Air Dry" and then adjust the temperature to 350 degrees F.
5. Set the timer for 20 min and press the "Start."
6. Then, close the door and touch "Rotate."
7. When the display shows "Add Food" arrange the rotisserie basket, on the rotisserie spit.
8. Then, close the door and touch "Rotate."
9. When Time to cook is complete, press the red lever to extrication the rod.
10. Remove from the Vortex and serve hot.

Ingredients:
- 1 pound Brussels Sprouts, ends trimmed and cut into bite-sized pieces
- 1 tbspn balsamic vinegar
- 1 tbspn olive oil
- Salt and ground black pepper, as required

Calories	Fat	Sugar	Protein	Carbs	Cholesterol
80	3.9 g	2.5 g	3.9 g	10.3 g	0 mg

Charming Spiced Zucchini

Prep Time	Time to cook	Serv
10 min	12 min	3

Directions:
1. In a bowl, add all the ingredients and toss to coat well.
2. Arrange the zucchini slices onto a cooking tray.
3. Arrange the drip pan at the bottom of the Instant Vortex Plus AirFryer Oven cooking chamber.
4. Select "Air Dry" and then adjust the temperature to 400 degrees F.
5. Set the timer for 12 min and press the "Start."
6. When the display shows "Add Food" insert the cooking tray in the center position.
7. When the display shows "Turn Food," do nothing.
8. When Time to cook is complete, remove the tray from Vortex and serve hot.

Ingredients:
- 1 pound zucchini, cut into ½-inch thick slices lengthwise
- 1 tbspn olive oil
- ½ tspn garlic powder
- ½ tspn cayenne pepper
- Salt and ground black pepper, as required

Calories	Fat	Sugar	Protein	Carbs	Cholesterol
67	5 g	2.8 g	2 g	5.6 g	0 mg

Green Beans with Carrots

Prep Time	Time to cook	Serv
15 min	10 min	3

Directions:
1. In a bowl, add all the ingredients and toss to coat well.
2. Place the vegetables in the rotisserie basket and attach the lid.
3. Arrange the drip pan at the bottom of the Instant Vortex Plus AirFryer Oven cooking chamber.
4. Select "Air Dry" and then adjust the temperature to 400 degrees F.
5. Set the timer for 10 min and press the "Start."
6. Then, close the door and touch "Rotate."
7. When the display shows "Add Food" arrange the rotisserie basket, on the rotisserie spit.
8. Then, close the door and touch "Rotate."
9. When Time to cook is complete, press the red lever to extrication the rod.
10. Remove from the Vortex and serve.

Ingredients:
- ½ pound green beans, trimmed
- ½ pound carrots, peeled and cut into sticks
- 1 tbspn olive oil
- Salt and ground black pepper, as required

Calories	Fat	Sugar	Protein	Carbs	Cholesterol
94	4.8 g	4.8 g	2 g	12.7 g	0 mg

Enchanting Mixed Veggies Combo

Prep Time	Time to cook	Serv
15 min	12 min	4

Directions:
1. In a bowl, add all the ingredients and toss to coat thoroughly.
2. Place the vegetables in the rotisserie basket and attach the lid.
3. Arrange the drip pan at the bottom of the Instant Vortex Plus AirFryer Oven cooking chamber.
4. Choose "Air Fry" and then adjust the temperature to 380 degrees F.
5. Maintain the timer for 18 min and press the "Start."
6. Then, close the door and touch "Rotate."
7. When the display shows "Add Food" arrange the rotisserie basket, on the rotisserie spit.
8. Then, close the door and touch "Rotate."
9. When Time to cook is complete, press the red lever to extrication the rod.
10. Remove from the Vortex and serve.

Ingredients:
- 1 cup baby carrots
- 1 cup broccoli florets
- 1 cup cauliflower florets
- 1 tbspn olive oil
- 1 tbspn Italian seasoning
- Salt and ground black pepper, as required

Calories	Fat	Sugar	Protein	Carbs	Cholesterol
66	4.7 g	2.7 g	1.4 g	5.7 g	2 mg

Garlic Zucchini Pate

Prep Time	Time to cook	Serv
10 min	27 min	3

Directions:
1. Peel the zucchini and grate it.
2. Now combine the grated zucchini with the salt and ground pepper and stir the zucchini.
3. Preheat the AirFryer to 390 degrees F.
4. Put the grated zucchini in the AirFryer basket tray.
5. Add olive oil and minced garlic clove and cook it for 8 min.
6. Next, stir the zucchini carefully and add butter.
7. Cook the zucchini pate for 4 min more at 400 degrees F.
8. The zucchini pate will be smooth and soft when the time has elapsed. Remove it from the AirFryer and allow it to cool to room temperature.
9. Enjoy!

Ingredients:
- 2 garlic cloves, minced
- 1 tbspn coconut butter
- 1 tspn salt
- 1/2 tspn ground black pepper
- 2 zucchini
- 1/2 tbspn olive oil

Calories	Fat	Sugar	Protein
238	8 g	3 g	7 g

Pretty Turnip Mash

Prep Time	Time to cook	Serv
10 min	24 min	3

Direction:
1. Preheat the AirFryer to 400 degrees F.
2. Peel the turnip and chop them.
3. Place the minced turnips in the AirFryer basket tray.
4. Add coconut butter, grated onion, salt, and coconut cream.
5. Cook the dish for 14 min. Allow the cooked turnip to chill for 5 min when the time has elapsed. Now use the hand blender to blend the turnip mixture into the mash.
6. Serve the cooked turnip mash warm.

Ingredients:
- Five turnip
- 3 ounces. coconut butter
- 1/2 white onion, grated
- 1 tspn salt
- 1 cup coconut cream

Calories	Fat	Sugar	Protein
23	6 g	2 g	6 g

Poultry

Buffalo Chicken Wings

Prep Time	Time to cook	Serv
15 min	20 min	7

Directions:
1. Whisk salt, brown sugar, Worcestershire sauce, butter, and hot sauce together and set to the side.
2. Dry wings and add to the AirFryer basket.
3. Cook 25 min at 380 degrees, tossing halfway through.
4. When the timer sounds, shake wings and bump up the temperature to 400 degrees and cook for another 5 min.
5. Take out wings and place them into a big bowl. Add sauce and toss well.
6. Serve alongside celery sticks!

Calories	Fat	Sugar	Protein
402	16 g	4 g	17 g

Ingredients:
- 1 tbspn. salt
- 1-2 tbspn. brown sugar
- 1 tbspn. Worcestershire sauce
- ½ C. vegan butter
- ½ C. cayenne pepper sauce
- 4 pounds of chicken wings

Soulful Chicken Fajita Rollups

Prep Time	Time to cook	Serv
5 min	10 min	7

Directions:
1. Mix oregano, cayenne pepper, garlic powder, cumin, and paprika along with a pinch or 2 of pepper and salt. Set to the side.
2. Slice chicken breasts lengthwise into 2 slices.
3. Between 2 pieces of parchment paper, add breast slices and pound till they are ¼-inch thick. With seasoning, liberally season both sides of chicken slices.
4. Put 2 strips of each color of bell pepper and a few onion slices onto chicken pieces. Roll up tightly and secure with toothpicks.
5. Repeat with remaining ingredients and sprinkle and rub mixture that is left over the chicken rolls.
6. Lightly grease your AirFryer basket and place 3 rollups into the fryer. Cook 12 min at 400 degrees.
7. Repeat with remaining rollups.
8. Serve with salad!

Calories	Fat	Sugar	Protein
189	14 g	1 g	11 g

Ingredients:
- ½ tbspn. oregano
- ½ tbspn. cayenne pepper
- 1 tbspn. cumin
- 1 tbspn. garlic powder
- 2 tbspn. paprika
- ½ sliced red onion
- ½ yellow bell pepper, sliced into strips
- ½ green bell pepper, sliced into strips
- ½ red bell pepper, sliced into strips
- 3 chicken breasts

Cute Rosemary Turkey Breast with Maple Mustard Glaze

Prep Time	Time to cook	Serv
5 min	15 min	6

Directions:
1. Mix pepper, salt, rosemary, garlic, and olive oil together. Spread herb mixture over turkey breast. Cover and chill 2 hours or overnight to marinade.
2. Make sure to remove from the fridge about half an hour before cooking.
3. Ensure your AirFryer is greased well and preheated to 400 degrees. Place loin into the fryer and cook 20 min.
4. While turkey cooks, melt butter in the microwave. Then add brown mustard and maple syrup.
5. Open fryer and spoon on butter mixture over turkey. Cook another 10 min.
6. Remove turkey from the fryer and let rest 5-10 min before attempting to slice.
7. Slice against the grain and enjoy it!

Ingredients:
- 1 tbspn. vegan butter
- 1 tbspn. st1-ground brown mustard
- ¼ C. pure maple syrup
- 1 tbspn. crushed pepper
- 2 tbspn. salt
- ½ tbspn. dried rosemary
- 2 dicedgarlic cloves
- ¼ C. olive oil
- 2.5 pounds turkey breast loin

Calories	Fat	Sugar	Protein
278	15 g	7 g	29 g

Hearty Mexican Chicken Burgers

Prep Time	Time to cook	Serv
5 min	20 min	7

Directions:
1. Ensure your AirFryer is preheated to 350 degrees.
2. Add seasonings to a blender. Slice cauliflower into florets and add to blender.
3. Pulse till mixture resembles that of breadcrumbs.
4. Take out ¾ of the cauliflower mixture and add to a bowl. Set to the side. In another bowl, beat your egg and set it to the side.
5. Remove skin and b1s from chicken breasts and add to blender with remaining cauliflower mixture. Season with pepper and salt.
6. Take out mixture and form into burger shapes. Roll each patty in cauliflower crumbs, then the egg, and back into bits again.
7. Place coated patties into the AirFryer, cooking 20 min.
8. Flip over at a 10-min mark. They are d1 when crispy!

Ingredients:
- 1 jalapeno pepper
- 1 tbspn. cayenne pepper
- 1 tbspn. mustard powder
- 1 tbspn. oregano
- 1 tbspn. thyme
- 3 tbspn. smoked paprika
- 1 beaten egg
- 1 small head of cauliflower
- 4 chicken breasts

Calories	Fat	Sugar	Protein
234	18 g	1 g	24 g

Crispy Southern Fried Chicken

Prep Time	Time to cook	Serv
10 min	20 min	4

Directions:
1. Ensure AirFryer is preheated to 350 degrees.
2. Layout chicken and season with pepper and salt on all sides.
3. Add all other ingredients to a blender, blending till a smooth-like breadcrumb mixture is created.
4. Place in a bowl and add a beaten egg to another container.
5. Dip chicken into breadcrumbs, then into the egg, and breadcrumbs once more.
6. Place coated drumsticks into the AirFryer and cook for 20 min.
7. Bump up the temperature to 390 degrees and cook for another 5 min till crispy.

Ingredients:
- 1 tbspn. cayenne pepper
- 2 tbspn. mustard powder
- 2 tbspn. oregano
- 2 tbspn. thyme
- 3 tbspn. coconut milk
- 1 beaten egg
- ¼ C. cauliflower
- ¼ C. gluten-free oats
- Eight chicken drumsticks

Calories	Fat	Sugar	Protein
504	18 g	5 g	35 g

Scrummy AirFryer Turkey Breast

Prep Time	Time to cook	Serv
5 min	10 min	7

Directions:
1. Preheat AirFryer to 350 degrees.
2. Season turkey with pepper, salt, and other desired seasonings.
3. Place turkey in the AirFryer basket.
4. Cook 60 min. The meat should be at 165 degrees when d1.
5. Allow resting 10-15 min before slicing. Enjoy!

Ingredients:
- Pepper and salt
- 1 oven-ready turkey breast
- Turkey seasonings of choice

Calories	Fat	Sugar	Protein
212	12 g	0 g	24 g

Chicken Kabobs

Prep Time	Time to cook	Serv
15 min	10 min	4

Directions:
1. Chop up chicken into cubes, seasoning with a few sprays of olive oil, pepper, and salt.
2. Dicedup bell peppers and cut mushrooms in half.
3. Mix soy sauce and honey till well combined.
4. Add sesame seeds and stir.
5. Skewer chicken, peppers, and mushrooms onto wooden skewers.
6. Ensure AirFryer is preheated to 388 degrees. Coat kabobs with honey-soy sauce.
7. Place coated kabobs in the AirFryer basket and cook for 15-20 min.

Ingredients:
- 2 dicedchicken breasts
- 3 bell peppers
- Six mushrooms
- Sesame seeds
- 1/3 C. low-sodium soy sauce
- 1/3 C. raw honey

Calories	Fat	Sugar	Protein
296	13 g	1 g	17 g

Yummy Mustard Chicken Tenders

Prep Time	Time to cook	Serv
10 min	10 min	5

Directions:
1. Season tenders with pepper and salt.
2. Place a thin layer of mustard onto tenders and then dredge in flour and dip in egg.
3. Add to AirFryer and cook 10-15 min at 390 degrees till crispy.

Calories	Fat	Sugar	Protein
403	20 g	4 g	22 g

Ingredients:
- ½ C. coconut flour
- 1 tbspn. spicy brown mustard
- 2 beaten eggs
- 1 pound of chicken tenders

Appetizing Fried "Mock KFC" Chicken

Prep Time	Time to cook	Serv
15 min	10 min	5

Directions:
1. Wash and pat dry chicken thighs. Slice into small chunks.
2. Mash cloves and add them along with all spices in a blender. Blend until smooth and pour over chicken, adding milk and egg. Mix thoroughly.
3. Cover chicken and chill for 1 hour.
4. Add whey protein to a bowl and dredge coated chicken pieces. Shake excess powder.
5. Ensure your AirFryer is preheated to 390 degrees.
6. Add coated chicken and cook 20 min till crispy, making sure to turn halfway through cooking.

Calories	Fat	Sugar	Protein
521	21 g	6 g	36 g

Ingredients:
- 1 tbspn. chili flakes
- 1 tbspn. curcumin
- 1 tbspn. white pepper
- 1 tbspn. ginger powder
- 1 tbspn. garlic powder
- 1 tbspn. paprika
- 1 tbspn. powdered mustard
- 1 tbspn. pepper
- 1 tbspn. celery salt
- 1/3 tbspn. oregano
- ½ tbspn. basil
- ½ tbspn. thyme
- 2 garlic cloves
- 1 egg
- Six boneless, skinless chicken thighs
- 2 tbspn. unsweetened almond milk
- ¼ C. whey protein isolate powder

Cheesy Chicken Fritters

Prep Time	Time to cook	Serv
10 min	15 min	17

Directions:
1. Slice chicken breasts into 1/3" pieces and place in a bowl.
2. Add all remaining fritter ingredients to the pan and Stir.
3. Cover and chill 2 hours or overnight.
4. Ensure your AirFryer is preheated to 350 degrees. Spray the basket with a bit of olive oil.
5. Add marinated chicken to the AirFryer and cook for 20 min, making sure to turn halfway through the cooking process.

Calories	Fat	Sugar	Protein
467	27 g	3 g	21 g

Ingredients:
- Chicken Fritters:
- ½ tbspn. salt
- 1/8 tbspn. pepper
- 1 ½ tbspn. fresh dill
- 1 1/3 C. shredded mounceszarella cheese
- 1/3 C. coconut flour
- 1/3 C. vegan mayo
- 2 eggs
- 1 ½ pounds chicken breasts
- 1/8 tbspn. pepper
- ¼ tbspn. salt
- ½ tbspn. lemon juice
- 1 pressed garlic cloves
- 1/3 C. vegan mayo

Magical Salt and Pepper Chicken Wing Stir-Fry

Prep Time	Time to cook	Serv
15 min	15 min	14-20

Directions:
1. Coat AirFryer with oil.
2. Whisk pepper, salt, and egg white together till foamy.
3. Pat wings dry and add to the bowl of egg white mixture. Coat well. Let marinate at least 20 min.
4. Place coated wings in a big bowl and add starch. Dredge wings well. Shake off and add to the AirFryer basket.
5. Cook 25 min at 380 degrees. When timer sounds, bump up the temperature to 400 degrees and cook an additional 5 min till browned.
6. For the stir fry, remove seeds from jalapenos and chop up scallions. Add both to a bowl and set to the side.
7. Heat a wok with oil and add pepper, salt, scallions, and jalapenos. Cook 1 min. Add air fried chicken to skillet and toss with stir-fried veggies. Cook 60 seconds and devour!

Ingredients:
- ¾ C. potato starch
- ¼ tbspn. pepper
- ½ tbspn. salt
- 1 egg white
- 14-20 chicken wing pieces
- ¼ tbspn. pepper
- 1 tbspn. sea salt
- 2 tbspn. avocado oil
- 2 trimmed scallions
- 2 jalapeno peppers

Calories	Fat	Sugar	Protein
351	14 g	23 g	2 g

AirFryer Chicken Parmesan

Prep Time	Time to cook	Serv
15 min	15 min	4

Directions:
1. Ensure AirFryer is preheated to 360 degrees.
2. Spray the basket with olive oil.
3. Mix parmesan cheese and breadcrumbs together. Melt ghee.
4. Brush melted ghee onto the chicken and dip into breadcrumb mixture.
5. Place coated chicken in the AirFryer and top with olive oil.
6. Cook 2 breasts for 6 min and top each breast with a tbspnn of sauce and 1 ½ tbspnn of mounceszarella cheese.
7. Cook another 3 min to melt the cheese.
8. Keep cooked pieces warm as you repeat the process with remaining breasts.

Ingredients:
- ½ C. keto marinara
- 6 tbspn. mounceszarella cheese
- 1 tbspn. melted ghee
- 2 tbspn. grated parmesan cheese
- 6 tbspn. gluten-free seasoned breadcrumbs
- 2 8-ounce chicken breasts

Calories	Fat	Sugar	Protein
251	10 g	0 g	31 g

Great Jerk Chicken Wings

Prep Time	Time to cook	Serv
10 min	15 min	7

Directions:
1. Combine all ingredients except wings in a bowl.
2. Pour into a gallon bag and add chicken wings.
3. Chill 2-24 hours to marinate.
4. Ensure your AirFryer is preheated to 390 degrees.
5. Place chicken wings into a strainer to drain excess liquids.
6. Pour half of the wings into your AirFryer and cook 14-16 min, making sure to shake halfway through the cooking process.
7. Remove and repeat the process with remaining wings.

Calories	Fat	Sugar	Protein
374	14 g	1 g	33 g

Ingredients:
- 1 tbspn. salt
- ½ C. red wine vinegar
- 5 tbspn. lime juice
- 4 minced scallions
- 1 tbspn. grated ginger
- 2 tbspn. brown sugar
- 1 tbspn. minced thyme
- 1 tbspn. white pepper
- 1 tbspn. cayenne pepper
- 1 tbspn. cinnamon
- 1 tbspn. allspice
- 1 Habanero pepper
- Six minced garlic cloves
- 2 tbspn. low-sodium soy sauce
- 2 tbspn. olive oil
- 4 pounds of chicken wings

Crispy Panko Crusted Chicken Balls

Prep Time	Time to cook	Serv
20 min	25 min	6

Directions:
1. In a large bowl, combine the butter with garlic and parsley.
2. Divide and spoon 12 equal parts of the mixture on a baking sheet. Refrigerate for 20 min or until frouncesen.
3. Divide the ground chicken into 12 equal-sized parts, and press the center of each section to make an invention.
4. Add a spoon of butter mixture into the indention. Wrap the mix in the ground chicken part and shape it into a ball.
5. Repeat with remaining butter mixture and ground chicken parts. Set aside.
6. Whisk the eggs in a separate bowl. In a third bowl, mix the panko, paprika, black pepper, and salt.
7. Drop each chicken ball in the whisked eggs, then in the panko mixture.
8. Repeat the dredging process for 1 more time. Shake the excess off. Transfer all balls to a baking sheet; refrigerate for 10 min.
9. Spritz the AirFryer basket with cooking spray, put the balls in the basket. You may need to work in batches to avoid overcrowding.
10. Put the AirFryer lid on and cook in the preheated AirFryer at 400°F for 10 min.
11. Spritz the balls with cooking spray and turn the balls over when the lid screen indicates 'TURN FOOD' halfway through the Time to cook.
12. Remove the chicken balls from the basket. Serve warm with ketchup, if desired.

Ingredients:
- 1 package (19-ounce) ground chicken breast
- 1 cup panko bread crumbs
- ½ cup unsalted butter softened
- 2 cloves garlic, crushed
- 2 tbspns flat-leaf parsley, minced
- 2 eggs
- 1 tspn paprika
- Salt and ground black pepper, to taste
- Cooking spray

Calories	Fat	Carbohydrates	Protein
154	9.4 g	6.7 g	12.6 g

Gorgeous Bang Bang Chicken with Yogurt Sauce

Prep Time: 15 min
Time to cook: 15 min
Serv: 4

Directions:
1. In a bowl, whisk the egg, milk, and hot sauce together.
2. In a second bowl, mix the flour, tapioca starch, garlic, cumin, and salt. Set aside.
3. Dredge the chicken pieces in the egg mixture first, then in the flour mixture. Shake off the excess.
4. Spritz the AirFryer basket with cooking spray. Arrange them in the basket, and spritz with cooking spray.
5. Put the air fry lid on. Cook in the preheated AirFryer at 375ºF for 5 min, shaking the basket once halfway through or until the chicken is crisp outside and juicy inside.
6. Meanwhile, to make the yogurt sauce, in a small bowl, mix the Greek yogurt, hot sauce, and sweet chili sauce.

Ingredients:
- 1 pound boneless, skinless chicken breasts
- 1 egg ½ cup milk
- 1 tbspnn hot pepper sauce
- ½ cup flour
- ½ cup tapioca starch
- 1 tspn garlic, granulated
- ½ tspn cumin
- 1½ tspns salt

Yogurt Sauce:
- ¼ cup plain Greek yogurt
- 1 tspn hot sauce
- 3 tbspns sweet chili sauce

Calories	Fat	Carbohydrates	Protein
313	6.1 g	34.4 g	28.7 g

Charming Air-fried Chicken

Prep Time: 20 min
Time to cook: 20 min
Serv: 2

Directions:
1. In a bowl, evenly combine the butter, garlic, parsley, and salt. Half the butter mixture and place on a baking sheet to cool for 10 min.
2. On a clean work surface, season the chicken with salt and pepper. Place the halved butter in the center of each chicken breast. Roll the side up to wrap the butter mixture, then wrap them in plastic. Refrigerate for 30 min.
3. In a second bowl, combine the flour and beaten egg. In a third bowl, combine the bread crumbs and paprika.
4. Remove the chicken from the refrigerator. Dredge each chicken breast in the second bowl, then in the third bowl.
5. Spritz the AirFryer basket with cooking spray, arrange the breaded chicken in the basket.
6. Put the air fry lid on and cook in the preheated AirFryer at 400ºF for 10 min.
7. Spritz the chicken with cooking spray and flip when the lid screen indicates 'TURN FOOD' halfway through.
8. Transfer the cooked chicken to a platter and chill for 5 min. Slice to serve.

Ingredients:
- 2 (8-ounce) skinless, boneless chicken breast halves, pounded to the ¼-inch thickness
- 4 tbspns butter softened
- 1 clove garlic, diced
- 2 tbspns fresh flat-leaf parsley, minced
- 1 tspn salt
- Salt and ground black pepper to taste
- ½ cup all-purpose flour
- 1 egg, beaten
- 1 cup panko bread crumbs
- 1 tspn paprika
- Cooking spray

Calories	Fat	Carbohydrates	Protein
782	35.1 g	63.7 g	63.5 g

Pretzel Crusted Chicken Chunks

Prep Time	Time to cook	Serv
10 min	10 min	6

Directions:
1. Dredge the chicken chunks in it until well coated.
2. Mix the crushed pretzels, paprika, shallot powder, salt, and pepper well in another bowl. And then toss the chicken into the mixture to get a good coating.
3. Arrange the well-coated chunks in the AirFryer basket. Put the AirFryer lid on and cook in the preheated AirFryer at 375°F for 12 min, shaking the AirFryer basket when it shows 'TURN FOOD' on the lid screen during Time to cook.
4. In the meantime, in a third bowl, combine the vegetable broth with tomato paste,
5. Worcestershire sauce, apple cider vinegar, and cornstarch.
6. Heat a frying pan over medium-high heat. Add the olive oil, then stir in the jalapeño pepper and garlic, and stir-fry for 30 to 40 seconds.
7. Pour the cornstarch mixture in the pan and bring it to a simmer. Keep stirring.
8. When the sauce starts to thicken, put the air-fried chicken chunks and mustard in.
9. Simmer it for an additional 2 min.
10. Transfer them onto a platter and serve. Bon appetit!

Ingredients:
- 1½ pound chicken breasts, boneless, skinless, cut into bite-sized chunks
- ½ cup crushed pretzels
- 2 eggs
- 1 tspn paprika
- 1 tspn shallot powderea Salt
- ½ cup vegetable broth
- 3 tbspns tomato paste
- 3 tbspns Worcestershire sauce
- 1 tbspnn apple cider vinegar
- 1 tbspnn cornstarch
- 2 tbspns olive oil
- 1 jalapeño pepper, diced
- 2 garlic cloves, minced
- 1 tspn yellow mustard

Calories	Fat	Carbs	Protein
356	17.7 g	20.4 g	28.2 g

Dreamy Rustic Drumsticks with Tamari and Hot Sauce

Prep Time	Time to cook	Serv
25 min	15 min	6

Directions:
1. Spritz the AirFryer basket with the nonstick cooking spray.
2. Place the chicken drumsticks in the AirFryer basket.
3. Put the AirFryer lid on and cook in the preheated AirFryer at 375°F for 35 min.
4. Spritz the drumsticks with the nonstick cooking spray and flip when the lid screen indicates 'TURN FOOD' halfway through Time to cook.
5. Meanwhile, warm a saucepan over medium-low heat, then add oregano, tamari sauce, thyme, and hot sauce.
6. Cook for 2 to 4 min until it has a thick consistency. Transfer the cooked drumsticks to a plate.
7. Top with the sauce and serve.

Ingredients:
- Six chicken drumsticks
- Nonstick cooking spray

Sauce:
- ½ tspn dried oregano
- 3 tbspns tamari sauce
- 1 tspn dried thyme
- 6 ounces hot sauce

Calories	Fat	Carbohydrates	Protein
281	18.8 g	2.7 g	24.2 g

Crispy Chicken Tenders

Prep Time	Time to cook	Serv
10 min	15 min	4

Directions:
1. In a shallow bowl, beat egg.
2. Thoroughly mix the crushed chips, garlic powder, red pepper flakes, salt, and pepper in a separate bowl.
3. Rub the peanut oil all over the chicken tenders.
4. Dredge the chicken tenders in the egg mixture, then in the chip mixture. Shake off the excess.
5. Spritz the AirFryer basket with cooking spray.
6. Arrange the tenders in the basket.
7. Put the AirFryer lid on and cook in batches in the preheated AirFryer at 350°F for 12 to 13 min until cooked through.
8. Spritz the tenders with cooking spray and flip when the lid screen indicates 'TURN FOOD' halfway through the Time to cook.
9. Remove the tenders from the basket to a plate and serve garnished with peanuts.

Ingredients:
- 1 pounds chicken tenders
- 2 tbspns peanut oil
- 1 egg
- ½ cup tortilla chips, crushed
- ½ tspn garlic powder
- 1 tspn red pepper flakes
- Sea salt ground black pepper
- 2 tbspns peanuts, roasted and roughly minced
- Cooking spray

Calories	Fat	Carbohydrates	Protein
342	16.5 g	10.5 g	36.7 g

Pretty Turkey Tenders with Baby Potatoes

Prep Time	Time to cook	Serv
25 min	25 min	6

Direction:
1. In a bowl, rub 1 tspn of olive oil all over the turkey tenders and sprinkle the paprika, salt, and black pepper to season.
2. Pour the white wine on the tenders and top with tarragon. Wrap in plastic and refrigerate to marinate for half an hour.
3. Arrange the tenders in the basket.
4. Put the AirFryer lid on and cook in the preheated AirFryer at 350°F for 30 min.
5. Turn the bids over when it shows 'TURN FOOD' on the lid screen halfway through.
6. Remove tenders from the AirFryer basket to a plate.
7. Chill for 5 to 9 min.
8. Spray the remaining olive oil on the sides and bottom of the AirFryer basket and cook the baby potatoes at 375°F for 16 min.
9. Shake the bucket for at least 3 times during the cooking. Slice the turkey tenders to serve, with the baby potatoes.

Ingredients:
- 2 pounds turkey tenders
- 1 pound baby potatoes, rubbed
- 2 tspns olive oil
- 1 tspn smoked paprika
- Salt and ground black pepper, to taste
- 1 tbspnn fresh tarragon, minced
- 2 tbspns dry white wine

Calories	Fat	Carbohydrates	Protein
316	7.5 g	14.3 g	45.8 g

Lovely Chicken Alfredo Bake

Prep Time	Time to cook	Serv
10 min	25 min	6

Directions:
1. Whisk cream, broth, chicken, pasta, and all the Ingredients: in a casserole dish.
2. Press "Power Button" of Air Fry Oven and turn the dial to select the "Bake" mode.
3. Press the Time button and again turn the dial to set the Time to cook to 25 min.
4. Now push the Temp button and rotate the dial to set the temperature at 380 degrees F.
5. Once preheated, place the baking dish inside and close its lid.
6. Serve warm.

Calories	Fat	Carbohydrates	Protein
378	21 g	7.1 g	23 g

Ingredients:
- 1 tbspnn olive oil
- 3 chicken breasts, cubed
- salt, to taste
- Black pepper, to taste
- 4 cloves garlic, diced
- 2 ½ cups chicken broth
- 2 ½ cups heavy cream
- 1 cup penne pasta, uncooked
- 2 cups parmesan cheese
- 2 cups mounceszarella cheese
- 1 handful fresh parsley, minced

Flavorful Chicken Drumsticks

Prep Time	Time to cook	Serv
10 min	30 min	4

Directions:
1. Add all ingredients except chicken in a large mixing bowl and mix well.
2. Add chicken drumsticks to the bowl and mix until well coated.
3. Place chicken drumsticks on the instant vortex AirFryer rack air fry at 400 F for 15 min.
4. Turn chicken drumsticks to another side and cook for 15 min more.
5. Enjoy.

Calories	Fat	Carbohydrates	Protein
296	15.8 g	11.6 g	26.9 g

Ingredients:
- Eight chicken drumsticks
- ¼ tbspn cayenne pepper
- 1 tbspn onion powder
- 1 tbspn garlic powder
- 1 ½ tbspn honey
- 1 ½ tbspn fresh lemon juice
- 1 tbspn Worcestershire sauce
- ¼ cup soy sauce, low-sodium
- 1 tbspn sesame oil
- 2 tbspn olive oil
- ½ tbspn kosher salt

Healthy Air Fried Chicken

Prep Time	Time to cook	Serv
10 min	25 min	6

Directions:
1. Preheat the instant vortex AirFryer using bake mode at 390 F.
2. Add breadcrumbs, spices, and flour into the zip-lock bag and mix well.
3. In a bowl, mix chicken and buttermilk and let sit for 2 min.
4. Now put a single piece of chicken into the zip-lock bag and shake it until chicken is evenly coated with breadcrumb mixture.
5. Do this same with remaining chicken pieces.
6. Spray coated chicken with cooking spray.
7. Place chicken into the bottom tray of instant vortex AirFryer and bake for 25 min.
8. Enjoy.

Ingredients:
- Six chicken drumsticks, rinse and pat dry with a paper towel
- 1 tbspn ginger
- 1 tbspn onion powder
- 1 tbspn garlic powder
- 1 tbspn paprika
- 1 cup buttermilk
- ¼ cup brown sugar
- ½ cup breadcrumbs
- 1 cup all-purpose flour
- ½ tbspn pepper
- 1 tbspn salt

Calories	Fat	Carbohydrates	Protein
234	3.8 g	31.5 g	17.6 g

Enjoyable Parmesan Garlic Chicken Wings

Prep Time	Time to cook	Serv
10 min	21 min	4

Directions:
1. Arrange chicken wings on prepared vortex AirFryer tray and air fry at 400 F for 7 min.
2. Turn chicken wings to the other side and air fry for 7 min more.
3. Turn chicken wings again and air fry for another 7 min.
4. In a mixing bowl, mix cheese, butter, parsley, garlic, pepper, and salt.
5. Once chicken wings are d1, then transfer in mixing bowl and toss well with cheese mixture until well coated.
6. Enjoy.

Ingredients
- 1 lb chicken wings
- 1 tbspn parsley
- 2 tbspn garlic, diced
- ¾ cup parmesan cheese, grated
- 1 tbspn butter, melted
- ¼ tbspn pepper
- 1 tbspn salt

Calories	Fat	Carbohydrates	Protein
398	20.3 g	1.5 g	45.2 g

Healthy Chicken Popcorn

Prep Time	Time to cook	Serv
10 min	10 min	4

Directions:
1. Season chicken pieces with pepper and salt.
2. Mix all-purpose flour in a medium bowl, and baking powder.
3. In another mixing bowl, mix egg, buttermilk, and Tabasco sauce.
4. Coat chicken with flour mixture, then dip chicken into the egg mixture, then again coat with flour mixture.
5. Place coated chicken pieces on prepared vortex AirFryer tray.
6. Spray painted chicken pieces with cooking spray. Air fry chicken popcorn at 400 F for min.
7. Turn chicken popcorn to another side and air fry for 5 min more.
8. Enjoy.

Ingredients:
- 1 lb chicken breast, skinless, boneless, and cut into 1-inch pieces
- 1 egg, lightly beaten
- ½ tbspn Tabasco sauce
- 1 cup buttermilk
- 1 tbspn baking powder
- 1 cup all-purpose flour
- ½ tbspn pepper
- 1 tbspn salt

Calories	Fat	Carbohydrates	Protein
285	4.8 g	27.6 g	30.7 g

Beautiful Oregano Whole Chicken

Prep Time	Time to cook	Serv
10 min	18 min	7

Directions:
1. Rub the black pepper and salt evenly over the chicken. In a mixing bowl, combine cayenne, paprika, garlic powder, onion powder, oregano, and thyme.
2. Add the chicken and coat well.
3. Grease AirFryer Basket with some cooking spray.
4. Add the chicken pieces.
5. Place AirFryer AirFryer Crisp over kitchen platform.
6. Press Air Fry, set the temperature to 400°F and set the timer to 5 min to preheat.
7. Press "Start" and allow it to preheat for 5 min.
8. In the inner pot, place the AirFryer basket.
9. Close the Crisp Lid and press the "Air Fry" setting. Set temperature to 350°F and set the timer to 18 min. Press "Start."
10. Halfway down, open the Crisp Lid, shake the basket and close the lid to continue cooking for the remaining time.
11. Open the Crisp Lid after Time to cook is over.
12. Serve warm with your choice of dip.

Ingredients:
- cut into eight pieces,
- 3-pound whole chicken
- 2 tspns onion powder
- 2 tspns garlic powder
- 1 tspn oregano dried
- 1 tbspnn thyme, dried
- ½ tspn ground black pepper
- ½ tspn kosher salt
- 1 tspn paprika, smoked
- ¼ tspn cayenne

Calories	Fat	Carbohydrates	Protein
208	5 g	3 g	34 g

Herbed Turkey Breast

Prep Time	Time to cook	Serv
10 min	50 min	6

Directions:
1. In a bowl, mix butter, garlic, sage, rosemary, thyme, lemon zest, pepper, and salt.
2. Rub the butter mixture all over the turkey breast.
3. Place turkey breast into the bottom rack of instant vortex AirFryer and cook at 350 F for 20 min.
4. Turn turkey breast to the other side and cook for 30 min more or until the internal temperature of turkey breast reaches 160 F.
5. Slice and serve.

Calories	Fat	Carbohydrates	Protein
294	9.7 g	11.1 g	39 g

Ingredients:
- 3 lbs turkey breast
- 3 garlic cloves, diced
- 1 tbspn fresh sage leaves, minced
- 1 tbspn rosemary leaves, minced
- 1 tbspn fresh thyme
- 3 tbspn butter
- 1 tbspn lemon zest, grated
- ½ tbspn pepper
- 1 tbspn kosher salt

Wonderful Mustard Turkey

Prep Time	Time to cook	Serv
10 min	35 min	4

Directions:
1. Season the turkey with black pepper and salt. Evenly rub the thyme, rosemary, and sage over the turkey.
2. Combine the melted butter in a mixing bowl, Dijon mustard, maple syrup.
3. Grease AirFryer Basket with some cooking spray. Add the seasoned turkey.
4. Place AirFryer AirFryer Crisp platform. Press AirFryer, set the temperature to 400°F and set the timer to 5 min to preheat. Press "Start" and allow it to preheat for 5 min.
5. In the inner pot, place the AirFryer basket.
6. Close the Crisp Lid and press the "Air Fry" setting. Set temperature to 390°F and set the timer to 35 min. Press "Start."
7. Halfway down, open the Crisp Lid, shake the basket and close the lid to continue cooking for the remaining time.
8. Open the Crisp Lid after Time to cook is over. Spread the maple syrup over the turkey and Air Fry for 2-3 more min.
9. Serve warm.

Calories	Fat	Carbohydrates	Protein
426	18 g	14 g	48 g

Ingredients:
- 2-pound turkey breast
- 1 tspn coarsely minced sage
- 1 tspn minced thyme
- 1 tspn finely minced rosemary
- 1 tbspn butter
- ¾ tspn ground black pepper
- ¼ cup maple syrup
- 2 tbspns Dijon mustard
- ½ tspn kosher salt

Delicious Rotisserie Chicken

Prep Time	Time to cook	Serv
10 min	50 min	6

Directions:
1. Mix garlic powder, olive oil, buttermilk, pepper, and salt in a large zip-lock bag.
2. Add whole chicken in bag. Seal bag and marinate the chicken overnight.
3. Remove marinated chicken from bag and season with pepper and salt.
4. Place marinated chicken on the rotisserie spit and inset into the instant vortex AirFryer oven.
5. Air fry chicken to 380 F for 50 min or until the internal temperature of chicken reaches 165 F.
6. Enjoy.

Ingredients:
- 3 lbs whole chicken
- ¾ tbspn garlic powder
- ¼ cup olive oil
- 2 cups buttermilk
- Pepper
- Salt

Calories	Fat	Carbohydrates	Protein
537	25.9 g	4.2 g	68.4 g

Perfect Lemon Chicken Potatoes

Prep Time	Time to cook	Serv
10 min	20 min	6

Directions:
1. In a mixing bowl, whisk the lemon juice, olive oil, garlic, parsley, oregano, pepper, lemon zest, and salt.
2. Place AirFryer AirFryer Crisp over kitchen platform. In the inner pot, add the broth and chicken. Arrange the potatoes on top and pour the lemon mixture.
3. Close the Pressure Lid and press the "Pressure" setting. Set the "Hi" pressure level and set the timer to 15 min. Press "Start."
4. AirFryer will start building pressure. Quick-extrication pressure after Time to cook is over (just press the button on the lid), and open the cover.
5. Add the chicken mixture to a serving plate along with the lemon sauce.
6. Add back the chicken to the pot. Close the Crisp Lid and press the "Air Fry" setting. Set temperature to 400°F and set the timer to 4 min. Press "Start."
7. Halfway down, open the Crisp Lid, shake the basket and close the lid to continue cooking for the remaining time.
8. Open the Crisp Lid after Time to cook is over.
9. Add the chicken to the potato mixture and serve warm.

Ingredients:
- ½ cup chicken broth
- 12 chicken thighs, b1-in
- 1 ½ pound yellow potatoes, quartered
- ⅓ cup olive oil
- ⅓ cup lemon juice
- 1 tspn lemon zest
- 1 tspn dried parsley
- 1 tspn black pepper
- 1 tbspnn garlic, diced
- 2 tspns dried oregano
- 2 tspns kosher salt
- Lemon wedges to serve

Calories	Fat	Carbohydrates	Protein
612	38.5 g	23 g	43 g

Chicken Kebabs

Prep Time	Time to cook	Serv
10 min	20 min	2

Direction:
1. Toss chicken and veggies with all the spices and seasoning in a bowl.
2. Alternatively, thread them on skewers and place these skewers in the AirFryer basket.
3. Press "Power Button" of Air Fry Oven and turn the dial to select the "Air Fry" mode.
4. Press the Time button and again turn the dial to set the Time to cook to 20 min.
5. Now push the Temp button and rotate the dial to set the temperature at 350 degrees F.
6. Once preheated, place the baking dish inside and close its lid.
7. Flip the skewers when cooked halfway through then resume cooking.
8. Serve warm.

Calories	Fat	Carbohydrates	Protein
327	3.5 g	33.6 g	24.5 g

Ingredients
- 16 ounces skinless chicken breasts, cubed
- 2 tbspns soy sauce
- ½ zucchini sliced
- 1 tbspnn chicken seasoning
- 1 tspn bbq seasoning
- salt and pepper to taste
- ½ green pepper sliced
- ½ red pepper sliced
- ½ yellow pepper sliced
- ¼ red onion sliced
- 4 cherry tomatoes
- cooking spray

Fabulous Asian Chicken Kebabs

Prep Time	Time to cook	Serv
10 min	12 min	6

Direction:
1. Toss chicken and veggies with all the spices and seasoning in a bowl.
2. Alternatively, thread them on skewers and place these skewers in the AirFryer basket.
3. Press "Power Button" of Air Fry Oven and turn the dial to select the "Air Fry" mode.
4. Press the Time button and again turn the dial to set the Time to cook to 12 min.
5. Now push the Temp button and rotate the dial to set the temperature at 380 degrees F.
6. Once preheated, place the baking dish inside and close its lid.
7. Flip the skewers when cooked halfway through then resume cooking.
8. Serve warm.

Calories	Fat	Carbohydrates	Protein
353	7.5 g	10.4 g	13.1 g

Ingredients:
- 2 lbs. chicken breasts, cubed
- 1/2 cup soy sauce
- Six cloves garlic, crushed
- 1 tspn fresh ginger, grated
- 1/2 cup golden sweetener
- 1 red pepper, minced
- 1/2 red onion, minced
- Eight mushrooms halved
- 2 cups zucchini, minced

Kebab Tavuk Sheesh

Prep Time: 10 min
Time to cook: 10 min
Serv: 2

Direction:
1. Mix chicken with yogurt and all the seasonings in a bowl.
2. Marinate the yogurt chicken for 30 min in the refrigerator.
3. Thread chicken pieces on the skewers and place these skewers in the AirFryer basket.
4. Press "Power Button" of Air Fry Oven and turn the dial to select the "Air Fry" mode.
5. Press the Time button and again turn the dial to set the Time to cook to 10 min.
6. Now push the Temp button and rotate the dial to set the temperature at 370 degrees F.
7. Once preheated, place the baking dish inside and close its lid.
8. Flip the skewers when cooked halfway through then resume cooking.
9. Serve warm.

Ingredients:
- 1/4 cup plain yogurt
- 1 tbspnn garlic, diced
- 1 tbspnn tomato paste
- 1 tbspnn olive oil
- 1 tbspnn lemon juice
- 1 tspn salt
- 1 tspn ground cumin
- 1 tspn smoked paprika
- 1/2 tspn ground cinnamon
- 1/2 tspn ground black pepper
- 1/2 tspn cayenne
- 1 lb. boneless skinless chicken thighs, quartered

Calories	Fat	Carbohydrates	Protein
426	18 g	14 g	48 g

Delish Chicken Mushroom Kebab

Prep Time: 10 min
Time to cook: 15 min
Serv: 4

Direction:
1. Toss chicken, mushrooms and veggies with all the honey, and seasoning in a bowl.
2. Alternatively, thread them on skewers and place these skewers in the AirFryer basket.
3. Press "Power Button" of Air Fry Oven and turn the dial to select the "Air Fry" mode.
4. Press the Time button and again turn the dial to set the Time to cook to 15 min.
5. Now push the Temp button and rotate the dial to set the temperature at 350 degrees F.
6. Once preheated, place the baking dish inside and close its lid.
7. Flip the skewers when cooked halfway through then resume cooking.
8. Serve warm.

Ingredients:
- 1/3 cup honey
- 1/3 cup soy sauce
- Salt, to taste
- Six mushrooms chop in half
- 3 bell peppers, cubed
- 2 chicken breasts diced

Calories	Fat	Carbohydrates	Protein
457	19.1 g	18.9 g	48 g

Chicken Fajita Skewers

Prep Time: 10 min
Time to cook: 8 min
Serv: 2

Direction:
1. Toss chicken and veggies with all the spices and seasoning in a bowl.
2. Alternatively, thread them on skewers and place these skewers in the AirFryer basket.
3. Press "Power Button" of Air Fry Oven and turn the dial to select the "Air Fry" mode.
4. Press the Time button and again turn the dial to set the Time to cook to 8 min.
5. Now push the Temp button and rotate the dial to set the temperature at 360 degrees F.
6. Once preheated, place the baking dish inside and close its lid.
7. Flip the skewers when cooked halfway through then resume cooking.
8. Serve warm.

Calories	Fat	Carbohydrates	Protein
392	16.1 g	13.9 g	48 g

Ingredients:
- 1 lb. chicken breasts, diced
- 1 tbspnn lemon juice
- 1 tspn chili powder
- 1 tspn cumin
- 1 orange bell pepper, cut into squares
- 1 red bell pepper, cut into squares
- 2 tbspnn olive oil
- 1 tspn garlic powder
- 1 large red onion, cut into squares
- 1 tspn salt
- 1 tspn ground black pepper
- 1 tspn oregano
- 1 tspn parsley flakes
- 1 tspn paprika

Yummy Zucchini Chicken Kebabs

Prep Time: 10 min
Time to cook: 16 min
Serv: 4

Direction:
1. Toss chicken and veggies with all the spices and seasoning in a bowl.
2. Alternatively, thread them on skewers and place these skewers in the AirFryer basket.
3. Press "Power Button" of Air Fry Oven and turn the dial to select the "Air Fry" mode.
4. Press the Time button and again turn the dial to set the Time to cook to 16 min.
5. Now push the Temp button and rotate the dial to set the temperature at 380 degrees F.
6. Once preheated, place the baking dish inside and close its lid.
7. Flip the skewers when cooked halfway through then resume cooking.
8. Serve warm.

Calories	Fat	Carbohydrates	Protein
321	7.4 g	19.4 g	37.2 g

Ingredients:
- 1 large zucchini, cut into squares
- 2 chicken breasts boneless, skinless, cubed
- 1 onion yellow, cut into squares
- 1.5 cup grape tomatoes
- 1 clove garlic diced
- 1 lemon juiced
- 1/4 c olive oil
- 1 tbspnn olive oil
- 2 tbspns red wine vinegar
- 1 tspn oregano

Easy Chicken Soy Skewers

Prep Time	Time to cook	Serv
10 min	7 min	4

Direction:
1. Toss chicken with all the sauces and seasonings in a baking pan.
2. Press "Power Button" of Air Fry Oven and turn the dial to select the "Air Fry" mode.
3. Press the Time button and again turn the dial to set the Time to cook to 7 min.
4. Now push the Temp button and rotate the dial to set the temperature at 390 degrees F.
5. Once preheated, place the baking dish inside and close its lid.
6. Serve warm.

Ingredients:
- 1-lb. boneless chicken tenders, diced
- 1/2 cup soy sauce
- 1/2 cup pineapple juice
- 1/4 cup sesame seed oil
- 4 garlic cloves, minced
- 4 scallions, minced
- 1 tbspnn grated ginger
- 2 tspns toasted sesame seeds
- black pepper

Calories	Fat	Carbohydrates	Protein
248	15.7 g	31.4 g	24.9 g

Enjoyable Basil-Garlic Breaded Chicken Bake

Prep Time	Time to cook	Serv
5 min	25 min	2

Directions:
1. In a shallow bowl, whisk well egg substitute and place flour in a separate bowl.
2. Dip chicken in flour, then egg, and then flour. In a small bowl, whisk fresh butter, bread crumbs, and cheese.
3. Sprinkle over chicken.
4. Lightly grease the baking pan of the AirFryer with cooking spray.
5. Place breaded chicken on the bottom of the pan.
6. Cover with foil.
7. For 20 min, cook at 390°F. Meanwhile, in a bowl whisk well-remaining ingredient.
8. Remove foil from pan and then pour over chicken the remaining Ingredients.
9. Cook for 8 min.
10. Enjoy.

Ingredients:
- 2 boneless skinless chicken breast halves (4 ounces each)
- 1 tbspnn butter, melted
- 1 large tomato, seeded and minced
- 2 garlic cloves, diced
- 1 1/2 tbspns dicedfresh basil
- 1/2 tbspnn olive oil
- 1/2 tspn salt
- 1/4 cup all-purpose flour
- 1/4 cup egg substitute
- 1/4 cup grated Parmesan cheese
- 1/4 cup dry bread crumbs
- 1/4 tspn pepper

Calories	Fat	Carbohydrates	Protein
311	11 g	22 g	31 g

Finger-licking Chicken Alfredo Bake

Prep Time	Time to cook	Serv
10 min	25 min	6

Direction:
1. Whisk cream, broth, chicken, pasta, and all the ingredients in a casserole dish.
2. Press "Power Button" of Air Fry Oven and turn the dial to select the "Bake" mode.
3. Press the Time button and again turn the dial to set the Time to cook to 25 min.
4. Now push the Temp button and rotate the dial to set the temperature at 380 degrees F.
5. Once preheated, place the baking dish inside and close its lid.
6. Serve warm.

Calories	Fat	Carbohydrates	Protein
378	21 g	7.1 g	23 g

Ingredients:
- 1 tbspnn olive oil
- 3 chicken breasts, cubed salt, to taste
- Black pepper, to taste
- 4 cloves garlic, diced
- 2 ½ cups chicken broth
- 2 ½ cups heavy cream
- 1 cup penne pasta, uncooked
- 2 cups parmesan cheese
- 2 cups mounceszarella cheese
- 1 handful fresh parsley, minced

Roasted Goose

Prep Time	Time to cook	Serv
10 min	40 min	12

Directions:
1. Place the goose in a baking tray and whisk the rest of the ingredients in a bowl.
2. Pour this thick sauce over the goose and brush it liberally.
3. Press "Power Button" of Air Fry Oven and turn the dial to select the "Air Roast" mode.
4. Press the Time button and again turn the dial to set the Time to cook to 40 min.
5. Now push the Temp button and rotate the dial to set the temperature at 355 degrees F.
6. Once preheated, place the casserole dish inside and close its lid.
7. Serve warm.

Calories	Fat	Carbohydrates	Protein
231	20.1 g	20.1 g	14.6 g

Ingredients:
- 8 lbs. goose
- Juice of a lemon
- Salt and pepper
- 1/2 yellow onion, peeled and minced
- 1 head garlic, peeled and minced
- 1/2 cup wine
- 1 tspn dried thyme

Holyday Roast Goose

Prep Time	Time to cook	Serv
10 min	60 min	12

Directions:
1. Place the goose in a baking dish and brush it with syrup.
2. Set the lemon and lime slices on top of the goose.
3. Add all the herbs and spice powder over the lemon slices.
4. Press "Power Button" of Air Fry Oven and turn the dial to select the "Air Roast" mode.
5. Press the Time button and again turn the dial to set the Time to cook to 60 min.
6. Now push the Temp button and rotate the dial to set the temperature at 375 degrees F.
7. Once preheated, place the baking dish inside and close its lid.
8. Serve warm.

Calories	Fat	Carbohydrates	Protein
472	11.1g	19.9 g	13.5 g

Ingredients:
- 2 goose
- 2 lemons, sliced
- 1 ½ lime, sliced
- ½ tspn Chinese five-spice powder
- ½ handful parsley, minced
- ½ handful sprigs, minced
- ½ handful thyme, minced
- ½ handful sage, minced
- 1 ½ tbspnn clear honey
- ½ tbspnn thyme leaves

Almond Flour Coco-Milk Battered Chicken

Prep Time	Time to cook	Serv
5 min	30 min	4

Directions:
1. Preheat the AirFryer oven for 5 min.
2. Mix the egg and coconut milk in a bowl.
3. Soak the chicken thighs in the beaten egg mixture.
4. In a mixing bowl, combine the almond flour, Cajun seasoning, salt, and pepper.
5. Dredge the chicken thighs in the almond flour mixture.
6. Place in the AirFryer basket.
7. Cook for 30 min at 350°F.

Calories	Fat	Carbohydrates	Protein
590	38 g	3.2 g	32.5 g

Ingredients:
- ¼ cup of coconut milk
- ½ cup almond flour
- 1 ½ tbspnn old bay Cajun seasoning
- 1 egg, beaten
- 4 small chicken thighs
- Salt and pepper to taste

Fantastic Buffalo Chicken Wings

Prep Time	Time to cook	Serv
5 min	30 min	8

Directions:
1. Whisk salt, brown sugar, Worcestershire sauce, butter, and hot sauce together and set to the side.
2. Dry wings and add to the AirFryer basket.
3. Set temperature to 380°F, and set time to 25 min. Cook is tossing halfway through.
4. When the timer sounds, shake wings and bump up the temperature to 400 degrees and cook for another 5 min.
5. Take out wings and place them into a big bowl.
6. Add sauce and toss well.
7. Serve alongside celery sticks.

Calories	Fat	Sugar	Protein
402	18 g	22 g	17 g

Ingredients:
- 1 tbspn. salt
- 1-2 tbspn. brown sugar
- 1 tbspn. Worcestershire sauce
- ½ C. vegan butter
- ½ C. cayenne pepper sauce
- 4 pounds of chicken wings

Honey and Wine Chicken Breasts

Prep Time	Time to cook	Serv
5 min	15 min	4

Directions:
1. Firstly, pat the chicken breasts dry.
2. Lightly coat them with the melted butter.
3. Then, add the remaining ingredients.
4. Transfer them to the AirFryer basket; bake about 15 min at 330 degrees F.
5. Serve warm and enjoy!

Calories	Fat	Sugar	Protein
189	14 g	1g	11 g

Ingredients:
- 2 chicken breasts, rinsed and halved
- 1 tbspnn melted butter
- 1/2 tspn ground pepper
- 3/4 tspn salt
- 1 tspn paprika
- 1 tspn dried rosemary
- 2 tbspns dry white wine
- 1 tbspnn honey

Great Lemon-Pepper Chicken Wings

Prep Time	Time to cook	Serv
10 min	20 min	4

Directions:
1. Place the sides in a sealable plastic bag.
2. Drizzle the sides with the lemon juice.
3. Season the teams with the garlic powder, onion powder, and salt and pepper to taste.
4. Seal the bag. Shake thoroughly to combine the seasonings and coat the wings.
5. Pour the buttermilk and the flour into separate bowls large enough to dip the wings.
6. Spray the AirFryer oven basket with cooking oil.
7. 1 at a time, dip the wings in the buttermilk and then the flour.
8. Place the wings in the AirFryer oven basket. It is okay to stack them on top of each other.
9. Spray the sides with cooking oil, being sure to spray the bottom layer.
10. Set temperature to 360°F and cook for 5 min.
11. Remove the basket and shake it to ensure all of the pieces will cook thoroughly.
12. Return the basket to the AirFryer oven and continue to cook the chicken.
13. Repeat shaking every 5 min until a total of 20 min has passed.
14. Cool before serving.

Calories	Fat	Sugar	Protein
347	12 g	1 g	46 g

Ingredients:
- 1/8 C. water
- ½ tbspn. salt
- 4 tbspn. dicedgarlic
- ¼ C. vegan butter
- ¼ C. raw honey
- ¾ C. almond flour
- 16 chicken wings

Magnificent Crispy Honey Garlic Chicken Wings

Prep Time	Time to cook	Serv
10 min	25 min	8

Directions:
1. Rinse off and dry chicken wings well.
2. Spray AirFryer basket with olive oil.
3. Coat chicken wings with almond flour and add coated sides to the AirFryer.
4. Pour into the Oven basket.
5. Place the basket on the middle shelf of the AirFryer oven.
6. Set temperature to 380 F, and set time to 25 min.
7. Cook is shaking every 5 min.
8. When the timer goes off, cook 5-10 min at 400 degrees till the skin becomes crispy and dry.
9. As chicken cooks, melt butter in a saucepan and add garlic.
10. Sauté garlic 5 min.
11. Add salt and honey, simmer 20 min. Often stir, so the sauce does not burn.
12. Add a bit of water after 15 min to ensure the sauce does not harden.
13. Take out chicken wings from the AirFryer and coat in sauce. Enjoy!

Ingredients:
- Eight whole chicken wings
- Juice of ½ lemon
- ½ tspn garlic powder
- 1 tspn onion powder
- Salt
- Pepper
- ¼ cup low-fat buttermilk
- ½ cup all-purpose flour
- Cooking oil

Calories	Fat	Sugar	Protein
435	19 g	6 g	31 g

Mexican Chicken Burgers

Prep Time	Time to cook	Serv
10 min	10 min	6

Directions:
1. Ensure your AirFryer oven is preheated to 350 degrees.
2. Add seasonings to a blender. Slice cauliflower into florets and add to blender.
3. Pulse till mixture resembles that of breadcrumbs.
4. Take out ¾ of the cauliflower mixture and add to a bowl. Set to the side. In another bowl, beat your egg and set it to the side.
5. Remove skin and b1s from chicken breasts and add to blender with remaining cauliflower mixture. Season with pepper and salt.
6. Take out mixture and form into burger shapes.
7. Roll each patty in cauliflower crumbs, then the egg, and back into bits again.
8. Place coated patties into the Oven rack/basket.
9. Place the Rack on the middle-shelf of the AirFryer oven.
10. Set temperature to 350°F and set time to 10 min. Flip over at a 10-min mark.
11. They are d1 when crispy.

Ingredients:
- 1 jalapeno pepper
- 1 tbspn. cayenne pepper
- 1 tbspn. mustard powder
- 1 tbspn. oregano
- 1 tbspn. thyme
- 3 tbspn. smoked paprika
- 1 beaten egg
- 1 small head of cauliflower
- 4 chicken breasts

Calories	Fat	Sugar	Protein
234	18 g	1 g	24 g

Yummy BBQ Chicken Recipe from Greece

Prep Time	Time to cook	Serv
10 min	25 min	4

Directions:
1. In a shallow dish, mix well rosemary, pepper, salt, oregano, lemon juice, lemon zest, feta cheese, and yogurt.
2. Add chicken and toss well to coat.
3. Marinate in the ref for 3 hours.
4. Thread bell pepper, onion, and chicken pieces in skewers.
5. Place on a skewer rack.
6. For 12 min, cook on 360°F. Halfway through Time to cook, turnover skewers.
7. If needed, cook in batches.
8. Enjoy.

Calories	Fat	Sugar	Protein
242	7.5 g	6 g	31 g

Ingredients:
- 1 (8 ounces) container fat-free plain yogurt
- 2 tbspns fresh lemon juice
- 2 tspns dried oregano
- 1-pound skinless, boneless chicken breast halves - cut into 1-inch pieces
- 1 large red onion, cut into wedges
- 1/2 tspn lemon zest
- 1/2 tspn salt
- 1 large green bell pepper
- cut into 1 1/2-inch piece
- 1/3 cup crumbled feta cheese with basil and sun-dried tomatoes
- 1/4 tspn ground black pepper
- 1/4 tspn crushed dried rosemary

Caesar Marinated Grilled Chicken

Prep Time	Time to cook	Serv
10 min	24 min	3

Direcions:
1. In a shallow dish, mix well chicken, 2 tbspns Caesar dressing, parmesan, and breadcrumbs. Mix well with hands.
2. Form into 1-inch oval patties.
3. Thread chicken pieces in skewers. Place on skewer rack in AirFryer oven.
4. For 12 min, cook on 360°F. Halfway through Time to cook, turnover skewers. If needed, cook in batches.
5. Enjoy on a bed of lettuce and sprinkle with croutons and extra dressing.

Calories	Fat	Sugar	Protein
339	18.9 g	1 g	32.6 g

Ingredients:
- ¼ cup crouton
- 1 tspn lemon zest. Form into ovals, skewer, and grill.
- 1/2 cup Parmesan
- 1/4 cup breadcrumbs
- 1-pound ground chicken
- 2 tbspns Caesar dressing and more for drizzling
- 2-4 romaine leaves

Adorable Fried Chicken Livers

Prep Time	Time to cook	Serv
5 min	10 min	4

Directions:
1. Clean and rinse the livers, pat dry.
2. Beat eggs in a shallow bowl and mix in milk.
3. In another bowl, combine flour, cornmeal, and seasoning, mixing until even.
4. Dip the livers in the egg mix, then toss them in the flour mix.
5. Pour into the Oven rack/basket.
6. Place the Rack on the middle-shelf of the AirFryer oven.
7. Set temperature to 375°F, and set time to 10 min.
8. Toss at least once halfway through.

Calories	Fat	Sugar	Protein
409	11 g	2 g	36 g

Ingredients:
- 1 pound chicken livers
- 1 cup flour
- 1/2 cup cornmeal
- 2 tspns your favorite seasoning blend
- 3 eggs
- 2 tbspns milk

Crispy Southern Fried Chicken

Prep Time	Time to cook	Serv
10 min	25 min	4

Directions:
1. Ensure the AirFryer oven is preheated to 350 degrees.
2. Layout chicken and season with pepper and salt on all sides.
3. Add all other ingredients to a blender, blending till a smooth-like breadcrumb mixture is created. Place in a bowl and add a beaten egg to another container.
4. Dip chicken into breadcrumbs, then into the egg, and breadcrumbs once more.
5. Place coated drumsticks into the AirFryer basket. Set temperature to 350°F, and set time to 20 min and cook 20 min. Bump up the heat to 390 degrees and cook another 5 min till crispy.

Calories	Fat	Sugar	Protein
504	18 g	5 g	35 g

Ingredients:
- 1 tbspn. cayenne pepper
- 2 tbspn. mustard powder
- 2 tbspn. oregano
- 2 tbspn. thyme
- 3 tbspn. coconut milk
- 1 beaten egg
- ¼ C. cauliflower
- ¼ C. gluten-free oats
- Eight chicken drumsticks

Pretty Garlic Rosemary Roasted Cornish Hen

Prep Time	Time to cook	Serv
10 min	45 min	2

Directions:
1. Season the entire chicken with garlic, salt, and pepper.
2. Place in the AirFryer basket.
3. Cook for 30 min at 3300F.
4. Flip the chicken on the other side and cook for another 15 min.

Calories	Fat	Sugar	Protein
166	4.3g	1.2 g	26.5 g

Ingredients:
- 1 tbspn rosemary
- 1 whole Cornish game hen
- 4 cloves of garlic, diced
- Salt and pepper to taste

Ginger-Garam Masala Rubbed Chicken

Prep Time	Time to cook	Serv
10 min	50 min	8

Directions:
1. Preheat the AirFryer to 350oF.
2. Place all ingredients in a baking dish that will fit in the AirFryer.
3. Stir to combine.
4. Place in the AirFryer.
5. Cook for 50 min.
6. Halfway through Time to cook, turn over chicken pieces, and stir to mix.

Calories	Fat	Sugar	Protein
236	13 g	1.3 g	25.1 g

Ingredients:
- 2 tbspns olive oil
- 1 whole chicken, sliced into eight pieces
- 1 thumb-size ginger, grated
- 1 tspn turmeric powder
- 1 tspn garam masala
- 1 tspn coriander powder
- 1 cup of coconut milk
- 1 bell pepper, seeded and julienned

Tasty Chicken Cordon Bleu

Prep Time	Time to cook	Serv
5 min	30 min	2

Directions:
1. Season the chicken with parsley, salt, and pepper to taste.
2. Place the cheese and ham in the middle of the chicken and roll.
3. Secure with a toothpick.
4. Soak the rolled-up chicken in egg and dredge in almond flour.
5. Place in the AirFryer.
6. Cook for 30 min at 3500F.
7. Turnover chicken after 20 min of Time to cook.

Calories	Fat	Sugar	Protein
458	19.1 g	1.8 g	64 g

Ingredients:
- ¼ cup almond flour
- 1 slice cheddar cheese
- 1 slice of ham
- 1 small egg, beaten
- 1 tspn parsley
- 2 chicken breasts, butterflied
- Salt and pepper to taste

Perfect Southern Style Fried Chicken

Prep Time	Time to cook	Serv
5 min	35 min	2

Directions:
1. Preheat the AirFryer to 350oF.
2. Put all ingredients in a bowl, except for chicken.
3. Give a good stir.
4. Add chicken and cover well with batter.
5. Place chicken in the AirFryer.
6. Cook for 35 min. After 20 min, turn over chicken.

Calories	Fat	Sugar	Protein
321	8.3 g	1.4 g	32.6 g

Ingredients:
- 2-pcs chicken leg quarters
- 1 tspn salt
- 1 tspn pepper
- 1 tspn paprika
- 1 tspn garlic powder
- ½ cup coconut flour

Chicken Marinated in Coconut Milk with Ginger-Cilantro

Prep Time	Time to cook	Serv
10 min	25 min	4

Directions:
1. Place the ingredients all together in a bowl and stir to coat the chicken with all ingredients.
2. Allow to marinate and leave it on the fridge for 2 hours.
3. Preheat the AirFryer to 400oF.
4. Place the chicken pieces in the AirFryer basket.
5. Cook for 25 min at 4000F.
6. Turnover of chicken pieces after 17 min has elapsed.

Calories	Fat	Sugar	Protein
173	6.8 g	1.2 g	24 g

Ingredients:
- Salt and pepper to taste
- 1-pound chicken tenders, cut in half
- 1 tspn turmeric
- 1 tspn smoked paprika
- 1 tspn garam masala
- 1 tbspnn dicedgarlic
- 1 tbspnn grated ginger
- ½ cup of coconut milk
- ¼ cup cilantro leaves, minced

Tasty Turkey Meatballs in Cranberry Sauce

Prep Time	Time to cook	Serv
5 min	25 min	4

Directions:
1. In a bowl, mix well with hands the turkey, ground bacon, and a tbspn of salt.
2. Evenly form into 16 equal-sized balls.
3. In a small saucepan boil, cranberry sauce, barbecue sauce, water, cider vinegar, and a dash or 2 of salt.
4. Mix well and simmer for 3 min.
5. Preheat AIRFRYER AirFryer to 360oF.
6. For 15 min, cook meatballs and shake basket halfway through Time to cook.
7. Pour sauce over cooked meatballs, Enjoy.

Ingredients:
- 2 tspns cider vinegar
- 1-pound ground turkey 1/4-pound ground bacon
- 1/3 cup cranberry sauce
- 1 tbspn salt and more to taste
- 1 1/2 tbspns barbecue sauce
- 1 ½ tbspns water

Calories	Fat	Sugar	Protein
329	19.9 g	11 g	25.9 g

Creamy Chicken Breasts Bake

Prep Time	Time to cook	Serv
4 min	25 min	4

Directions:
1. Preheat the AirFryer for 5 min.
2. Put on the breast chicken in a baking dish that will fit in the AirFryer.
3. Add the olive oil and cream cheese.
4. Season with salt and pepper to taste.
5. Place the baking dish with the chicken and cook for 25 min at 3500F.
6. Sprinkle crumbled bacon after.

Ingredients:
- ¼ cup olive oil
- 1 block cream cheese
- 2 chicken breasts
- Eight slices of bacon, fried and crumbled
- Salt and pepper to taste

Calories	Fat	Sugar	Protein
557	44.2 g	2.6 g	35.7 g

Lovely Chicken Pot Pie

Prep Time	Time to cook	Serv
5 min	30 min	4

Directions:
1. Preheat the AirFryer to 325F.
2. Place 1 tbspnn butter, broccoli, onion, garlic, coconut milk, chicken broth, and ground chicken in a baking dish that will fit in the AirFryer. Season with salt and pepper to taste.
3. In a mixing bowl, combine the 2.5 tbspns butter, coconut flour, and eggs.
4. Sprinkle the top of the chicken and broccoli mixture with the coconut flour dough evenly.
5. Place the dish in the AirFryer.
6. Cook for 30 min at 325F.

Ingredients:
- Salt and pepper to taste
- 2 eggs
- 2 cloves of garlic, diced
- 2 ½ tbspns butter, melted
- 1-pound ground chicken
- 1/3 cup coconut flour
- 1 tbspnn butter
- 1 cup chicken broth
- ¾ cup of coconut milk
- ½ cup broccoli, minced
- ¼ small onion, minced

Calories	Fat	Sugar	Protein
436	35 g	3.1 g	26.3 g

Butter-Lemon on Chicken Thighs

Prep Time	Time to cook	Serv
4 min	35 min	4

Directions:
1. Preheat the AirFryer to 325oF.
2. Combine all ingredients in a baking dish.
3. Make sure that all lumps are removed.
4. Place the baking dish in the AirFryer chamber.
5. Cook for 35 min at 3250F.
6. After 25 min of Time to cook, turn over chicken pieces, and mix sauce well.

Calories	Fat	Sugar	Protein
391	30.9 g	2.3 g	22.4 g

Ingredients:
- 1/2 cup almond flour
- ½ cup chicken stock
- 1 egg, beaten
- 1 small onion, diced
- 1-pound chicken thighs
- 2 tbspns capers
- 1 tbspnn olive oil 2 tbspns butter
- Juice from 1 lemon, freshly squeezed
- Salt and pepper to taste

Magical Garlicky-Dijon Chicken Thighs

Prep Time	Time to cook	Serv
5 min	25 min	4

Directions:
1. Place all ingredients in a Ziploc bag.
2. Allowing to marinate in the fridge for at least 2 hours.
3. Preheat the AirFryer to 350oF.
4. Place the chicken in the fryer basket.
5. Cook for 25 min at 3500F.
6. After 15 min of cooking, turnover thighs.

Calories	Fat	Sugar	Protein
318	25.7 g	0.6 g	19.1 g

Ingredients:
- Salt and pepper to taste
- 2 tspns herbs de Provence
- 2 tbspnn olive oil
- 1-pound chicken thighs
- 1 tbspnn Dijon mustard
- 1 tbspnn cider vinegar

Air Fried Turkey with Maple Mustard Glaze

Prep Time	Time to cook	Serv
10 min	30 min	4

Direction:
1. Preheat the fryer to 350 degrees.
2. Brush the entire turkey with olive oil.
3. Combine seasonings and toss to mix.
4. Rub the seasonings over the turkey and put it in the fryer, frying for 25 min.
5. Turn it on 1 side and fry for another 12 min.
6. Turn it on the other side and cook for 12 more min.
7. Melting butter in a bowl and mix in syrup and mustard.
8. Return the turkey to its upright position and brush the syrup mix over the turkey.
9. Cook for five more min before serving.

Calories	Fat	Sugar	Protein
469	8.7 g	6 g	70.4 g

Ingredients:
- 2 tspns Olive Oil
- 3 pound Whole Turkey Breast
- 1 tspn Dried Thyme
- 1/2 tspn Dried Sage
- 1/2 tspn Smoked Paprika
- 1 tspn salt
- 1/2 tspn Black Pepper
- 1/4 cup Maple Syrup
- 2 tbspnn Dijon Mustard
- 1 tbspnn butter

Easy and Healthy Chicken Strips

Prep Time	Time to cook	Serv
10 min	10 min	2

Direction:
1. Separate the egg and remove the yolk.
2. Cutting the chicken breasts into strips and with salt and pepper.
3. Set up your flour, egg whites, and bread crumbs in 3 separate shallow bowls.
4. Cover the chicken in flour, dip it in egg, then dredge it through the bread crumbs.
5. Cook at 350 degrees for 10 min.

Ingredients:
- 12 ounces Chicken Breasts
- 1 Egg
- 1/8 cup Flour
- 1/2 cup Panko Bread Crumbs
- Salt and Pepper to taste

Calories	Fat	Sugar	Protein
490	16.3 g	5 g	56.4 g

Chicken Fajita Roll-Ups

Prep Time	Time to cook	Serv
25 min	10 min	6

Direction:
1. Cut the bell pepper halves vertically into thin strips.
2. Mix all of your spices.
3. Half each chicken breast through the middle to create 2 breasts from 1. Pound each breast half flat.
4. Seasoning both sides of each piece of chicken with the spice blend.
5. Place 2 bell pepper strips of each color and a few pieces of onion in the center of each piece of chicken.
6. Roll the chicken up around the peppers and onions and use 1 or 2 toothpicks to hold the roll up shut.
7. Preheat your fryer to 400 degrees.
8. Spray each roll-up with cooking spray and cook 3 at a time for 10 min.

Ingredients:
- 3 Chicken Breasts
- 1/2 Red, Green, and Yellow Bell Pepper
- 1/2 Red Onion
- 2 tspns Paprika
- 1 tspn Garlic Powder
- 1 tspn Cumin Powder
- 1/2 tspn Cayenne
- 1/2 tspn Oregano
- Salt and Pepper to taste
- Cooking Spray
- Toothpicks

Calories	Fat	Sugar	Protein
145	8.1 g	3 g	7.8 g

Fantastic Mounceszarella Turkey Rolls

Prep Time	Time to cook	Serv
4 min	10 min	4

Directions:
1. Preheat your AirFryer to 390°F. Place the slices of mounceszarella cheese, tomato, and basil onto each slice of turkey. Roll up and tie with a chive shoot. Place into an AirFryer and cook for 10-min. Serve warm.

Ingredients:
- 4 slices of turkey breast
- 4 chive shoots (for tying rolls)
- 1 tomato, sliced
- ½ cup basil, fresh, minced
- 1 cup mounceszarella, sliced

Calories	Fat	Carbs	Protein
296	12.4 g	10.2 g	16.2 g

Chicken Kabobs

Prep Time	Time to cook	Serv
15 min	15 min	2

Direction:
1. Cut the chicken breast into cubes.
2. Spray the cubes with cooking spray and season with salt and pepper.
3. Transfer to a bowl and mix chicken with honey, soy sauce, and sesame seeds.
4. Cut Mushrooms in half.
5. Preheat your fryer to 340 degrees.
6. Add chicken, peppers, and mushrooms onto kabob skewers (metal skewers work better in an AirFryer), alternating each 1 until the skewers are full.
7. Cook for 20 min, turning the kabobs at the halfway mark.

Ingredients:
- 2 Chicken Breasts
- 1/3 cup Honey
- 1/3 cup Soy Sauce
- Sesame Seeds
- 6 Mushrooms
- 1 each Red, Yellow, and Green Bell Pepper
- Cooking Spray
- Salt to taste

Calories	Fat	Carbs	Protein
377	3.1 g	65.1 g	27.5 g

Savory Tandoori Chicken

Prep Time	Time to cook	Serv
25 min	30 min	2

Direction:
1. Wash the chicken legs and cut a few slits in each 1.
2. Mix ginger paste, garlic paste, and salt.
3. Put the chicken in a bowl and coat with the ginger paste mix.
4. Set the chicken in the fridge for 15 min.
5. While the chicken marinates, mix all the other ingredients.
6. Pour the marinade over the chicken and return to the fridge for at least 10 hours.
7. Preheat the fryer to 360 degrees.
8. Cook the chicken for 30 min, turning halfway through.

Ingredients:
- 4 Chicken Legs
- 3 tspns Ginger Paste
- 3 tspns Garlic Paste
- Salt to taste
- 3 tbspns Lemon Juice
- 2 tbspnn Tandoori Masala Powder
- 1 tspn Roasted Cumin Powder
- 1 tspn Garam Masala Powder
- 2 tspns Red Chili Powder
- 1 tspn Turmeric Powder
- 4 tbspns Hung Curd
- 2 tspns Kasuri Methi
- 1 tspn Black Pepper
- 2 tspns Coriander Powder

Calories	Fat	Carbs	Protein
526	16.4 g	80.1 g	21.1 g

Crispy Coconut Chicken

Prep Time	Time to cook	Serv
15 min	15 min	4

Direction:
1. Beat the eggs and cut the chicken into strips.
2. Mix cornstarch, salt, and pepper in a separate bowl.
3. Place your coconut in a third shallow bowl or plate.
4. Roll the chicken in the cornstarch mix.
5. Put the chicken in the egg and roll it in coconut.
6. Preheat the fryer to 360 degrees.
7. Cook for 15 min, flipping halfway through.

Ingredients:
- 1/2 cup Cornstarch
- 1/4 tspn salt
- 1/8 tspn Pepper
- 3 Eggs
- 4 cups of Sweetened Coconut Flakes
- 4 medium boneless

Calories	Fat	Carbs	Protein
820	43 g	66.5 g	38.8 g

Scrummy Bacon-Wrapped Stuffed Chicken

Prep Time	Time to cook	Serv
10 min	30 min	4

Direction:
1. Put all the cream cheese in a mixing bowl and allow it to soften.
2. Mix the cheddar cheese and cream cheese.
3. Put the cheese mixture into equal-sized logs.
4. Wrap each log in plastic wrap and place them in the freezer for 10 min.
5. Cut a slit into each chicken breast from the top, but be careful not to cut through the bottom.
6. Wrapping the 2 pieces of bacon around each breast.
7. Place the breasts in the fryer and sprinkle with parsley.
8. Cook at 360 for 30 min, flipping halfway through.

Calories	Fat	Carbs	Protein
424	25.4 g	1 g	43.4 g

Ingredients:
- 4 ounces Cream Cheese
- 1/2 cup Shredded Cheddar Cheese
- 4 – 4 ounce Chicken Breasts
- Eight slices Thin Cut Bacon
- 1 tbspnn Parsley

Homemade Chicken Nuggets

Prep Time	Time to cook	Serv
10 min	10 min	4

Direction:
1. Put chicken, olive oil, salt, and pepper in a bowl and toss to coat.
2. Mix the breadcrumbs and parmesan in a bowl.
3. Toss the chicken in the breadcrumb mixture.
4. Placing the chicken in the basket and put with olive oil spray.
5. Preheat the fryer to 400 degrees.
6. Cook for 10 min, tossing halfway through.

Calories	Fat	Carbs	Protein
147	4.6 g	10.2 g	16 g

Ingredients:
- 2 – 8-ounce Skinless Boneless Chicken Breasts
- Salt and Pepper to taste
- 2 tspns Olive Oil
- Six tbspns Italian Seasoned Breadcrumbs
- 2 tbspns Panko Bread Crumbs
- 2 tbspns Parmesan Cheese
- Olive Oil Spray

Appetizing Buffalo Chicken Meatballs

Prep Time	Time to cook	Serv
10 min	10 min	4

Direction:
1. Dicedthe garlic.
2. Combine garlic, ranch seasoning, and breadcrumbs in a large bowl.
3. Add the chicken and knead the ingredients together.
4. Roll into small balls.
5. Cook for 360 degrees for 5 min.
6. Toss the meatballs in the hot sauce and cook for another 5 min.
7. Mix ranch and blue cheese crumbles.
8. Drizzle ranch mix over meatballs before serving.

Calories	Fat	Carbs	Protein
419	12.9 g	11.4 g	37.3 g

Ingredients:
- 1 pound Ground Chicken
- 4 Garlic Cloves
- 1 package Ranch Seasoning
- 1 cup Seasoned Breadcrumbs
- 1 cup Hot Sauce
- 1 cup Ranch Dressing
- 1/2 cup Blue Cheese Crumbles

Perfect Chicken Wontons

Prep Time	Time to cook	Serv
12 min	25 min	4

Direction:
1. Finely dicedall of your vegetables, beans, and chicken into the smallest pieces possible.
2. Mix flour, salt, and a little hot water to create a stiff dough. Cover and set aside.
3. Beat the egg in a large bowl.
4. Add all other ingredients except for the sesame seed oil to the egg bowl and mix well.
5. Add the sesame seed oil to the mix and mix again.
6. Roll your dough flat and use a cookie cutter to cut it into circles about 6 inches in diameter.
7. Preheat the fryer to 360 degrees.
8. Scoop a little mixture into the center of each circle.
9. Use your fingers to wet the edges of the circles.
10. Fold them over the stuffing and press to close.
11. Cook in the fryer for 12 min, flipping them after 7 min.

Ingredients:
- 1 cup All-Purpose Flour
- 1/4 pound Boneless Skinless Chicken Breast
- 1 Egg
- 1 Green Onion
- 1 tbspnn French beans
- 1 tbspnn carrots
- 1/2 tspn Pepper Powder
- 1/4 tspn Soy Sauce
- 1/2 tspn Cornstarch
- 1 tspn Sesame Seed Oil

Calories	Fat	Carbs	Protein
208	4.7 g	26.8 g	13.5 g

Turkey & Cheese Calz1

Prep Time	Time to cook	Serv
5 min	10 min	4

Directions:
1. Roll the pizza dough out into small circles, the same size as a small pizza. Add thyme, oregano, basil into a bowl with tomato sauce, and mix well. Pour a small amount of sauce onto your pizza bases and spread across the surface. Add the turkey, bacon, and cheese. Brush the edge of dough with beaten egg, then fold over and pinch to seal. Brush the outside with more egg. Place into the AirFryer and cook at 350°F for 10-min. Serve warm.

Ingredients:
- 1 free-range egg, beaten
- ¼ cup mounceszarella cheese, grated
- 1 cup cheddar cheese, grated
- 1-ounce bacon, minced, cooked
- Cooked turkey, shredded
- 4 tbspns tomato sauce
- Salt and pepper to taste
- 1 tspn thyme
- 1 tspn basil
- 1 tspn oregano
- 1 package frouncesen pizza dough

Calories	Fat	Carbs	Protein
289	11.2 g	10.3 g	11.4 g

Toothsome Turkey & Avocado Burrito

Prep Time	Time to cook	Serv
4 min	10 min	2

Directions:
1. Whisk the eggs, then add some salt and pepper. Spray the inside of your AirFryer tray with cooking spray and pour in the egg mixture. Cook for 5-min at 390°F. Scrape into a clean bowl. Divide the eggs between the 2 tortillas, followed by the turkey, avocado, pepper, cheese, and salsa. Roll up carefully. Spray inside of the AirFryer again and place the burritos inside of it. Cook at 350°F for 5-min. Serve warm.

Ingredients:
- 4 free-range eggs
- 8-slices turkey breast, cooked
- 4 tbspns salsa
- ¼ cup mounceszarella cheese, grated
- ½ cup avocado, sliced
- ½ red bell pepper, sliced
- 2 x tortillas
- Salt and pepper to taste

Calories	Fat	Carbs	Protein
289	11.2 g	9.7 g	12.3 g

Turkey Sausage Patties

Prep Time	Time to cook	Serv
2 min	4 min	6

Directions:
1. Preheat your AirFryer to 375°F. Add half of the oil along with onion and garlic to the AirFryer. Air fry for 1-min, then add fennel seeds then transfer to plate. In a mixing bowl, mix paprika, ground turkey, nutmeg, chives, vinegar, salt pepper, and onion. Mix well and form patties. Add the remaining oil to your AirFryer and air fry patties for 3-min. Serve on buns.

Ingredients:
- 1 tspn olive oil
- 1 small onion, diced
- 1 large garlic clove, minced
- Salt and pepper to taste
- 1 tbspnn vinegar
- 1 tbspnn chives, minced
- ¾ tspn paprika
- Pinch of nutmeg
- 1 lb. lean ground turkey
- 1 tspn fennel seeds

Calories	Fat	Carbs	Protein
302	12.2 g	10.2 g	16.3 g

Tasty Chicken Quesadilla

Prep Time	Time to cook	Serv
5 min	5 min	1

Direction:
1. Dicedup your pepper and onion.
2. Spray the bottom of your basket with cooking spray.
3. Preheat your fryer to 370 degrees.
4. Place 1 tortilla down on the bottom of the basket.
5. Sprinkle on cheese, place a few chicken strips down, sprinkle on vegetables, then sprinkle on more cheese.
6. Cover with another tortilla shell and spray with cooking spray.
7. Cook for 5 min.
8. The outside should be crispy when you take it out.

Ingredients:
- Soft Taco Shells
- Chicken Fajita Strips
- 1/4 Green Pepper
- 1/4 White Onion Shredded Mexican Cheese
- Cooking Spray

Calories	Fat	Sugar	Protein
222	12.8 g	2.1 g	19.3 g

Wonderful Chicken Popcorn

Prep Time	Time to cook	Serv
10 min	10 min	6

Directions:
1. In a small bowl, mix together coconut flour, pepper, and salt. In another bowl, whisk eggs until combined.
2. Take 1 more bowl and mix together pork panko, paprika, garlic powder, and onion powder.
3. Add chicken pieces in a large mixing bowl. Sprinkle coconut flour mixture over chicken and toss well.
4. Dip chicken pieces in the egg mixture and coat with pork panko mixture and place on a plate.
5. Spray AirFryer basket with cooking spray.
6. Preheat the AirFryer to 400 F.
7. Add half prepared chicken in AirFryer basket and cook for 10-12 min.
8. Shake basket halfway through.
9. Cook remaining half using the same method.
10. Enjoy.

Calories	Fat	Carbs	Protein
265	11 g	3 g	35 g

Ingredients:
- 4 eggs
- 1 1/2 lbs chicken breasts, cut into small chunks
- 1 tbspn paprika
- 1/2 tbspn garlic powder
- 1 tbspn onion powder
- 2 1/2 cups pork rind, crushed
- 1/4 cup coconut flour
- Pepper
- Salt

Tasty Whole Chicken

Prep Time	Time to cook	Serv
10 min	50 min	4

Directions:
1. In a small bowl, mix together Italian seasoning, garlic powder, onion powder, paprika, pepper, and salt.
2. Rub spice mixture from inside and outside of the chicken. Place chicken breast side down in AirFryer basket.
3. Roast chicken for 30 min at 360 F.
4. Turn chicken and roast for 20 min more or internal temperature of chicken reaches at 165 F.
5. Enjoy.

Calories	Fat	Carbs	Protein
356	25 g	1 g	30 g

Ingredients:
- 3 lbs whole chicken, remove giblets and pat dry chicken
- 1 tbspn Italian seasoning
- 1/2 tbspn garlic powder
- 1/2 tbspn onion powder
- 1/4 tbspn paprika
- 1/4 tbspn pepper
- 1 1/2 tbspn salt

Fast & Easy Meatballs

Prep Time	Time to cook	Serv
10 min	10 min	4

Directions:
1. Add all ingredients into the large mixing bowl and mix until well combined.
2. Make small balls from mixture and place in the AirFryer basket.
3. Cook meatballs for 10 min at 400 F.
4. Enjoy.

Calories	Fat	Carbs	Protein
253	10 g	2 g	35 g

Ingredients:
- 1 lb ground chicken
- 1 egg, lightly beaten
- 1/2 cup mounceszarella cheese, shredded
- 1 1/2 tbspn taco seasoning
- 3 garlic cloves, diced
- 3 tbspn fresh parsley, minced
- 1 small onion, diced
- Pepper
- Salt

Lemon Pepper Chicken Wings

Prep Time	Time to cook	Serv
10 min	16 min	4

Directions:
1. Add chicken wings into the large mixing bowl.
2. Add remaining ingredients over chicken and toss well to coat.
3. Place chicken wings in the AirFryer basket.
4. Cook chicken wings for 8 min at 400 F.
5. Turn chicken wings to another side and cook for 8 min more.
6. Enjoy.

Ingredients:
- 1 lb chicken wings
- 1 tbspn lemon pepper
- 1 tbspn olive oil
- 1 tbspn salt

Calories	Fat	Carbs	Protein
247	11 g	0.3 g	32 g

Enchanting BBQ Chicken Wings

Prep Time	Time to cook	Serv
10 min	20 min	4

Directions:
1. In a large bowl, toss chicken wings with garlic powder, oil, paprika, pepper, and salt.
2. Preheat the AirFryer to 360 F.
3. Add chicken wings in AirFryer basket and cook for 12 min.
4. Turn chicken wings to another side and cook for 5 min more.
5. Remove chicken wings from the AirFryer and toss with BBQ sauce.
6. Return chicken wings in an AirFryer basket and cook for 2 min more.
7. Enjoy.

Ingredients:
- 1 1/2 lbs chicken wings
- 2 tbspn unsweetened BBQ sauce
- 1 tbspn paprika
- 1 tbspn olive oil
- 1 tbspn garlic powder
- Pepper
- Salt

Calories	Fat	Carbs	Protein
372	16.2 g	4.3 g	49.4 g

Simple & Crispy Chicken Wings

Prep Time	Time to cook	Serv
5 min	20 min	8

Directions:
1. Toss chicken wings with oil and place in the AirFryer basket.
2. Cook chicken wings at 370 F for 15 min.
3. Shake basket and cook at 400 F for 5 min more.
4. Season chicken wings with pepper and salt.
5. Enjoy.

Ingredients:
- 1 1/2 lbs chicken wings
- 2 tbspn olive oil
- Pepper
- Salt

Calories	Fat	Carbs	Protein
192	9.8 g	0 g	24.6 g

Scrummy Chicken Nuggets

Prep Time	Time to cook	Serv
10 min	12 min	4

Directions:
1. Preheat the AirFryer to 400 F.
2. Toss chicken with oil and salt in a bowl until well coated.
3. Add coconut flour and ginger in a zip-lock bag and shake to mix.
4. Add chicken to the bag and shake well to coat. In a large bowl, add egg whites.
5. Add chicken in egg whites and toss until well coated.
6. Add sesame seeds in a large zip-lock bag.
7. Shake excess egg off from chicken and add chicken in sesame seed bag.
8. Shake bag until chicken well coated with sesame seeds.
9. Spray AirFryer basket with cooking spray.
10. Place chicken in AirFryer basket and cook for 6 min.
11. Turn chicken to another side and cook for 6 min more.
12. Enjoy.

Ingredients:
- 1 lb chicken breast, skinless, boneless and cut into chunks
- 6 tbspn sesame seeds, toasted
- 4 egg whites
- 1/2 tbspn ground ginger
- 1/4 cup coconut flour
- 1 tbspn sesame oil
- Pinch of salt

Calories	Fat	Carbs	Protein
265	11.5 g	8.6 g	31.1 g

Italian Seasoned Chicken Tenders

Prep Time	Time to cook	Serv
10 min	10 min	2

Directions:
1. Preheat the AirFryer to 400 F.
2. Season chicken with pepper and salt.
3. In a medium bowl, whisk eggs to combine.
4. In a shallow dish, mix together almond flour, all seasonings, and flaxseed.
5. Dip chicken into the egg then coats with almond flour mixture and place on a plate.
6. Spray AirFryer basket with cooking spray.
7. Place half chicken tenders in AirFryer basket and cook for 10 min.
8. Turn halfway through.
9. Cook remaining chicken tenders using same steps.
10. Enjoy.

Ingredients:
- 2 eggs, lightly beaten
- 1 1/2 lbs chicken tenders
- 1/2 tbspn onion powder
- 1/2 tbspn garlic powder
- 1 tbspn paprika
- 1 tbspn Italian seasoning
- 2 tbspn ground flax seed
- 1 cup almond flour
- 1/2 tbspn pepper
- 1 tbspn sea salt

Calories	Fat	Carbs	Protein
315	21 g	12 g	17 g

American Chicken Wings

Prep Time	Time to cook	Serv
10 min	40 min	4

Directions:
1. Spray AirFryer basket with cooking spray.
2. Add chicken wings in AirFryer basket and cook for 25 min at 380 F.
3. Shake basket after every 5 min.
4. After 25 min turn temperature to 400 F and cook for 10-15 min more.
5. Meanwhile, in a large bowl, mix together all sauce ingredients.
6. Add cooked chicken wings in a sauce bowl and toss well to coat.
7. Enjoy.

Calories	Fat	Carbs	Protein
593	34.4g	1.6 g	66.2 g

Ingredients:
- 2 lbs chicken wings
- For sauce:
- 1/4 tbspn Tabasco
- 1/4 tbspn Worcestershire sauce 6 tbspn butter, melted
- 12 ounces hot sauce

Pretty Fried Chicken

Prep Time	Time to cook	Serv
10 min	40 min	10

Directions:
1. Add chicken in a large mixing bowl.
2. Add milk and vinegar over chicken and place in the refrigerator for 2 hours. I a shallow dish, mix together pork rinds, white pepper, ginger, garlic salt, paprika, mustard, pepper, celery salt, oregano, basil, thyme, and salt.
3. Coat AirFryer basket with coconut oil. Coat each chicken piece with pork rind mixture and place on a plate.
4. Place half coated chicken in the AirFryer basket.
5. Cook chicken at 360 F for 10 min then turn chicken to another side and cook for 10 min more or until internal temperature reaches at 165 F.
6. Cook remaining chicken using the same method.
7. Enjoy.

Calories	Fat	Carbs	Protein
539	37 g	1 g	45 g

Ingredients:
- 5 lbs chicken, about 10 pieces
- 1 tbspn coconut oil
- 2 1/2 tbspn white pepper
- 1 tbspn ground ginger
- 1 1/2 tbspn garlic salt
- 1 tbspn paprika
- 1 tbspn dried mustard
- 1 tbspn pepper
- 1 tbspn celery salt
- 1/3 tbspn oregano
- 1/2 tbspn basil
- 1/2 tbspn thyme
- 2 cups pork rinds, crushed
- 1 tbspn vinegar
- 1 cup unsweetened almond milk
- 1/2 tbspn salt

Gorgeous Cornish Hen

Prep Time	Time to cook	Serv
10 min	25 min	3

Directions:
1. Coat Cornish hen with olive oil and rub with paprika, garlic powder, pepper, and salt.
2. Place Cornish hen in the AirFryer basket.
3. Cook at 390 F for 25 min.
4. Turn halfway through.
5. Slice and serve.

Calories	Fat	Carbs	Protein
301	5 g	2 g	25 g

Ingredients:
- 1 Cornish hen, wash and pat dry
- 1 tbspn olive oil
- 1 tbspn smoked paprika
- 1/2 tbspn garlic powder
- Pepper
- Salt

Herb Seasoned Turkey Breast

Prep Time	Time to cook	Serv
10 min	35 min	4

Directions:
1. Spray AirFryer basket with cooking spray.
2. In a small bowl, mix together sage, rosemary, and thyme.
3. Season turkey breast with pepper and salt and rub with herb mixture.
4. Place turkey breast in AirFryer basket and cook at 390 F for 30-35 min.
5. Slice and serve.

Calories	Fat	Carbs	Protein
238	3.9 g	10 g	38.8 g

Ingredients:
- 2 lbs turkey breast
- 1 tbspn fresh sage, minced
- 1 tbspn fresh rosemary, minced
- 1 tbspn fresh thyme, minced
- Pepper
- Salt

Delicious Rotisserie Chicken

Prep Time	Time to cook	Serv
10 min	20 min	6

Directions:
1. Season chicken with pepper and salt.
2. In a bowl, mix together spices and herbs and rub spice mixture over chicken pieces.
3. Spray AirFryer basket with cooking spray.
4. Place chicken in an AirFryer basket and cook at 350 F for 10 min.
5. Turn chicken to another side and cook for 10 min more or until the internal temperature of chicken reaches 165 F.
6. Enjoy.

Calories	Fat	Carbs	Protein
350	7 g	1.8 g	66 g

Ingredients:
- 3 lbs chicken, cut into eight pieces
- 1/4 tbspn cayenne
- 1 tbspn paprika
- 2 tbspn onion powder
- 1 1/2 tbspn garlic powder
- 1 1/2 tbspn dried oregano
- 1/2 tbspn dried thyme
- Pepper Salt

Spicy Asian Chicken Thighs

Prep Time	Time to cook	Serv
10 min	20 min	4

Directios:
1. In a large bowl, whisk together ginger, lime juice, chili garlic sauce, oil, and soy sauce.
2. Add chicken in bowl and coat well with marinade and place in the refrigerator for 30 min.
3. Place marinated chicken in AirFryer basket and cook at 400 F for 15-20 min or until the internal temperature of chicken reaches at 165 F.
4. Turn chicken halfway through.
5. Enjoy.

Calories	Fat	Carbs	Protein
403	23.5 g	3.2 g	43.7 g

Ingredients:
- 4 chicken thighs, skin-on, and b1-in
- 2 tbspn ginger, grated
- 1 lime juice
- 2 tbspn chili garlic sauce
- 1/4 cup olive oil
- 1/3 cup soy sauce

Wonderful Chicken Vegetable Fry

Prep Time: 10 min | Time to cook: 15 min | Serv: 2

Directions:
1. Add all ingredients into the large bowl and toss well.
2. Transfer chicken mixture into the AirFryer basket and cook at 375 F for 15 min.
3. Shake the basket halfway through.
4. Enjoy.

Calories	Fat	Carbs	Protein
185	8 g	5 g	20 g

Ingredients:
- 6 ounces chicken breast, boneless and cut into cubes
- 1/4 tbspn dried thyme
- 1/2 tbspn garlic powder
- 1 tbspn dried oregano
- 1/4 onion, sliced
- 1/2 bell pepper, minced
- 1/2 zucchini, minced
- 1 tbspn olive oil

Cilantro Lime Chicken

Prep Time: 10 min | Time to cook: 20 min | Serv: 4

Directions:
1. Whisk together cilantro, seasoning, soy sauce, lime juice, olive oil, pepper, and salt in a large bowl.
2. Add chicken into the bowl and coat well with marinade and place in the refrigerator for overnight. Spray AirFryer basket with cooking spray.
3. Place marinated chicken into the AirFryer basket and cook at 400 F for 10 min.
4. Turn chicken to another side and cook for 10 min more.
5. Enjoy.

Calories	Fat	Carbs	Protein
444	18 g	0.8 g	65.8 g

Ingredients:
- 2 lbs chicken thighs, boneless
- 2 tbspn fresh cilantro, minced
- 1 tbspn Montreal chicken seasoning
- 1 tbspn soy sauce
- 1/2 lime juice
- 1 tbspn olive oil
- Pepper
- Salt

Pleasant Chicken with Mushrooms

Prep Time: 10 min | Time to cook: 24 min | Serv: 4

Directions:
1. Preheat the AirFryer to 370 F.
2. Spray AirFryer baking dish with cooking spray.
3. Place chicken breasts into the baking dish and top with sun-dried tomatoes, mushrooms, mayonnaise, and salt. Mix well.
4. Place the dish in the AirFryer and cook for 24 min.
5. Enjoy.

Calories	Fat	Carbs	Protein
561	26.8 g	9 g	65 g

Ingredients:
- 2 lbs chicken breasts, halved
- 1/3 cup sun-dried tomatoes
- 8 ounces mushrooms, sliced
- 1/2 cup mayonnaise
- 1 tbspn salt

Tasty Meatloaf

Prep Time	Time to cook	Serv
10 min	32 min	8

Directions:
1. Preheat the AirFryer to 370 F.
2. Add all ingredients into the large bowl and mix until well combined.
3. Transfer bowl mixture to the silic1 loaf pan and place in the AirFryer.
4. Cook for 32 min.
5. Enjoy.

Calories	Fat	Carbs	Protein
350	19.5 g	4 g	43 g

Ingredients:
- 2 eggs
- 1/2 cup parmesan cheese, grated
- 1/2 cup marinara sauce, without sugar
- 1 cup cottage cheese
- 1 lb mounceszarella cheese, cut into cubes
- 2 lbs ground turkey
- 2 tbspn Italian seasoning
- 1/4 cup basil pesto
- 1 tbspn salt

Yummy Meatloaf

Prep Time	Time to cook	Serv
10 min	28 min	8

Directions:
1. Preheat the AirFryer to 370 F.
2. In a large bowl, combine together all ingredients then transfer into the silicon loaf pan.
3. Place the loaf pan in the AirFryer and cook for 25-28 min.
4. Enjoy.

Calories	Fat	Carbs	Protein
301	17 g	3 g	35.5 g

Ingredients:
- 1 egg
- 1 tbspn chili powder
- 1 tbspn garlic powder
- 1 tbspn garlic, diced
- 2 lbs ground turkey
- 2 ounces BBQ sauce, sugar-free
- 1 tbspn ground mustard
- 1 tbspn onion, diced
- 1 cup cheddar cheese, shredded
- 1 tbspn salt

Chili Garlic Chicken Wings

Prep Time	Time to cook	Serv
10 min	35 min	4

Directions:
1. Preheat the AirFryer to 370 F.
2. In a large bowl, add all ingredients except chicken wings and mix well.
3. Add chicken wings into the bowl coat well.
4. Spray AirFryer basket with cooking spray.
5. Add chicken wings into the AirFryer basket. (In batches)
6. Cook for 35-40 min.
7. Shake halfway through.
8. Enjoy.

Calories	Fat	Carbs	Protein
440	17.1 g	1 g	65 g

Ingredients:
- 2 lbs chicken wings
- 1/8 tbspn paprika
- 2 tbspn seasoned salt
- 1/2 cup coconut flour
- 1/4 tbspn garlic powder
- 1/4 tbspn chili powder

Finger-licking Garlic Chicken

Prep Time	Time to cook	Serv
10 min	32 min	4

Directions:
1. Preheat the AirFryer to 400 F.
2. Add all ingredients into the large mixing bowl and toss well.
3. Transfer chicken wings into the AirFryer basket and cook for 32 min.
4. Toss halfway through.
5. Enjoy.

Calories	Fat	Carbs	Protein
560	31 g	3 g	63 g

Ingredients:
- 2 lbs chicken drumsticks
- 1 fresh lemon juice
- 9 garlic cloves, sliced
- 4 tbspn butter, melted
- 2 tbspn parsley, minced
- 2 tbspn olive oil
- Pepper
- Salt

Beef

Spicy grilled steak

Prep Time	Time to cook	Serv
7 min	8 min	4

Directions:
1. In a small bowl, thoroughly mix the salsa, chipotle pepper, cider vinegar, cumin, black pepper, and red pepper flakes. Rub this mixture into both sides of each steak piece. Let stand for 15 min at room temperature.
2. Grill the steaks in the AirFryer, 2 at a time, for 6 to 9 min, or until they reach at least 145°f on a meat thermometer.

Calories	Fat	Fiber	Protein	Carbohydrates	Sodium
160	6 g	0 g	24 g	5.7 g	2 mg

Ingredients:
- 2 tbspns low-Sodium salsa
- 1 tbspnn dicedchipotle pepper
- 1 tbspnn apple cider vinegar
- 1 tspn ground cumin
- ⅛ tspn freshly ground black pepper
- ⅛ tspn red pepper flakes
- ¾ pound sirloin tip steak, cut into 4 pieces and gently pounded to about ⅓ inch thick

Toothsome Greek vegetable skillet

Prep Time	Time to cook	Serv
10 min	19 min	4

Directions:
1. In a 6-by-2-inch metal pan, crumble the beef. Time to cook: in the AirFryer for 3 to 7 min, stirring once during cooking, until browned. Drain off any fat or liquid.
2. Add the tomatoes, onion, and garlic to the pan. Air-fry for 4 to 8 min more, or until the onion is tender.
3. Add the spinach, lemon juice, and beef broth. Air-fry for 2 to 4 min more, or until the spinach is wilted.
4. Sprinkle with the feta cheese and serve immediately.

Calories	Fat	Fiber	Protein	Carbohydrates	Sodium
97	1 g	1 g	15 g	5 g	123 mg

Ingredients:
- ½ pound 96 percent lean ground beef
- 2 medium tomatoes, minced
- 1 onion, minced
- 2 garlic cloves, diced
- 2 cups fresh baby spinach
- 2 tbspns freshly squeezed lemon juice
- ⅓ cup low-Sodium beef broth
- 2 tbspns crumbled low-Sodium feta cheese

Light herbed meatballs

Prep Time	Time to cook	Serv
10 min	15 min	24

Directions:
1. In a 6-by-2-inch pan, combine the onion, garlic, and olive oil. Air-fry for 2 to 4 min, or until the vegetables are crisp-tender.
2. Transfer the vegetables to a medium bowl and add the breadcrumbs, milk, marjoram, and basil. Mix well.
3. Add the ground beef. With your hands, work the mixture gently but thoroughly until combined. Form the meat mixture into about 24 (1-inch) meatballs.
4. Bake the meatballs, in batches, in the AirFryer basket for 12 to 17 min, or until they reach 160°f on a meat thermometer. Serve immediately.

Calories	Fat	Fiber	Protein	Carbohydrates	Sodium
190	6 g	1 g	25 g	8 g	120 mg

Ingredients:
- 1 medium onion, diced
- 2 garlic cloves, diced
- 1 tspn olive oil
- 1 slice low-sodium whole-wheat bread, crumbled
- 3 tbspns 1 percent milk
- 1 tspn dried marjoram
- 1 tspn dried basil
- 1-pound 96 percent lean ground beef

Marvelous Sirloin steak

Prep Time	Time to cook	Serv
5 min	15 min	6

Directions:
1. Switch on the AirFryer, insert fryer basket, grease it with olive oil, then shut with its lid, set the fryer at 392 degrees f, and preheat for 5 min.
2. Meanwhile, pat dries the steaks, then brush with oil and then season well with steak seasoning until coated on both sides.
3. Open the fryer, add steaks in it, close with its lid and cook for 10 min until nicely golden and crispy, flipping the steaks halfway through the frying.
4. When AirFryer beeps, open its lid, transfer steaks onto a serving plate.

Ingredients:
- 2 sirloin steaks, grass-fed
- 1 tbspnn olive oil
- 2 tbspns steak seasoning

Calories	Fat	Fiber	Protein	Carbs
253.6	18.1 g	0.1 g	21.1 g	0.2 g

Meatloaf

Prep Time	Time to cook	Serv
10 min	20 min	4

Directions:
1. Switch on the AirFryer, insert fryer basket, then shut with its lid, set the fryer at 360 degrees f, and preheat for 5 min.
2. Meanwhile, place all the ingredients in a bowl, stir until well mixed, then take an 8-inches round pan, grease it with oil, add the beef mixture in it, and spread it evenly.
3. Open the fryer, place the pan in it, close with its lid and cook for 15 min until the top is nicely golden and meatloaf is thoroughly cooked.
4. When AirFryer beeps, open its lid, take out the pan, then drain the excess Fat and take out the meatloaf.
5. Cut the meatloaf into 4 pieces.

Ingredients:
- 1-pound ground beef, grass-fed
- 1 tbspnn dicedgarlic
- 1 cup white onion, peeled and diced
- 1 tbspnn dicedginger
- 1/4 cup minced cilantro
- 2 tspns garam masala
- 1 tspn cayenne pepper
- 1 tspn salt
- 1/2 tspn ground cinnamon
- 1 tspn turmeric powder
- 1/8 tspn ground cardamom
- 2 eggs, pastured

Calories	Fat	Fiber	Protein	Carbs
260	13 g	1 g	26 g	6 g

Simple Rib Eye Steak

Prep Time	Time to cook	Serv
5 min	12 min	2

Directions:
1. Coat each steak evenly with butter and then, season with salt and black pepper.
2. Set the temperature of AirFryer to 392 degrees f. Grease an AirFryer basket.
3. Arrange steaks into the prepared AirFryer basket.
4. Air fry for about 8-12 min.
5. Remove from the AirFryer and transfer the steaks onto serving plates.

Ingredients:
- 2 (7-ounces) striploin steak
- 1½ tbspns butter softened
- Salt and ground black pepper, as required

Calories	Fat	Sugar	Protein	Carbohydrates	Sodium
595	37.6 g	0 g	58.1 g	0 g	452 mg

Double Cheeseburger

Prep Time	Time to cook	Serv
5 min	18 min	1

Directions:
1. Switch on the AirFryer, insert fryer basket, grease it with olive oil, then shut with its lid, set the fryer at 370 degrees f, and preheat for 5 min.
2. Meanwhile, season the patties well with onion powder, black pepper, and salt.
3. Open the fryer, add beef patties in it, close with its lid and cook for 12 min until nicely golden and cooked, flipping the patties halfway through the frying.
4. Then top the patties with a cheese slice and continue cooking for 1 min or until cheese melts.

Calories	Fat	Fiber	Protein	Carbs
670	50 g	0 g	39 g	0 g

Ingredients:
- 2 beef patties, pastured
- 1/8 tspn onion powder
- 2 slices of mounceszarella cheese, low Fat
- 1/8 tspn ground black pepper
- 1/8 tspn salt

AppetizingCrispy Sirloin Steak

Prep Time	Time to cook	Serv
15 min	10 min	2

Directions:
1. In a shallow bowl, place the flour.
2. Beat egg
3. Coat each steak with the white flour, then dip into beaten eggs, and finally, coat with panko mixture.
4. Set the temperature of AirFryer to 360 degrees f. Grease an AirFryer basket.
5. Arrange steaks into the prepared AirFryer basket.
6. Air fry for about 10 min.
7. Remove from the AirFryer and transfer the steaks onto the serving plates.

Calories	Fat	Sugar	Protein	Carbohydrates	Sodium
561	50.3 g	0.6 g	31.9 g	6.1 g	100 mg

Ingredients:
- 1 cup white flour
- 2 eggs
- 1 cup panko breadcrumbs
- 1 tspn garlic powder
- 1 tspn onion powder
- Salt and ground black pepper, as required
- 2 (6-ounces) sirloin steaks, pounded

Buttered Filet Mignon

Prep Time	Time to cook	Serv
10 min	14 min	4

Directions:
1. Coat each steak evenly with butter and then, season with salt and black pepper.
2. Set the temperature of AirFryer to 390 degrees f. Grease an AirFryer basket.
3. Arrange steaks into the prepared AirFryer basket.
4. Air fry for about 14 min, flipping once halfway through.
5. Remove from the AirFryer and transfer onto serving plates.
6. Serve hot.

Calories	Fat	Sugar	Protein	Carbohydrates	Sodium
403	22 g	0 g	48.7 g	0 g	228 mg

Ingredients:
- 2 (6-ounces) filet mignon steaks
- 1 tbspnn butter softened
- Salt and ground black pepper, as required

Savory Spiced & Herbed Skirt Steak

Prep Time	Time to cook	Serv
15 min	10 min	4

Directions:
1. In a bowl, mix the garlic, herbs, spices, oil, and vinegar.
2. In a resealable bag, place ¼ cup of the herb mixture and steaks.
3. Refrigerate for about 24 hours.
4. Reserve the remaining herb mixture in the refrigerator.
5. Take out the steaks from the fridge and place it at room temperature for about 30 min.
6. Set the temperature of AirFryer to 390 degrees f. Grease an AirFryer basket. Arrange steaks into the prepared AirFryer basket.
7. Air fry for about 8-10 min.
8. Remove from the AirFryer and place the steaks onto a cutting board for about 10 min before slicing.
9. Cut each steak into desired size slices and transfer onto a serving platter.
10. Top with reserved herb mixture and serve.

Ingredients:
- 3 garlic cloves, diced
- 1 cup fresh parsley leaves, finely minced
- 3 tbspns fresh oregano, finely minced
- 3 tbspns fresh mint leaves, finely minced
- 1 tbspnn ground cumin
- 2 tspns smoked paprika
- 1 tspn cayenne pepper
- 1 tspn red pepper flakes, crushed
- Salt and ground black pepper, as required
- ¾ cup olive oil
- 3 tbspns red wine vinegar
- 2 (8-ounces) skirt steaks

Calories	Fat	Sugar	Protein	Carbohydrates	Sodium
561	50.3 g	0.6 g	31.9 g	6.1 g	100 mg

Nourishing Steak With Bell Peppers

Prep Time	Time to cook	Serv
20 min	22 min	4

Directions:
1. In a large bowl, mix the oregano and spices.
2. Add the beef strips, bell peppers, onion, and oil. Mix until well combined.
3. Set the temperature of AirFryer to 390 degrees f. Grease an AirFryer basket.
4. Arrange steak strips mixture into the prepared AirFryer basket in 2 batches.
5. Air fry for about 10-11 min or until d1 completely.
6. Remove from the AirFryer and transfer the steak mixture onto serving plates.

Ingredients:
- 1 tspn dried oregano, crushed
- 1 tspn onion powder
- 1 tspn garlic powder
- 1 tspn red chili powder
- 1 tspn paprika
- Salt, to taste
- 1¼ pounds beef steak, cut into thin strips
- 2 green bell peppers, seeded and cubed
- 1 red bell pepper, seeded and cubed
- 1 red onion, sliced
- 2 tbspns olive oil

Calories	Fat	Sugar	Protein	Carbohydrates	Sodium
372	16.3 g	6.2 g	44.6 g	11.2 g	143 mg

Bacon-Wrapped Filet Mignon

Prep Time	Time to cook	Serv
15 min	15 min	2

Directions:
1. Wrap 1 bacon slice around each mignon steak and secure with a toothpick.
2. Season the steak evenly with salt and black pepper.
3. Then, coat each steak with avocado oil.
4. Set the temperature of AirFryer to 375 degrees f. Grease an AirFryer basket.
5. Arrange steaks into the prepared AirFryer basket.
6. Air fry for about 15 min, flipping once halfway through.
7. Remove from the AirFryer and transfer the steaks onto serving plates.
8. Serve hot.

Ingredients:
- 2 bacon slices
- 2 (6-ounces) filet mignon steaks
- Salt and ground black pepper, as required
- 1 tspn avocado oil

Calories	Fat	Sugar	Protein	Carbohydrates	Sodium
512	28.6 g	0 g	59.4 g	0.5 g	857 mg

Enchanting Beef Short Ribs

Prep Time	Time to cook	Serv
15 min	16 min	8

Directions:
1. In a resealable bag, put the ribs and all the above Ingredients
2. Refrigerate overnight.
3. Set the temperature of AirFryer to 380 degrees f. Grease an AirFryer basket.
4. Take out the short ribs from a resealable bag and arrange it into the prepared AirFryer basket in 2 batches in a single layer.
5. Air fry for about 8 min, flipping once halfway through.
6. Remove from AirFryer and transfer onto a serving platter.
7. Serve hot.

Ingredients:
- 4 pounds b1-in beef short ribs
- 1/3 small cup lions, minced
- 1 tbspnn fresh ginger, finely grated
- 1 cup low-Sodium soy sauce
- ½ cup of rice vinegar
- 1 tbspnn sriracha
- 2 tbspns Brown Sugar
- 1 tspn ground black pepper

Calories	Fat	Sugar	Protein	Carbohydrates	Sodium
507	20.5 g	2.8 g	67.3 g	6.3 g	1200 mg

Corned Beef

Prep Time	Time to cook	Serv
10 min	35 min	6

Directions:
1. Add butter into the AirFryer and set the container on sauté mode.
2. Add bacon to the pot and cook until bacon is crispy.
3. Add meat and cook until browned. Add remaining ingredients and Stir.
4. Seal fryer with lid and cook on manual high pressure for 35 min.
5. Once d1, then extrication pressure using the quick-extrication method than open the lid.
6. Stir and serve.

Ingredients:
- 2 1/4 lbs. corned beef, minced
- 1 onion, minced
- 2 celery stalks, minced
- 1/2 tbspn cumin
- 1 tbspn garlic powder
- 3 cups chicken broth
- 1 tbspn butter
- 2 bacon slices, diced
- 2 1/2 lbs cabbage, minced
- 1 carrot, sliced
- 1/2 tbspn salt

Calories	Fat	Sugar	Protein	Carbohydrates
316	20.1 g	5.9 g	22.8 g	11.1 g

Lovely Brussel Sprout Beef Chops

Prep Time	Time to cook	Serv
6 min	38 min	1

Directions:
1. Coat Beef chop with olive oil cooking spray; sprinkle it with salt and 1/4 tbspn. of the pepper. Mix oil, syrup, mustard, and remaining 1/4 tbspn. Pepper in a bowl; add Brussels sprouts; coat it. Put Beef chop on 1 side of the AirFryer toaster oven tray and painted Brussels sprouts on the other side. Heat AirFryer to 400°F, and cook until unless golden brown and Beef is prepared to the required temperature.

Ingredients:
- 8 ounces. Beef chops
- 6 ounces. Brussels sprouts
- Olive oil spray
- 1 tbspn. olive oil
- 1/8 tbspn. kosher salt
- 1 tbspn. maple syrup
- 1/2 tbspn. black pepper
- 1 tbspn. Dijon mustard

Calories	Fat	Carbs	Protein	Fiber
348	13 g	21 g	38 g	0.5 g

Dipping Sauce Beef Dumplings

Prep Time	Time to cook	Serv
10 min	50 min	6

Directions:
1. Pour canola oil in a skillet over medium to high heat. Put Bok choy and cook, often mixing, until unless wilted and mostly dry, 6 to 8 min. Put ginger and garlic; cook, constantly mixing, 1 min. Shift Bok choy mixture to a plate to cool it for 5 min. Pat down the mixture dry with a paper towel. Stir together ground Beef, Bok choy mixture, and crushed red pepper in a bowl. Put a dumpling wrapper on the work surface and spoon about 1 tbspn. Filling in the middle of the wrapper. Using your fingers, moisten the corners of the wrapper with water. Fold the wrapper over to make a half-moon shape, pressing corners to seal. Do the same with remaining wrappers and filling. Coat the AirFryer toaster oven tray with olive oil spray. Put six dumplings in a tray, leaving room between each; spray the dumplings with olive oil spray. Cook it at 375°F until lightly browned, 12 min, flipping dumplings over halfway through cooking. Do the same with remaining dumplings, keeping cooked dumplings warm. During the time, stir together rice vinegar, soy sauce, sesame oil, brown sugar, and scallions in a bowl until sugar is mixed. To eat, place 3 dumplings on each plate with 2 tbspn. Sauce.

Ingredients:
- 4 cups minced Bok choy
- 2 tbspn. Soy sauce
- 4 ounces ground Beef
- 1 tbspn. canola oil
- 1/4 tbspn. red pepper
- Olive oil spray
- 18 dumpling wrappers
- 1 tbspn. garlic
- 1 tbspn. toasted sesame oil
- 1/2 tbspn. brown sugar
- 1 tbspn. ginger
- 1 tbspn. minced Scallions
- 2 tbspn. rice vinegar

Calories	Fat	Carbs	Protein	Fiber
148	6 g	16 g	7 g	1 g

Delectable Kansas Farm Beef Chops

Prep Time	Time to cook	Serv
7 min	20 min	4

Directions:
1. Take a bowl that needs to be big enough to dip down the Beef chops put Beef rinds, parsley, paprika, onion and garlic powders, and allspice. Whisk until mixed well. Spray each Beef chop on both sides with olive oil spray, ensuring to cover it all as the Beef rinds are going to stick to the olive oil. Put each Beef chop in the Beef rind mixture, coating it entirely on both sides. Put Beef chops in AirFryer toaster oven, ensuring not to overcrowd. Set an AirFryer toaster oven to 400° for 12 min. Once d1, turn the Beef chop over and cook for another 5 min at 400° if needed.

Calories	Fat	Carbs	Protein	Fiber
291	24 g	1 g	40 g	0.5 g

Ingredients:
- 4 b1-in Beef chops
- 1 tbspn. paprika
- 1 tbspn. onion powder
- 1 tbspn. parsley
- 1 tbspn. garlic powder
- 1/8 tbspn. allspice
- Olive oil
- 2 cups finely crushed Beef rinds

Air Fry Mounceszarella Beef Brisket

Prep Time	Time to cook	Serv
18 min	28 min	3

Directions:
1. Dry Beef brisket using the paper towels and discard the paper towels. Brush olive oil over the beef brisket. Put seasonings, and mix Beef brisket to coat all of it with seasonings. Now open Beef brisket, line 4 pieces, and top with about 4 slices of tomatoes and 4 basil leaves. Close down Beef and seal it with 4 toothpicks at the corners of Beef. Do the same with other Beef. Spritz AirFryer basket with olive oil cooking spray. Lay the Beef. Spray the top of Beef with olive oil cooking spray for a golden color. Set down the temperature to 360 degrees F and the set timer for 28 min or a bit more for desired crispness and golden brown color. When time completes, remove Beef from baskets, and take out the toothpicks before serving. Garnish them with minced basil.

Calories	Fat	Carbs	Protein	Fiber
294	24 g	5 g	10 g	0.5 g

Ingredients:
- 3 tbspn. olive oil
- Eight basil leaves
- 8 ounces. Beef Brisket
- 2 tomatoes
- 1/2 tbspn. dried thyme
- 1/2 tbspn. salt
- 1 tbspn. dried oregano
- 1 tbspn. dried basil
- 1/2 tbspn. black pepper
- 4 ounces. mounceszarella cheese

Delightful Zucchini Lean Beef Burger

Prep Time	Time to cook	Serv
5 min	20 min	2

Directions:
1. Squeeze all the moisture very well from the zucchini with paper towels. In a bowl, mix the ground beef, zucchini, breadcrumbs, garlic, onion, salt, and pepper. Create five equal patties, 4 ounces. Each, 1/2 inch thick. Preheat the AirFryer toaster oven to 370F. Now cook in a single layer in 2 batches 10 min or cook until browned and cooked through from the center.

Calories	Fat	Carbs	Protein	Fiber
235	18 g	5 g	12 g	1 g

Ingredients:
- 6 ounces. zucchini
- Oil spray
- 1/4 cup breadcrumbs
- 1 clove garlic
- 1 tbspn. red onion
- 1 lb. lean beef
- 1 tbspn. kosher salt, pepper

Roasted Pepper Beef Prosciutto

Prep Time	Time to cook	Serv
20 min	40 min	8

Directions:
1. First, wash and dry the Beef cutlets very thoroughly with paper towels. Add breadcrumbs in a bowl and another second bowl, stir the olive oil, lemon juice, and pepper. Preheat the AirFryer toaster oven to 450°F. Slightly spray a baking dish with olive oil spray. Put each cutlet on a work surface such as a cutting board and lay 1/2 slice prosciutto, 1/2 slice cheese, 1 piece of roasted pepper, and 3 spinach leaves on 1 side of the Beef cutlet. Roll it and put seam side down on a dish. Dip down the Beef in the olive oil and lemon juice after that into the breadcrumbs. Do the same with the Beef left. Bake it 25 to 30 min or until your desired crispness.

Ingredients:
- 24 ounces. Beef cutlets
- Olive oil spray
- 12 ounces. sliced thin prosciutto
- 4 slices mounceszarella
- 22 ounces. roasted peppers
- 1 lemon
- 24 Spinach leaves
- 1 tbspn. olive oil
- 1/2 cup GF breadcrumbs
- Salt and fresh pepper

Calories	Fat	Carbs	Protein	Fiber
287	20 g	7 g	20 g	1 g

Adorable Creamy Beef Belly Rolls

Prep Time	Time to cook	Serv
10 min	35 min	8

Drections:
1. Add Beef belly in the slow cooker and put enough water or Beef broth to cover it well. Cook it high for 4 hours. Take it out and shred with 2 forks, remove the liquid. To prepare in the AirFryer, but at least 1 cup broth or water, enough to cover the Beef well. Cook it on the high pressure 15 min on natural extrication. Remove liquid and shred it with 2 forks. During the time, add the cream cheese and hot sauce together until it is smooth. Put the Beef, blue cheese, carrots, and scallions and Stir, makes 3 cups. Place egg roll wrapper at a time on a clean surface, points facing top and bottom like a diamond. Spread 3 tbspn. Of the buffalo dip mixture onto the bottom third of the wrapper. Dip down your finger in a bowl of water and rub it along the edges of the wrapper. Lift the nearest point to you and wrap it around the filling. Wrap the left and right corners in toward the center and continue to roll into a tight air cylinder. Left aside and do the same with remaining wrappers and filling. Spray all sides of the egg rolls with olive oil spray using your fingers to equally coat. Preheat the AirFryer toaster oven to 400F. Spritz a sheet pan with oil. Shift the egg rolls to the baking sheet and cook until unless browned and crisp, about 16 to 18 min, flipping halfway if needed. Eat immediately, with dipping sauce on the side, if required. You can cook it more for desired crispness.

Ingredients:
- 16 ounces. Beef Belly
- Olive oil spray
- 2 ounces. cream cheese
- 1/2 cup hot sauce
- 1/3 cup shredded carrots
- 1/2 cup blue cheese
- 1/3 cup minced Scallions
- 16 egg roll wrappers

Calories	Fat	Carbs	Protein	Fiber
287	20 g	7 g	20 g	1 g

Seasoned Bleu Cordon Beef Belly

Prep Time	Time to cook	Serv
10 min	35 min	6

Directions:
1. Preheat AirFryer toaster oven to 450°F. Spread a large baking sheet with cooking spray. Wash down and dry the Beef cutlets; lightly pound the Beef to make thinner and lightly season with salt and pepper. Lay the Beef on a plain surface and put a slice cheese and roll, setting them aside seam side down. In a bowl, stir eggs and egg whites along with water to make an egg wash. In a separate bowl, add breadcrumbs and parmesan cheese. Dip down the Beef into the egg wash after that into the breadcrumbs. Put Beef onto the baking sheet seems side down. Spray the top of the Beef with more olive oil spray and bake it to about 25 min, or until your desired crispness and golden brownish color.

Calories	Fat	Carbs	Protein	Fiber
379	24 g	8 g	24 g	2 g

Ingredients:
- 36 ounces. Beef belly
- 1/2 cup seasoned breadcrumb
- 2 large egg whites
- 1 large egg
- Salt and pepper
- Cooking spray
- 4.4 ounces. cheese

Exquisite Honey Mustard Cheesy Meatballs

Prep Time	Time to cook	Serv
15 min	15 min	8

Directions:
1. Preheat the AirFryer to 385 o F and grease an AirFryer basket.
2. Mix all the ingredients in a bowl until well combined.
3. Shape the mixture into equal-sized balls gently and arrange the meatballs in the AirFryer basket.
4. Cook for about 15 min and dish out to serve warm.

Calories	Fat	Sugar	Protein	Sodium
134	4.4 g	2.7 g	18.2 g	50 mg

Ingredients:
- 2 onions, minced
- 1 pound ground beef
- 4 tbspns fresh basil, minced
- 2 tbspns cheddar cheese, grated
- 2 tspns garlic paste
- 2 tspns honey
- Salt and black pepper, to taste
- 2 tspns mustard

Simple Beef Burgers

Prep Time	Time to cook	Serv
20 min	12 min	6

Directions:
1. Preheat the AirFryer to 390 F and grease an AirFryer basket.
2. Mix the beef, salt, and black pepper in a bowl.
3. Make small equal-sized patties from the beef mixture and arrange half of the patties in the AirFryer basket.
4. Cook for about 12 min and top each patty with 1 cheese slice.
5. Arrange the patties between rolls and drizzle with ketchup.
6. Repeat with the remaining batch and dish out to serve hot.

Calories	Fat	Sugar	Protein	Sodium
537	28.3 g	4.2 g	60.6 g	636 mg

Ingredients:
- 2 pounds ground beef
- 12 cheddar cheese slices
- 12 dinner rolls
- Six tbspns tomato ketchup
- Salt and black pepper, to taste

Garlic-Mustard Rubbed Roast Beef

Prep Time	Time to cook	Serv
20 min	2 hour	12

Directions:
1. In a mixing bowl, combine the garlic, almond flour, parsley, salt, and pepper. Heat a butter and olive oil in a skillet and brown the beef on all sides.
2. Rub the almond flour mixture all over the beef.
3. Brush with Dijon mustard.
4. Place the crusted beef in a baking dish.
5. Pour the beef broth slowly.
6. Place the baking dish with the bee in the AirFryer. Close.
7. Cook for 2 hours at 400 F.
8. Baste the beef with the sauce every 30 min.

Calories	Fat	Protein	Carbohydrates
310	20.3 g	24.6 g	7.2 g

Ingredients:
- ¼ cup Dijon mustard
- ¼ cup freshly parsley, minced
- ¼ cup unsalted butter
- 2 cups almond flour
- 2 tbspns olive oil
- 3 ½ cups beef broth
- 3 pounds boneless beef eye round roast
- 4 cloves of garlic, minced
- Salt and pepper to taste

Magical Garlic-Rosemary Rubbed Beef Rib Roast

Prep Time	Time to cook	Serv
20 min	2 hour	8

Directions
1. Preheat the AirFryer for 5 min.
2. Place all ingredients in a baking dish that will fit in the AirFryer.
3. Place the dish in the AirFryer and cook for 2 hours at 3250F.

Calories	Fat	Protein	Carbohydrates
320	20.7 g	32.4 g	0.9 g

Ingredients:
- 1 cup dried porcini mushrooms
- 1 medium shallot, minced
- 2 cloves of garlic, diced
- 2 cups of water
- 3 tbspns unsalted pepper
- 3 tbspns vegetable oil
- 4 sprigs of thyme
- Six ribs, beef rib roast
- Salt and pepper to taste

Ginger Soy Beef Recipe from the Orient

Prep Time	Time to cook	Serv
5 min	5 min	3

Instructions:
1. In a resealable bag, mix fresh ginger, garlic, green onions, barbecue sauce, soy sauce, sherry, and hoisin. Add steak and mix well. Remove excess air, seal, and marinate for at least 2 hours.
2. Thread steak into skewers and discard marinade.
3. For 5 min, cook on preheated 390 F AirFryer.
4. Enjoy.

Calories	Fat	Protein	Carbs
130	4.9 g	14.7 g	6.7 g

Ingredients:
- 2 tbspns soy sauce
- 1 green onion, minced
- 1 clove garlic, diced
- 1 tbspnn and 1-1/2 tspns hoisin sauce
- 1 tbspnn and 1-1/2 tspns sherry
- 1/2 tspn barbeque sauce
- 1-1/2 tspns dicedfresh ginger root
- 3/4-pound flank steak, thinly sliced

Gorgeous Ginger-Orange Beef Strips

Prep Time	Time to cook	Serv
5 min	25 min	3

Directions:
1. Preheat the AirFryer to 330F.
2. Season the steak slices with soy sauce and dust with cornstarch.
3. Place in the AirFryer basket and cook for 25 min.
4. Meanwhile, place in the skillet oil and heat over medium flame.
5. Sauté the garlic and ginger until fragrant.
6. Stir in the oranges, molasses, and rice vinegar. Season with salt and pepper to taste.
7. Once the meat is cooked, place in the skillet and stir to coat the sauce.
8. Drizzle with oil and garnish with scallions

Calories	Fat	Protein	Carbs
306	10.4 g	9.4 g	43.6 g

Ingredients:
- 1 ½ pound stir fry steak slices
- 1 ½ tspn sesame oil
- 1 navel oranges, segmented
- 1 tbspnn olive oil
- 1 tbspnn rice vinegar
- 1 tspn grated ginger
- 2 scallions, minced
- 3 cloves of garlic, diced
- 3 tbspns molasses
- 3 tbspns soy sauce
- Six tbspns cornstarch

Gravy Smothered Country Fried Steak

Prep Time	Time to cook	Serv
5 min	25 min	2

Directions:
1. Preheat the AirFryer to 330F.
2. The steak season with salt and pepper to taste.
3. Dip the steak in egg and dredge in flour mixture (comprised of flour, bread crumbs, onion powder, and garlic powder).
4. Put in the AirFryer and cook for 25 min.
5. Meanwhile, place the sausage meat in a saucepan and allow the fat to render. Stir in flour to form a roux and add milk. Season with salt and pepper to taste. Keep stirring until the sauce thickens.
6. Serve the steak with the milk gravy

Calories	Fat	Protein	Carbs
1048	48.7 g	64.2 g	88.1 g

Ingredients:
- 1 cup flour
- 1 cup panko bread crumbs
- 1 tspn garlic powder
- 1 tspn onion powder
- 2 cups of milk
- 2 tbspns flour
- 3 eggs, beaten
- 6 ounces ground sausage meat
- 6 ounces sirloin steak, pounded thin
- Salt and pepper to taste

Lovely Grilled Beef with Grated Daikon Radish

Prep Time	Time to cook	Serv
10 min	40 min	2

Directions:
1. Preheat the AirFryer to 390F.
2. Place the grill pan accessory in the AirFryer.
3. Season the steak with salt and pepper.
4. Brush with oil.
5. Grill for 20 min per piece and make sure to flip the beef halfway through the Time to cook
6. Preparing the dipping sauce by combining the soy and vinegar.
7. Serve the steak with the sauce and daikon radish.

Calories	Fat	Protein	Carbs
510	24 g	54 g	19.3 g

Ingredients:
- ¼ cup grated daikon radish
- ½ cup of rice wine vinegar
- ½ cup of soy sauce
- 1 tbspnn olive oil
- 2 strip steaks
- Salt and pepper to taste

Grilled Spicy Carne Asada

Prep Time	Time to cook	Serv
10 min	50 min	2

Directions:
1. put all ingredients in a Ziploc bag and marinate in the fridge for 2 hours.
2. Preheat the AirFryer to 390F.
3. Place the grill pan accessory in the AirFryer.
4. Grill the skirt steak for 20 min.
5. Flip the steak every 10 min for even grilling.

Calories	Fat	Protein	Carbs
697	45 g	32.7 g	10.2 g

Ingredients:
- 1 chipotle pepper, minced
- 1 dried ancho chilies, minced
- 1 tbspnn coriander seeds
- 1 tbspnn cumin
- 1 tbspns soy sauce
- 2 slices skirt steak
- 2 tbspns Asian fish sauce
- 2 tbspns brown sugar
- 2 tbspns of fresh lemon juice
- 2 tbspns olive oil
- 3 cloves of garlic, diced

Savory Grilled Steak on Tomato-Olive Salad

Prep Time	Time to cook	Serv
10 min	50 min	5

Directions:
1. Preheat the AirFryer to 390F.
2. Place the grill pan accessory in the AirFryer.
3. Season the steak with salt, pepper, paprika, and cayenne pepper. Brush with oil
4. Place on the grill pan and cook for 45 to 50 min.
5. Meanwhile, prepare the salad by mixing the remaining ingredients.
6. Serve the beef with salad.

Calories	Fat	Protein	Carbs
351	22 g	30 g	8 g

Ingredients:
- ¼ cup extra virgin olive oil
- ¼ tspn cayenne pepper
- ½ cup green olives, pitted and sliced
- 1 cup red onion, minced
- 1 tbspnn oil
- 1 tspn paprika
- 2 ½ pound flank
- 2 pounds cherry tomatoes halved
- 2 tbspns Sherry vinegar
- Salt and pepper to taste

Grilled Tri-Tip over Beet Salad

Prep Time	Time to cook	Serv
10 min	45 min	6

Directions:
1. Preheat the AirFryer to 390F.
2. Place the grill pan accessory in the AirFryer.
3. Season the tri-tip with salt and pepper. Drizzle with oil.
4. Grill for 15 min per batch.
5. Meanwhile, prepare the salad by tossing the rest of the ingredients in a salad bowl.
6. Toss in the grilled tri-trip and drizzle with more balsamic vinegar.

Calories	Fat	Protein	Carbs
221	7.7 g	17.2 g	20 g

Ingredients:
- 1 bunch arugula, torn
- 1 bunch scallions, minced
- 1-pound tri-tip, sliced
- 2 tbspns olive oil
- 3 beets, peeled and sliced thinly
- 3 tbspns balsamic vinegar
- Salt and pepper to taste

Magnificent Meatloaf Sliders

Prep Time	Time to cook	Serv
10 min	10 min	8

Directions:
1. Add all ingredients into the mixing bowl and mix until well combined.
2. Make the equal shape of patties from mixture and place on a plate. Place in refrigerator for 10 min.
3. Spray AirFryer basket with cooking spray.
4. Preheat the AirFryer to 360 F.
5. Place prepared patties in AirFryer basket and cook for 10 min.
6. Enjoy.

Calories	Fat	Sugar	Protein	Carbohydrates	Cholesterol
228	16 g	2 g	13 g	6 g	80 mg

Ingredients:
- 1 lb ground beef
- 1/2 tbspn dried tarragon
- 1 tbspn Italian seasoning
- 1 tbspn Worcestershire sauce
- 1/4 cup ketchup
- 1/4 cup coconut flour
- 1/2 cup almond flour
- 1 garlic clove, diced
- 1/4 cup onion, minced
- 2 eggs, lightly beaten
- 1/4 tbspn pepper
- 1/2 tbspn sea salt

Fast & Easy Steak

Prep Time	Time to cook	Serv
10 min	7 min	2

Directions:
1. Add steak, liquid smoke, and soy sauce in a zip-lock bag and shake well.
2. Season steak with seasonings and place in the refrigerator for overnight.
3. Place marinated steak in AirFryer basket and cook at 375 F for 5 min.
4. Turn steak to another side and cook for 2 min more.
5. Enjoy.

Calories	Fat	Sugar	Protein	Carbohydrates	Cholesterol
356	8.7 g	0.2 g	62.2 g	1.4 g	153 mg

Ingredients:
- 12 ounces steaks
- 1/2 tbspn unsweetened cocoa powder
- 1 tbspn Montreal steak seasoning
- 1 tbspn liquid smoke
- 1 tbspn soy sauce
- Pepper
- Salt

Excellent Cheeseburger

Prep Time	Time to cook	Serv
5 min	12 min	2

Directions:
1. In a bowl, mix together ground beef, onion powder, pepper, and salt.
2. Make 2 equal shapes of patties from meat mixture and place in the AirFryer basket.
3. Cook patties at 370 F for 12 min. Turn patties halfway through.
4. Once AirFryer timer goes off then place cheese slices on top of each patty and close the AirFryer basket for 1 min.
5. Enjoy.

Calories	Fat	Sugar	Protein	Cholesterol
325	16.4 g	0.3 g	41.4 g	131 mg

Ingredients:
- 1/2 lb ground beef
- 1/4 tbspn onion powder
- 2 cheese slices
- 1/4 tbspn pepper
- 1/8 tbspn salt

Steak Bites with Mushrooms

Prep Time	Time to cook	Serv
10 min	18 min	3

Directions:
1. Add all ingredients into the large mixing bowl and toss well.
2. Spray AirFryer basket with cooking spray.
3. Preheat the AirFryer to 400 F.
4. Add steak mushroom mixture into the AirFryer basket and cook at 400 F for 15-18 min. Shake basket twice.
5. Enjoy.

Calories	Fat	Sugar	Protein	Cholesterol
388	15.5 g	1.8 g	57.1 g	156 mg

Ingredients:
- 1 lb steaks, cut into 1/2-inch cubes
- 1/2 tbspn garlic powder
- 1 tbspn Worcestershire sauce
- 2 tbspn butter, melted
- 8 ounces mushrooms, sliced
- Pepper
- Salt

Easy AirFryer Steak

Prep Time	Time to cook	Serv
10 min	18 min	2

Directions:
1. Coat steaks with oil and season with garlic powder, pepper, and salt.
2. Preheat the AirFryer to 400 F.
3. Place steaks in AirFryer basket and cook for 15-18 min. Turn halfway through.

Calories	Sugar	Protein	Carbohydrates	Cholesterol
363	0.3 g	61.7 g	1.1 g	153 mg

Ingredients:
- 12 ounces steaks, 3/4-inch thick
- 1 tbspn garlic powder
- 1 tbspn olive oil
- Pepper
- Salt

Steak Fajitas

Prep Time	Time to cook	Serv
10 min	15 min	6

Directions:
1. Line AirFryer basket with aluminum foil.
2. Add all ingredients large bowl and toss until well coated.
3. Transfer fajita mixture into the AirFryer basket and cook at 390 F for 5 min.
4. Toss well and cook for 5-10 min more.
5. Enjoy.

Calories	Fat	Sugar	Protein	Carbohydrates	Cholesterol
304	17 g	4 g	22 g	15 g	73 mg

Ingredients:
- 1 lb steak, sliced
- 1 tbspn olive oil
- 1 tbspn fajita seasoning, gluten-free
- 1/2 cup onion, sliced
- 3 bell peppers, sliced

Great Beef Roast

Prep Time	Time to cook	Serv
10 min	35 min	7

Directions:
1. Coat roast with olive oil.
2. Mix together thyme, garlic powder, pepper, and salt and rub all over roast.
3. Place roast into the AirFryer basket and cook at 400 F for 20 min.
4. Spray roast with cooking spray and cook for 15 min more.
5. Slice and serve.

Ingredients:
- 2 lbs beef roast
- 1 tbspn olive oil
- 1 tbspn thyme
- 2 tbspn garlic powder
- 1/4 tbspn pepper
- 1 tbspn kosher salt

Tasty Cheeseburgers

Prep Time	Time to cook	Serv
10 min	12 min	4

Directions:
1. Spray AirFryer basket with cooking spray.
2. In a bowl, mix together ground beef, Italian seasoning, pepper, and salt.
3. Make 4 equal shapes of patties from meat mixture and place into the AirFryer basket.
4. Cook at 375 F for 5 min. Turn patties to another side and cook for 5 min more.
5. Place cheese slices on top of each patty and cook for 2 min more.
6. Enjoy.

Ingredients:
- 1 lb ground beef
- 4 cheddar cheese slices
- 1/2 tbspn Italian seasoning
- Pepper
- Salt

Calories	Fat	Sugar	Protein	Cholesterol
325	16.5 g	0.2 g	41.4 g	131 mg

Asian Sirloin Steaks

Prep Time	Time to cook	Serv
10 min	20 min	2

Directions:
1. Add steaks in a large zip-lock bag along with remaining ingredients. Shake well and place in the refrigerator for overnight.
2. Spray AirFryer basket with cooking spray.
3. Place marinated steaks in AirFryer basket and cook at 400 F for 10 min.
4. Turn steaks to another side and cook for 10-15 min more.
5. Enjoy.

Ingredients:
- 12 ounces sirloin steaks
- 1 tbspn garlic, diced
- 1 tbspn ginger, grated
- 1/2 tbspn Worcestershire sauce
- 1 1/2 tbspn soy sauce
- 2 tbspn erythritol
- Pepper
- Salt

Calories	Fat	Sugar	Protein	Carbohydrates	Cholesterol
342	10 g	1 g	52 g	5 g	152 mg

Pretty Soft & Juicy Beef Kabobs

Prep Time	Time to cook	Serv
10 min	10 min	4

Directions:
1. In a medium bowl, mix together soy sauce and sour cream.
2. Add beef into the bowl and coat well and place in the refrigerator for overnight.
3. Thread marinated beef, bell peppers, and onions onto the soaked wooden skewers.
4. Place in AirFryer basket and cook at 400 F for 10 min. Turn halfway through.
5. Enjoy.

Ingredients:
- 1 lb beef, cut into chunks
- 1 bell pepper, cut into 1-inch pieces
- 2 tbspn soy sauce
- 1/3 cup sour cream
- 1/2 onion, cut into 1-inch pieces

Calories	Fat	Sugar	Protein	Carbohydrates	Cholesterol
251	15 g	2 g	23 g	4 g	85 mg

Asian Flavors Beef Broccoli

Prep Time	Time to cook	Serv
10 min	15 min	3

Directions:
1. Add all ingredients except sesame seeds into the large mixing bowl and toss well.
2. Place bowl in the refrigerator for 1 hour.
3. Add marinated steak and broccoli into the AirFryer basket and cook at 350 F for 15 min.
4. Shake basket 2-3 times while cooking.
5. Garnish with sesame seeds and serve.

Ingredients:
- 1/2 lb steak, cut into strips
- 1 tbspn garlic, diced
- 1 tbspn ginger, diced
- 2 tbspn sesame oil
- 2 tbspn soy sauce
- 4 tbspn oyster sauce
- 1 lb broccoli florets
- 1 tbspn sesame seeds, toasted

Calories	Fat	Sugar	Protein	Carbohydrates	Cholesterol
265	14 g	2 g	21 g	12.5 g	45 mg

Juicy Rib Eye Steak

Prep Time	Time to cook	Serv
10 min	14 min	2

Directions:
1. Coat steaks with oil and season with garlic powder, onion powder, pepper, and salt.
2. Preheat the AirFryer to 400 F.
3. Place steaks into the AirFryer basket and cook for 14 min.
4. Turn halfway through.
5. Enjoy.

Ingredients:
- 2 medium rib-eye steaks
- 1/4 tbspn garlic powder
- 1/4 tbspn onion powder
- 1 tbspn olive oil
- Pepper
- Salt

Calories	Fat	Sugar	Protein	Cholesterol
469	31 g	0.5 g	44 g	135 mg

Scrumptious Stuffed Peppers

Prep Time	Time to cook	Serv
10 min	8 min	2

Directions:
1. Preheat the AirFryer to 390 F.
2. Sauté garlic and onion in the olive oil in a small pan until softened.
3. Add meat, 1/4 cup tomato sauce, Worcestershire sauce, half cheese, pepper, and salt and Stir to combine.
4. Stuff meat mixture into each pepper and top with remaining cheese and tomato sauce.
5. Spray AirFryer basket with cooking spray.
6. Place stuffed peppers into the AirFryer basket and cook for 15-20 min.
7. Enjoy.

Ingredients:
- 2 bell peppers, remove stems and seeds
- 4 ounces cheddar cheese, shredded
- 1 1/2 tbspn Worcestershire sauce
- 1/2 cup tomato sauce
- 8 ounces ground beef
- 1 tbspn olive oil
- 1 garlic clove, diced
- 1/2 onion, minced
- 1/2 tbspn pepper
- 1/2 tbspn salt

Calories	Fat	Sugar	Protein	Cholesterol
530	28.7 g	10.8 g	51 g	161 mg

Italian Marvelous Sausage Meatballs

Prep Time	Time to cook	Serv
10 min	15 min	8

Directions:
1. Add all ingredients into the large mixing bowl and mix until well combined.
2. Spray AirFryer basket with cooking spray. Make meatballs from bowl mixture and place into the AirFryer basket.
3. Cook at 350 F for 15 min.
4. Enjoy.

Calories	Fat	Sugar	Protein	Cholesterol
334	21.9 g	0.3 g	31.4 g	143 mg

Ingredients:
- 1 lb Italian sausage
- 1 lb ground beef
- 1/2 tbspn Italian seasoning
- 1/2 tbspn red pepper flakes
- 1 1/2 cups parmesan cheese, grated
- 2 egg, lightly beaten
- 2 tbspn parsley, minced
- 2 garlic cloves, diced
- 1/4 cup onion, diced
- Pepper
- Salt

Seductive Meatballs

Prep Time	Time to cook	Serv
10 min	20 min	8

Directions:
1. Preheat the AirFryer to 370 F.
2. Spray AirFryer basket with cooking spray.
3. Add all ingredients into the large bowl and mix until well combined.
4. Make small balls from mixture and place into the AirFryer basket and cook for 20 min.
5. Enjoy.

Calories	Fat	Sugar	Protein	Carbohydrates	Cholesterol
325	16 g	1 g	40 g	6 g	125 mg

Ingredients:
- 2 lbs ground beef
- 3 eggs, lightly
- 1/2 cup fresh parsley, diced
- 1 tbspn cinnamon
- 2 tbspn dried oregano
- 2 tbspn cumin
- 1 cup almond flour
- 4 garlic cloves, diced
- 1 onion, grated
- 1 tbspn pepper
- 2 tbspn salt

Soulful Mushrooms Meatballs

Prep Time	Time to cook	Serv
10 min	20 min	2

Directions:
1. In a mixing bowl, combine together all ingredients until well combined.
2. Make small balls from meat mixture and place into the AirFryer basket.
3. Cook at 350 F for 20 min.
4. Enjoy.

Calories	Fat	Sugar	Protein	Carbohydrates	Cholesterol
269	8 g	2 g	34 g	10 g	105 mg

Ingredients:
- 1/2 lb ground beef
- 2 tbspn onion, minced
- 2 mushrooms, diced
- 1/4 tbspn pepper
- 1 tbspn parsley, minced
- 1/4 cup almond flour
- 1/2 tbspn salt

Glorious Meatloaf

Prep Time	Time to cook	Serv
10 min	25 min	2

Directions:
1. Preheat the AirFryer to 400 F.
2. In a large bowl, mix together all ingredients until well combined.
3. Transfer meat mixture into the small silic1 loaf pan.
4. Place pan into the AirFryer and cook for 25 min.
5. Slice and serve.

Ingredients:
- 1/2 lb ground beef
- 1 tbspn chorizo, minced
- 1 1/2 tbspn almond flour
- 1 egg, lightly beaten
- 2 mushroom, sliced
- 1/2 tbspn fresh thyme
- 1/2 small onion, minced
- Pepper
- Salt

Enjoyable Kabab

Prep Time	Time to cook	Serv
10 min	10 min	2

Directions:
1. Add all ingredients into the bowl and mix well combined.
2. Divide mixture into the 2 equal portions and give it to kabab shape.
3. Place kababs into the AirFryer basket and cook at 370 F for 10 min.
4. Enjoy.

Calories	Fat	Sugar	Protein	Carbohydrates	Cholesterol
245	11 g	0 g	35 g	1 g	103 mg

Ingredients:
- 1/2 lb ground beef
- 1 tbspn parsley, minced
- 1/2 tbspn olive oil
- 1 1/2 tbspn kabab spice mix
- 1/2 tbspn garlic, diced
- 1/2 tbspn salt

Exciting Beef Satay

Prep Time	Time to cook	Serv
10 min	8 min	2

Directions:
1. Add all ingredients into the zip-lock bag and shake well. Place into the fridge for 1 hour.
2. Add marinated meat into the AirFryer basket and cook at 400 F for 8 min. Turn halfway through.
3. Enjoy.

Calories	Fat	Sugar	Protein	Carbohydrates	Cholesterol
690	36 g	6 g	74 g	10 g	205 mg

Ingredients:
- 1 lb beef flank steak, sliced into long strips
- 1 tbspn hot sauce
- 1 tbspn Swerve
- 1 tbspn garlic, diced
- 1 tbspn ginger, diced
- 1 tbspn soy sauce
- 1/2 cup cilantro, minced
- 1 tbspn ground coriander
- 1 tbspn fish sauce
- 2 tbspn olive oil

Scrummy Meatloaf

Prep Time	Time to cook	Serv
10 min	15 min	2

Directions:
1. In a large bowl, mix together all the ingredients until well combined.
2. Place meat mixture into silicon meatloaf pan and place in the AirFryer basket.
3. Cook at 360 F for 15 min.
4. Slice and serve.

Calories	Fat	Sugar	Protein	Carbohydrates	Cholesterol
265	10 g	2 g	38 g	5 g	180 mg

Ingredients:
- 1 egg, lightly beaten
- 1/2 lb ground beef
- 1/2 tbspn cayenne
- 1/2 tbspn turmeric
- 1 tbspn garam masala
- 1/2 tbspn garlic, diced
- 1/2 tbspn ginger, diced
- 1 tbspn cilantro, minced
- 1/2 cup onion, minced
- 1/8 tbspn ground cardamom
- 1/4 tbspn ground cinnamon
- 1/2 tbspn salt

Fantastic Burger

Prep Time	Time to cook	Serv
10 min	10 min	2

Directions:
1. In a large bowl, mix together all ingredients until well combined. Place in refrigerator for 1 hour.
2. Make patties from beef mixture and place into the AirFryer basket.
3. Cook at 360 F for 10 min.
4. Enjoy.

Ingredients:
- 1/2 lb ground beef
- 1 tbspn swerve
- 1 tbspn ginger, diced
- 1/2 tbspn soy sauce
- 1 tbspn gochujang
- 1 tbspn green onion, minced
- 1/2 tbspn sesame oil
- 1/4 tbspn salt

Great Garlic Butter Steak

Prep Time	Time to cook	Serv
5 min	6 min	2

Directions:
1. Season steaks with Italian seasoning, pepper, and salt.
2. Rub steaks with garlic butter and place into the AirFryer basket and cook at 350 F for 6 min.

Calories	Fat	Sugar	Protein	Carbohydrates	Cholesterol
120	8 g	0 g	10 g	0 g	6 mg

Ingredients:
- 2 steaks
- 2 tbspn garlic butter
- 1/4 tbspn Italian seasoning
- Pepper
- Salt

Unbelievable Beef Patties

Prep Time	Time to cook	Serv
10 min	10 min	2

Directions:
1. Spray AirFryer basket with cooking spray.
2. Add all ingredients into the large bowl and mix until well combined.
3. Make small patties from mixture and place into the AirFryer basket.
4. Cook at 350 F for 10 min.

Calories	Fat	Sugar	Protein	Carbohydrates	Cholesterol
220	7 g	1 g	35 g	2 g	100 mg

Ingredients:
- 1/2 lb ground beef
- 1/4 tbspn garlic powder
- 2 drops liquid smoke
- 1/2 tbspn hot sauce
- 1/2 tbspn Worcestershire sauce
- 1/2 tbspn dried parsley
- 1/4 tbspn pepper
- 1/4 tbspn onion powder
- 1/4 tbspn cayenne
- 1/2 tbspn chili powder
- 1/4 tbspn salt

Magical Sirloin Steaks

Prep Time	Time to cook	Serv
10 min	15 min	4

Directions:
1. Add all ingredients except steak into the blender and blend until smooth.
2. Place meat into the bowl and pour the blended mixture over meat and coat well.
3. Place in refrigerator for 1 hour.
4. Place marinated meat into the AirFryer and cook for 15 min at 330 F. Turn meat halfway through.

Calories	Fat	Sugar	Protein	Carbohydrates	Cholesterol
150	4 g	1 g	25 g	6 g	45 mg

Ingredients:
- 1 lb lamb sirloin steaks, boneless
- 1 tbspn garam masala
- 4 garlic cloves
- 3/4 tbspn ginger
- 1/2 onion
- 1 tbspn cayenne
- 1/2 tbspn ground cardamom
- 1 tbspn ground cinnamon
- 1 tbspn ground fennel
- 1 tbspn salt

Fabulous Steak with Cheese Butter

Prep Time	Time to cook	Serv
10 min	8 min	2

Directions:
1. Preheat the AirFryer to 400 F.
2. Mix together garlic powder, pepper, and salt and rub over the steaks.
3. Spray AirFryer basket with cooking spray.
4. Place steak in the AirFryer basket and cook for 4-5 min on each side.
5. Top with blue butter cheese.

Ingredients:
- 2 rib-eye steaks
- 2 tbspn garlic powder
- 2 1/2 tbspn blue cheese butter
- 1 tbspn pepper
- 2 tbspn kosher salt

Dreamy Montreal Steak

Prep Time	Time to cook	Serv
5 min	7 min	2

Directions:
1. Add steak, liquid smoke, soy sauce, and steak seasonings into the large zip-lock bag. Coat well and place in the refrigerator for overnight.
2. Spray AirFryer basket with cooking spray.
3. Place marinated steaks into the AirFryer
4. Cook at 375 F for 7 min. Turn after 5 min to another side.

Calories	Fat	Sugar	Protein	Carbohydrates	Cholesterol
355	9 g	0.3 g	62 g	1 g	80 mg

Ingredients:
- 12 ounces steak
- 1/2 tbspn liquid smoke
- 1 tbspn soy sauce
- 1/2 tbspn cocoa powder
- 1 tbspn Montreal steak seasoning
- Pepper
- Salt

Savory Juicy & Tender Steak

Prep Time	Time to cook	Serv
10 min	12 min	2

Directions:
1. In a bowl, mix together butter, Worcestershire sauce, garlic, parsley, and salt and place in the refrigerator.
2. Preheat the AirFryer to 400 F.
3. Season steak with pepper and salt.
4. Place seasoned steak in the AirFryer and cook for 12 min. Turn halfway through.
5. Remove steak from AirFryer and top with butter mixture.

Calories	Fat	Sugar	Protein	Carbohydrates	Cholesterol
590	57 g	0.5 g	16 g	3 g	423 mg

Ingredients:
- 2 rib-eye steak
- 3 tbspn fresh parsley, minced
- 1 stick butter, softened
- 1 1/2 tbspn Worcestershire sauce
- 3 garlic cloves, diced
- Pepper
- Salt

Rosemary Beef Roast

Prep Time	Time to cook	Serv
10 min	45 min	6

Directions:
1. Preheat the AirFryer to 360 F.
2. Mix together oil, rosemary, thyme, pepper, and salt and rub over the meat.
3. Place meat in the AirFryer and cook for 45 min.

Calories	Fat	Sugar	Protein	Carbohydrates	Cholesterol
300	12 g	0 g	46 g	0.5 g	123 mg

Ingredients:
- 2 lbs beef roast
- 1 tbspn olive oil
- 1 tbspn rosemary
- 1 tbspn thyme
- 1/4 tbspn pepper
- 1 tbspn salt

Adorable Air Fried Steak

Prep Time	Time to cook	Serv
10 min	10 min	2

Directions:
1. Preheat the AirFryer to 350 F.
2. Coat steak with olive oil and season with steak seasoning, pepper, and salt.
3. Spray AirFryer basket with cooking spray and place steak in the AirFryer basket.
4. Cook for 10 min. Turn halfway through.
5. Slice and serve.

Ingredients:
- 2 sirloin steaks
- 2 tbspn olive oil
- 2 tbspn steak seasoning
- Pepper
- Salt

Enchanting Beef Broccoli

Prep Time	Time to cook	Serv
10 min	10 min	4

Directions:
1. Spray AirFryer basket with cooking spray.
2. Add all ingredients except broccoli into the large bowl and toss well.
3. Add bowl mixture into the AirFryer basket and cook at 360 F for 10 min.
4. Serve with broccoli and enjoy.

Calories	Fat	Sugar	Protein	Carbohydrates	Cholesterol
230	5 g	3 g	36 g	7 g	125 mg

Ingredients:
- 1 lb round beef cubes
- 1/2 medium onion, diced
- 1 tbspn Worcestershire sauce
- 1/2 lb broccoli florets, steamed
- 1 tbspn olive oil
- 1 tbspn onion powder
- 1 tbspn garlic powder
- Pepper
- Salt

Charming Kabab

Prep Time	Time to cook	Serv
10 min	10 min	4

Directions:
1. Add all ingredients into the bowl and mix until combined. Place in the fridge for 60 min.
2. Divide meat mixture into 4 sections and wrap around 4 soaked wooden skewers.
3. Spray AirFryer basket with cooking spray.
4. Place kabab into the AirFryer and cook at 370 F for 10 min.

Ingredients:
- 1 lb ground beef
- 1/4 cup fresh parsley, minced
- 1 tbspn olive oil
- 2 tbspn kabab spice mix
- 1 tbspn garlic, diced
- 1 tbspn salt

Yummy Broccoli Beef

Prep Time	Time to cook	Serv
10 min	12 min	5

Directions:
1. In a small bowl, combine together oyster sauce, stevia, soy sauce, sherry, arrowroot, and sesame oil.
2. Add broccoli and meat in a large bowl.
3. Pour oyster sauce mixture over meat and broccoli and toss well. Place in the fridge for 60 min.
4. Add marinated meat broccoli to the AirFryer basket. Drizzle with olive oil and sprinkle with ginger and garlic.
5. Cook at 360 F for 12 min.

Calories	Fat	Sugar	Protein	Carbohydrates	Cholesterol
302	20 g	2 g	24 g	8 g	142 mg

Ingredients:
- 1 lb round steak, cut into strips
- 1 lb broccoli florets
- 5 drops liquid stevia
- 1 tbspn soy sauce
- 1/3 cup sherry
- 2 tbspn sesame oil
- 1/3 cup oyster sauce
- 1 garlic clove, diced
- 1 tbspn ginger, sliced
- 1 tbspn arrowroot powder
- 1 tbspn olive oil

Pretty Spiced Steak

Prep Time	Time to cook	Serv
10 min	9 min	3

Directions:
1. In a small bowl, mix together all ingredients except steak.
2. Rub spice mixture over the steak and let marinate the steak for 20 min.
3. Spray AirFryer basket with cooking spray.
4. Preheat the AirFryer to 390 F.
5. Place marinated steak in the AirFryer and cook for 9 min.

Ingredients:
- 1 lb rib eye steak
- 1/2 tbspn chipotle powder
- 1/4 tbspn paprika
- 1/4 tbspn onion powder
- 1/2 tbspn garlic powder
- 1 tbspn chili powder
- 1/4 tbspn black pepper
- 1 tbspn coffee powder
- 1/8 tbspn cocoa powder
- 1/8 tbspn coriander powder
- 1 1/2 tbspn sea salt

Appetizing Burger Patties

Prep Time	Time to cook	Serv
10 min	45 min	4

Directions:
1. Add all ingredients into the large bowl and mix until combined.
2. Spray AirFryer basket with cooking spray.
3. Make patties from meat mixture and place into the AirFryer basket.
4. Cook at 390 F for 25 min then turn patties to another side and cook at 350 F for 20 min more.

Calories	Fat	Sugar	Protein	Carbohydrates	Cholesterol
175	7 g	2 g	25 g	1 g	125 mg

Ingredients:
- 10 ounces ground beef
- 1 tbspn dried basil
- 1 tbspn mustard
- 1 tbspn tomato paste
- 1 ounces cheddar cheese
- 1 tbspn mixed herbs
- 1 tbspn garlic puree
- Pepper
- Salt

Wonderful Asian Beef

Prep Time	Time to cook	Serv
10 min	20 min	4

Directions:
1. Spray AirFryer basket with cooking spray.
2. Toss beef and xanthan gum together.
3. Add beef into the AirFryer basket and cook at 390F for 20 min.
4. Toss halfway through.
5. Meanwhile, in a saucepan add remaining ingredients except for green onion and heat over low heat.
6. When sauce begins to boiling then remove from heat.
7. Add cooked meat into the saucepan and stir to coat. Let sit in for 5 min.
8. Garnish with green onion and serve.

Calories	Fat	Sugar	Protein	Carbohydrates	Cholesterol
295	15 g	0.4 g	35 g	6 g	42 mg

Ingredients:
- 1 lb beef tips, sliced
- 1/4 cup green onion, minced
- 2 tbspn garlic, diced
- 2 tbspn sesame oil
- 1 tbspn fish sauce
- 2 tbspn coconut aminos
- 1 tbspn xanthan gum
- 2 red chili peppers, sliced
- 2 tbspn water
- 1 tbspn ginger, sliced

Pork

Delectable Pork satay

Prep Time	Time to cook	Serv
15 min	10 min	4

Directions:
1. In a medium bowl, mix the pork, onion, garlic, jalapeño, lime juice, coconut milk, peanut butter, and curry powder until well combined.
2. Thread the pork onto about eight bamboo or metal skewers.
3. Grill for 9 to 14 min, brushing once with the reserved marinade until the pork reaches at least 145°f on a meat thermometer.
4. Discard any remaining marinade.
5. Serve immediately.

Calories	Fat	Fiber	Protein	Carbohydrates	Sodium
194	7 g	1 g	25 g	7 g	65 mg

Ingredients:
- 1 (1-pound) pork tenderloin, cut into 1½-inch cubes
- ¼ cup dicedonion
- 2 garlic cloves, diced
- 1 jalapeño pepper, diced
- 2 tbspns freshly squeezed lime juice
- 2 tbspns coconut milk
- 2 tbspns unsalted peanut butter
- 2 tspns curry powder

Hearty Crispy mustard pork tenderloin

Prep Time	Time to cook	Serv
10 min	15 min	4

Directions:
1. On a plate, mix the breadcrumbs, walnuts, and cornstarch. Dip the mustard-coated pork into the crumb mixture to coat.
2. Air-fry the pork for 12 to 16 min, or until it registers at least 145°f on a meat thermometer. Slice to serve.

Calories	Fat	Fiber	Protein	Carbohydrates	Sodium
239	9 g	2 g	26 g	15 g	118 mg

Ingredients:
- 3 tbspns low-Sodium grainy mustard
- 2 tspns olive oil
- ¼ tspn dry mustard powder
- 1 (1-pound) pork tenderloin, silver skin, and excess fat trimmed and discarded
- 2 slices low-sodium whole-wheat bread, crumbled
- ¼ cup ground walnuts
- 2 tbspns cornstarch

Exquisite Apple pork tenderloin

Prep Time	Time to cook	Serv
10 min	20 min	4

Directions:
1. Rub each piece of pork with the apple butter and olive oil.
2. In a medium metal bowl, mix the pork, apples, celery, onion, marjoram, and apple juice.
3. Place the bowl into the AirFryer and roast for 14 to 19 min or until the pork reaches at least 145°f on a meat thermometer, and the apples and vegetables are tender. Stir once during cooking. Serve immediately.

Calories	Fat	Fiber	Protein	Carbohydrates	Sodium
213	5 g	3 g	24 g	20 g	88 mg

Ingredients:
- 1 (1-pound) pork tenderloin, cut into 4 pieces
- 1 tbspn apple butter
- 2 tspns olive oil
- 2 granny smith apples or Jonagold apples, sliced
- 3 celery stalks, sliced
- 1 onion, sliced ½ tspn dried marjoram
- ⅓ cup apple juice

Glorious grilled pork tenderloin

Prep Time	Time to cook	Serv
15 min	10 min	4

Directions:
1. Stir in the honey, lemon juice, and olive oil until well mixed.
2. Spread the honey mixture over the pork and let stand for 10 min at room temperature.
3. Roast the tenderloin in the AirFryer basket for 9 to 11 min, or until the pork registers at least 145°f on a meat thermometer. Slice the meat to serve.

Calories	Fat	Fiber	Protein	Carbohydrates	Sodium
177	5 g	1 g	23 g	10 g	61 mg

Ingredients:
- 1 tbspn packed Brown Sugar
- 2 tspns espresso powder
- 1 tspn ground paprika
- ½ tspn dried marjoram
- 1 tbspn honey
- 1 tbspn freshly squeezed lemon juice
- 2 tspns olive oil
- 1 (1-pound) pork tenderloin

Delightful Pork chops

Prep Time	Time to cook	Serv
15 min	15 min	5

Directions:
1. Switch on the AirFryer, insert fryer basket, grease it with olive oil, then shut with its lid, set the fryer at 350 degrees f, and preheat for 5 min.
2. Meanwhile, place bread slices in a food processor and pulse until the mixture resembles crumbs.
3. Tip the breadcrumbs in a shallow dish, add parsley, ½ tspn salt, ¼ tspn ground black pepper, and stir until mixed.
4. Place flour in another shallow dish, add remaining salt and black pepper, along with pork seasoning, and stir until mixed.
5. Crack the egg in a bowl, pour in apple juice, and whisk until combined.
6. Working on 1 pork chop at a time, first coat it into the flour mixture, then dip into egg and then evenly coat with breadcrumbs mixture.
7. Open the fryer, add coated pork chops in it in a single layer, close with its lid and cook for 10 min until nicely golden and toasted, flipping the pork chops halfway through the frying.
8. When AirFryer beeps, open its lid, transfer pork chops onto a serving plate and serve.

Calories	Fat	Fiber	Protein	Carbs
441	22.3 g	0.5 g	30.6 g	10 g

Ingredients:
- 4 slices of almond bread
- Five pork chops, b1-in, pastured
- ounces coconut flour
- 1 tspn salt
- 3 tbspns parsley
- ½ tspn ground black pepper
- 1 tbspn pork seasoning
- 2 tbspns olive oil
- 1/3 cup apple juice, unsweetened
- 1 egg, pastured

Lovely Pork belly

Prep Time: 20 min
Time to cook: 40 min
Serv: 4

Directions:
1. Cut the pork belly evenly into 3 pieces, place them in an AirFryer, and add remaining ingredients.
2. Switch on the AirFryer, then shut it with lid and cook the pork belly for 15 min at high pressure.
3. Rake out the pork by tongs and let it drain and dry for 10 min.
4. Then switch on the AirFryer, insert fryer basket, grease it with olive oil, then shut with its lid, set the fryer at 400 degrees f, and preheat for 5 min.
5. While the AirFryer preheats, cut each piece of the pork into 2 long slices.
6. Open the fryer, add pork slices in it, close with its lid and cook for 15 min until nicely golden and crispy, flipping the pork halfway through the frying.
7. When AirFryer beeps, open its lid, transfer pork slices onto a serving plate.

Ingredients:
- 1-pound pork belly, pastured
- Six cloves of garlic, peeled
- 1 tspn ground black pepper
- 1 tspn salt
- 2 tbspns soy sauce
- 2 bay leaves
- 3 cups of water

Calories	Fat	Fiber	Protein	Carbs
594	60 g	0 g	11 g	2 g

Gordeous Teriyaki Pork

Prep Time: 10 min
Time to cook: 40 min
Serv: 4

Directions:
1. Put and mix all remaining ingredients in a small bowl except main meat and stock.
2. Pour the stock into the AirFryer.
3. Place meat into the pot then pours bowl mixture over the pork.
4. Seal fryer with lid and cook on manual high pressure for 45 min.
5. Once d1, then allow to extrication pressure naturally then open the lid.
6. Enjoy.

Ingredients:
- 2 lb. pork loin
- 1/2 tbspn onion powder
- 1 tbspn ground ginger
- 2 tbspn brown sugar
- 1/2 cup water
- 1/4 cup soy sauce
- 1 cup chicken stock
- 1 1/2 tbspn honey
- 2 garlic cloves, crushed

Calories	Fat	Sugar	Protein	Cholesterol
606	31.8 g	11.4 g	63.3 g	181 mg

Admirable Ribs

Prep Time: 10 min
Time to cook: 40 min
Serv: 4

Directions:
1. Mix all rub ingredients in a bowl and rub over meat.
2. Pour the stock into the AirFryer then place ribs into the container.
3. Seal fryer with lid and cook on high pressure for 45 min.
4. Once d1, then allow to extrication pressure naturally then open the lid.
5. Stir and serve.

Ingredients:
- 2 3/4 lbs. country-style pork ribs

Dry rub:
- 1 tbspn garlic powder
- 1 tbspn brown sugar
- 1 tbspn cumin
- 1 tbspn pepper
- 1 cup chicken stock
- 1 tbspn cayenne pepper
- 1 tbspn paprika
- 1 tbspn onion powder
- 1 tbspn salt

Fantastic Pork Curry

Prep Time	Time to cook	Serv
10 min	37 min	8

Directions:
1. Add oil into the pot and set the container on sauté mode.
2. Season meat with pepper and salt. Add chicken to the pot and cook until browned.
3. Add remaining ingredients and stir everything well.
4. Seal pot with lid and cook on soup/stew mode for 30 min.
5. Once d1, then extrication pressure using the quick-extrication method than open the lid.
6. Stir and serve.

Calories	Fat	Sugar	Protein	Cholesterol
877	68.6 g	2.9 g	56.5 g	204 mg

Ingredients:
- 4 lbs. pork shoulder, boneless and cut into chunks
- 2 garlic cloves, diced
- 1 onion, minced
- 3 cups chicken broth
- 2 cups of coconut milk
- 1/2 tbspn turmeric
- 2 tbspn olive oil
- 1/2 tbspn ground cumin
- 1 1/2 tbspn curry paste
- 2 tbspn fresh ginger, grated
- Pepper
- Salt

Cufe Pork Posole

Prep Time	Time to cook	Serv
10 min	30 min	8

Directions:
1. Mix all ingredients into the instant fryer and Stir.
2. Seal fryer with lid and cook on manual high pressure for 30 min.
3. Once d1, then allow to extrication pressure naturally then open the lid.
4. Stir and serve.

Calories	Fat	Sugar	Protein	Cholesterol
620	30.3 g	3.1 g	49.4 g	156 mg

Ingredients:
- 1 lb. pork shoulder, cut into cubes
- 1 tbspn dried oregano
- 3 tbspn chili sauce
- 24 ounces posole
- 1 cup of water
- 2 tbspn chili powder
- 1 tbspn ground cumin
- 2 garlic cloves
- 1 tbspn salt

Luscious Sauerkraut Pork

Prep Time	Time to cook	Serv
10 min	40 min	8

Directions:
1. Season pork loin with pepper and salt.
2. Put some oil into the fryer and set the pot on sauté mode.
3. Sear meat until lightly browned.
4. Add stock, garlic, onions, and apples to the pot. Pour sauerkraut on top.
5. Fryer with lid and cook on high pressure for 40 min.
6. Once d1, then allow to extrication pressure naturally for 10 min then extrication using the quick-extrication method. Open the lid.
7. Enjoy.

Calories	Fat	Sugar	Protein	Cholesterol
322	17.8 g	4.5 g	31.8 g	91 mg

Ingredients:
- 2 lbs pork loin
- 3 garlic cloves, diced
- 14 ounces sauerkraut, drained
- 1 tbspn olive oil
- 1 onion, sliced
- 1 apple, sliced
- 1 cup chicken stock
- Pepper
- Salt

Yummy Pork Adobo

Prep Time	Time to cook	Serv
10 min	35 min	4

Directions:
1. Add oil in the AirFryer and set the container on sauté mode.
2. Add meat and cook until browned. Season with pepper and salt.
3. Add onions, bay leaf, peppercorns, and garlic.
4. Mix vinegar, water, and soy sauce and pour over meat.
5. Fryer with lid and cook on high pressure for 10 min.
6. Once d1, then extrication pressure using the quick-extrication method than open the lid.
7. Set pot on sauté mode and cook for 15-20 min.
8. Enjoy.

Calories	Fat	Sugar	Protein	Cholesterol
712	26.3 g	1.5 g	107.2 g	313 mg

Ingredients:
- 3 lbs pork butt, cut into cubes
- 1/4 cup water
- 3 tbspn soy sauce
- 1 onion, sliced
- 1 tbspn olive oil
- 1/4 cup vinegar
- 1 bay leaf
- 1 tbspn peppercorns
- 3 garlic cloves, crushed
- Pepper
- Salt

Fantastic Pork Chops

Prep Time	Time to cook	Serv
10 min	15 min	4

Directions:
1. Season pork chops with pepper and salt.
2. Add oil in the AirFryer and set the container on sauté mode.
3. Add pork chops to the pot and sear until lightly browned. Transfer pork chops to a plate.
4. Add broth to the pot then place the trivet in the container.
5. Place pork chops on top of the trivet.
6. Seal pot with lid and cook on meat mode for 5 min.
7. Once d1, then allow to extrication pressure naturally for 10 min then extrication using the quick-extrication method. Open the lid.
8. Enjoy.

Calories	Fat	Sugar	Protein	Cholesterol
289	23.5 g	0.2 g	18.2 g	69 mg

Ingredients:
- 4 pork loin chops, b1-in
- 1 cup chicken stock
- 1 tbspn olive oil
- 1/4 tbspn pepper
- 1/2 tbspn salt

Great Garlicky Pork Roast

Prep Time	Time to cook	Serv
10 min	35 min	2

Directions:
1. Mix all ingredients into the instant fryer and Stir.
2. Seal pot with lid and cook on meat mode for 35 min.
3. Once d1, then allow to extrication pressure naturally then open the lid.
4. Stir and serve.

Calories	Fat	Sugar	Protein	Cholesterol
578	47.1 g	0.4 g	36.3 g	138 mg

Ingredients:
- 1 lb. pork roast
- 1 tbspn basil
- 1 1/2 tbspn soy sauce
- 2 tbspn grated parmesan cheese
- 2 tbspn honey
- 3 garlic cloves, diced
- 1/2 cup chicken stock
- 1/2 tbspn corn-starch
- 1/2 tbspn olive oil
- Salt

Dreamy Herbed Pork Burgers

Prep Time	Time to cook	Serv
15 min	45 min	8

Directions:
1. Preheat the AirFryer to 395 F and grease an AirFryer basket.
2. Mix all the ingredients in a bowl except cheese and buns.
3. Make eight equal-sized patties from the pork mixture and arrange thee patties in the AirFryer basket.
4. Cook for about 45 min, flipping once in between and arrange the patties in buns with cheese to serve.

Calories	Fat	Sugar	Protein	Sodium
289	6.5 g	4.9 g	28.7 g	384 mg

Ingredients:
- 2 small onions, minced
- 21-ounce ground pork
- 2 tspns fresh basil, minced
- Eight burger buns
- ½ cup cheddar cheese, grated
- 2 tspns mustard
- 2 tspns garlic puree
- 2 tspns tomato puree
- Salt and ground black pepper
- 2 tspns dried mixed herbs, crushed

Cute Chinese Style Pork Meatballs

Prep Time	Time to cook	Serv
15 min	20 min	3

Directions:
1. Preheat the AirFryer to 390 F and grease an AirFryer basket.
2. Mix all the ingredients in a bowl except cornstarch and oil until well combined.
3. Place the cornstarch through a shallow dish and shape the mixture into equal-sized balls and roll the meatballs evenly into the cornstarch mixture and arrange in the AirFryer basket.
4. Cook for about 10 min and dish out to serve warm.

Calories	Fat	Sugar	Protein	Sodium
171	6.6 g	0.7 g	16.9 g	254 mg

Ingredients:
- 1 egg, beaten
- 6-ounce ground pork
- ¼ cup cornstarch
- 1 tspn oyster sauce
- ½ tbspnn light soy sauce
- ½ tspn sesame oil
- ¼ tspn five-spice powder
- ½ tbspnn olive oil
- ¼ tspn brown sugar

Savory Ginger, Garlic 'n Pork Dumplings

Prep Time	Time to cook	Serv
5 min	15 min	8

Directions:
1. Heat oil in a skillet and sauté the ginger and garlic until fragrant. Stir in the ground pork and cook for 5 min.
2. Stir in the bok choy and crushed red pepper. Season with salt and pepper to taste. Allow cooling.
3. Put all the meat mixture in the middle of the dumpling wrappers. Fold the wrappers to seal the meat mixture in.
4. Place the bok choy in the grill pan.
5. Cook the dumplings in the AirFryer at 330F for 15 min.
6. Preparing the dipping sauce by mixing the remaining ingredients in a bowl.

Calories	Fat	Carbs	Protein
137	5 g	16 g	7 g

Ingredients:
- ¼ tspn crushed red pepper
- ½ tspn sugar
- 1 tbspnn minced fresh ginger
- 1 tbspnn minced garlic
- 1 tspn canola oil
- 1 tspn toasted sesame oil
- 18 dumpling wrappers
- 2 tbspns rice vinegar
- 2 tspns soy sauce
- 4 cups bok choy, minced
- 4 ounces ground pork

Seductive Grilled Prosciutto-Wrapped Fig

Prep Time: 5 min
Time to cook: 8 min
Serv: 2

Directions:
1. Wrap a prosciutto slice around 1 slice of fid and then thread into the skewer. Repeat process for remaining Ingredients. Place on skewer rack in an AirFryer.
2. For 8 min, cook on 390F. Halfway through Time to cook, turnover skewers.
3. Enjoy.

Calories	Fat	Carbs	Protein
277	10 g	10.7 g	36 g

Ingredients:
- 2 whole figs, sliced in quarters
- Eight prosciutto slices
- Pepper and salt to taste

Tasty Grilled Sausages with BBQ Sauce

Prep Time: 10 min
Time to cook: 30 min
Serv: 3

Directions:
1. Preheat the AirFryer to 390F.
2. Place the grill pan accessory in the AirFryer.
3. Place the sausage links and grill for 30 min.
4. Flip halfway through the Time to cook.
5. Before serving brush with prepared BBQ sauce.

Calories	Fat	Carbs	Protein
265	14.2 g	6.4 g	27.7 g

Ingredients:
- ½ cup prepared BBQ sauce
- Six sausage links for Cooking

Lovely Crisp Pork Chops

Prep Time: 10 min
Time to cook: 12 min
Serv: 6

Directions:
1. Preheat the AirFryer to 360 F.
2. Add all ingredients except pork chops in a zip-lock bag.
3. Add pork chops in the bag. Seal bag and shake well to coat pork chops.
4. Remove pork chops from zip-lock bag and place in the AirFryer basket.
5. Cook pork chops for 10-12 min.
6. Enjoy.

Calories	Fat	Sugar	Protein	Cholesterol
230	11 g	0.2 g	27 g	79 mg

Ingredients:
- 1 1/2 lbs pork chops, boneless
- 1 tbspn paprika
- 1 tbspn creole seasoning
- 1 tbspn garlic powder
- 1/4 cup parmesan cheese, grated
- 1/3 cup almond flour

Sweet Parmesan Pork Chops

Prep Time	Time to cook	Serv
10 min	15 min	4

Directions:
1. Preheat the AirFryer to 400 F.
2. Season pork chops with pepper and salt.
3. Add pork rind in food processor and process until crumbs form.
4. Mix together pork rind crumbs and seasoning in a large bowl.
5. Place egg in a separate bowl.
6. Dip pork chops in egg mixture then coat with pork crumb mixture and place in the AirFryer basket.
7. Cook pork chops for 12-15 min.
8. Enjoy.

Calories	Fat	Sugar	Protein	Cholesterol
329	24 g	0.4 g	23 g	158 mg

Ingredients:
- 4 pork chops, boneless
- 4 tbspn parmesan cheese, grated
- 1 cup pork rind
- 2 eggs, lightly beaten
- 1/2 tbspn chili powder
- 1/2 tbspn onion powder
- 1 tbspn paprika
- 1/4 tbspn pepper
- 1/2 tbspn salt

Simple Pork Chops

Prep Time	Time to cook	Serv
10 min	9 min	4

Directions:
1. Brush pork chops with olive oil.
2. In a bowl, mix together parmesan cheese and spices.
3. Spray AirFryer basket with cooking spray.
4. Coat pork chops with parmesan cheese mixture and place in the AirFryer basket.
5. Cook pork chops at 375 F for 9 min. Turn halfway through.
6. Enjoy.

Calories	Sugar	Protein	Carbohydrates	Cholesterol
332	0.3 g	19.3 g	1.1 g	71 mg

Ingredients:
- 4 pork chops, boneless
- 1 tbspn onion powder
- 1 tbspn smoked paprika
- 1/2 cup parmesan cheese, grated
- 2 tbspn olive oil
- 1/2 tbspn pepper
- 1 tbspn kosher salt

Quick Pork Chops

Prep Time	Time to cook	Serv
10 min	14 min	3

Directions:
1. Coat pork chops with olive oil and season with paprika, garlic powder, pepper, and salt.
2. Place pork chops in AirFryer basket and cook at 380 F for 10-14 min. Turn halfway through.
3. Enjoy.

Calories	Sugar	Protein	Carbohydrates	Cholesterol
285	0.1 g	18.1 g	0.5 g	69 mg

Ingredients:
- 3 pork chops, rinsed and pat dry
- 1/4 tbspn smoked paprika
- 1/2 tbspn garlic powder
- 2 tbspn olive oil
- Pepper
- Salt

Magnificent Pork with Mushrooms

Prep Time	Time to cook	Serv
10 min	18 min	4

Directions:
1. Preheat the AirFryer to 400 F.
2. Cut pork chops into the 3/4-inch cubes and place in a large mixing bowl.
3. Add remaining ingredients into the bowl and toss well.
4. Transfer pork and mushroom mixture into the AirFryer basket and cook for 15-18 min. Shake basket halfway through.
5. Enjoy.

Calories	Sugar	Protein	Carbohydrates	Cholesterol
428	1.1 g	27.5 g	2.2 g	113 mg

Ingredients:
- 1 lb pork chops, rinsed and pat dry
- 1/2 tbspn garlic powder
- 1 tbspn soy sauce
- 2 tbspn butter, melted
- 8 ounces mushrooms, halved
- Pepper
- Salt

Quick Bratwurst with Vegetables

Prep Time	Time to cook	Serv
10 min	20 min	6

Directions:
1. Add all ingredients into the large mixing bowl and toss well.
2. Line AirFryer basket with foil.
3. Add vegetable and bratwurst mixture into the AirFryer basket and cook at 390 F for 10 min.
4. Toss well and cook for 10 min more.
5. Enjoy.

Calories	Fat	Sugar	Protein	Carbohydrates	Cholesterol
63	4 g	2 g	2 g	4 g	10 mg

Ingredients:
- 1 package bratwurst, sliced 1/2-inch rounds
- 1/2 tbspn Cajun seasoning
- 1/4 cup onion, diced
- 2 bell pepper, sliced

Enchanting Cheesy & Juicy Pork Chops

Prep Time	Time to cook	Serv
10 min	8 min	2

Directions:
1. Preheat the AirFryer to 350 F.
2. Rub pork chops with garlic powder and salt and place in the AirFryer basket.
3. Cook pork chops for 4 min.
4. Turn pork chops to another side and cook for 2 min.
5. Add cheese on top of pork chops and cook for 2 min more.
6. Enjoy.

Calories	Fat	Sugar	Protein	Carbohydrates	Cholesterol
465	22 g	0.6 g	61 g	2 g	190 mg

Ingredients:
- 4 pork chops
- 1/4 cup cheddar cheese, shredded
- 1/2 tbspn garlic powder
- 1/2 tbspn salt

Delectable Pork Bites

Prep Time	Time to cook	Serv
10 min	21 min	6

Directions:
1. In a shallow bowl, whisk eggs.
2. In a shallow dish, mix together almond flour, coriander, paprika, lemon zest, and salt.
3. Dip each pork cube in egg then coat with almond flour mixture.
4. Preheat the AirFryer to 365 F.
5. Spray AirFryer basket with cooking spray.
6. Add coated pork cubes into the AirFryer basket and cook for 14 min.
7. Turn pork cubes to another side and cook for 7 min more.
8. Enjoy.

Ingredients:
- 2 eggs, lightly beaten
- 1 lb pork tenderloin, cut into cubes
- ¼ cup almond flour
- ½ tbspn ground coriander
- ½ tbspn paprika
- ½ tbspn lemon zest
- ½ tbspn kosher salt

Calories	Fat	Sugar	Protein	Carbohydrates	Cholesterol
135	4 g	0.1 g	21 g	0.2 g	111 mg

Fantastic Pork Tenderloin

Prep Time	Time to cook	Serv
10 min	15 min	3

Directions:
1. In a small bowl, mix together saffron, onion powder, garlic powder, cinnamon, and sage.
2. Rub pork tenderloin with the saffron mixture.
3. Now rub pork tenderloin with garlic and vinegar and let sit for 10 min.
4. Preheat the AirFryer to 320 F.
5. Place pork tenderloin into the AirFryer and top with butter.
6. Cook for 15 min.
7. Slice and serve.

Ingredients:
- 1 lb pork tenderloin
- 1 tbspn vinegar
- 2 garlic cloves, diced
- 3 tbspn butter
- ½ tbspn onion powder
- ½ tbspn garlic powder
- ½ tbspn cinnamon
- 1 tbspn sage
- ½ tbspn saffron

Calories	Fat	Sugar	Protein	Carbohydrates	Cholesterol
327	16 g	0.3 g	40 g	2 g	140 mg

Pretty Pesto Pork Chops

Prep Time	Time to cook	Serv
10 min	18 min	5

Directions:
1. Spray pork chops with cooking spray.
2. Coat pork chops with pesto and sprinkles with almond flour.
3. Place pork chops into the AirFryer basket and cook at 350 F for 18 min.
4. Enjoy.

Ingredients:
- 5 pork chops
- 3 tbspn basil pesto
- 2 tbspn almond flour
- 1 tbspn olive oil

Calories	Fat	Sugar	Protein	Carbohydrates	Cholesterol
321	26 g	0.5 g	21 g	3 g	241 mg

Beautiful Garlic Thyme Pork Chops

Prep Time	Time to cook	Serv
10 min	15 min	8

Directions:
1. Preheat the AirFryer to 400 F.
2. Spray AirFryer basket with cooking spray.
3. In a bowl, mix together butter, spices, cheese, and coconut oil.
4. Rub butter mixture on top of pork chops and place into the AirFryer basket.
5. Cook for 10 min. Turn to another side and cook for 10 min more.
6. Enjoy.

Calories	Fat	Sugar	Protein	Carbohydrates	Cholesterol
355	29 g	0 g	23 g	2 g	125 mg

Ingredients:
- 8 pork chops, boneless
- 5 garlic cloves, diced
- 1 cup parmesan cheese
- 2 tbspn butter, melted
- 1 tbspn thyme
- 1 tbspn parsley
- 2 tbspn coconut oil
- 1/4 tbspn pepper
- 1/2 tbspn sea salt

Easy Pork Strips

Prep Time	Time to cook	Serv
10 min	10 min	2

Directions:
1. Tenderize meat and season with pepper and salt.
2. In a bowl, mix together sweetener, soy sauce, and vinegar. Add ginger and garlic and set aside.
3. Add pork chops into the marinade mixture and marinate for 2 hours.
4. Preheat the AirFryer to 350 F.
5. Add marinated meat into the AirFryer and cook for 5 min on each side.
6. Cut into strips and serve.

Calories	Fat	Sugar	Protein	Cholesterol
551	39.8 g	8.8 g	36.6 g	138 mg

Ingredients:
- 4 pork loin chops
- 1 tbspn swerve
- 1 tbspn soy sauce
- 1/8 tbspn ground ginger
- 1 garlic clove, minced
- 1/2 tbspn balsamic vinegar

Sweet BBQ Ribs

Prep Time	Time to cook	Serv
10 min	30 min	2

Directions:
1. Preheat the AirFryer to 350 F.
2. Add all ingredients into the large bowl and mix well to coat. Place into the fridge for 1 hour.
3. Add marinated ribs into the AirFryer basket and cook for 15 min.
4. Turn ribs to another side and cook for 15 min more.
5. Enjoy.

Calories	Fat	Sugar	Protein	Carbohydrates	Cholesterol
697	42 g	8 g	60 g	12 g	235 mg

Ingredients:
- 1 lb pork ribs
- 1/2 tbspn five-spice powder
- 1 tbspn swerve
- 4 tbspn BBQ sauce, sugar-free
- 3 garlic cloves, minced
- 1 tbspn soy sauce
- 1 tbspn pepper
- 1 tbspn sesame oil
- 1 tbspn salt

Soulful Grilled Pork Shoulder

Prep Time	Time to cook	Serv
10 min	15 min	2

Directions:
1. In a large bowl, mix together all ingredients and place in the refrigerator for 60 min.
2. Place AirFryer grill pan into the AirFryer.
3. Add pork mixture into the AirFryer and cook at 400 F for 15 min. Turn halfway through.
4. Enjoy.

Calories	Fat	Sugar	Protein	Cholesterol
405	30 g	3 g	28 g	105 mg

Ingredients:
- 1/2 lb pork shoulder, cut into 1/2-inch slices
- 1/2 tbspn Swerve
- 1/2 tbspn sesame oil
- 1/2 tbspn rice wine
- 1/2 tbspn soy sauce
- 1 tbspn green onion, sliced
- 1/2 tbspn sesame seeds
- 1/4 tbspn cayenne pepper
- 1/2 tbspn garlic, diced
- 1/2 tbspn ginger, diced
- 1 tbspn gochujang
- 1/2 onion, sliced

Dreamy Coconut Butter Pork Chops

Prep Time	Time to cook	Serv
10 min	15 min	2

Directions:
1. Preheat the AirFryer to 350 F.
2. In a large bowl, mix together garlic, coconut butter, coconut oil, parsley, basil, rosemary, pepper, and salt.
3. Rub garlic mixture over pork chops. Place in the refrigerator for 2 hours.
4. Place marinated pork chops into the AirFryer basket and cook for 7 min.
5. Turn pork chops to another side and cook for 8 min.
6. Enjoy.

Calories	Fat	Sugar	Protein	Cholesterol
620	53 g	1 g	37 g	140 mg

Ingredients:
- 4 pork chops
- 1 tbspn coconut oil
- 1 tbspn coconut butter
- 1 tbspn dried parsley
- 1/4 tbspn dried basil
- 1/4 tbspn rosemary
- 3 garlic cloves, diced
- Pepper
- Salt

Fabulous BBQ Chops

Prep Time	Time to cook	Serv
10 min	10 min	2

Directions:
1. Preheat the AirFryer to 350 F for 5 min.
2. Season pork chops with pepper and salt.
3. In a bowl, combine together swerve, soy sauce, garlic, ground ginger, and vinegar.
4. Add pork chops in a bowl and coat well and place in the refrigerator for 2 hours.
5. Place marinated pork chops in AirFryer basket and cook for 10 min. Turn pork chops to another side halfway through.
6. Enjoy.

Calories	Fat	Sugar	Protein	Cholesterol
295	19.9 g	8 g	19 g	70 mg

Ingredients:
- 2 pork loin chops
- 1 tbspn swerve
- 1/2 tbspn balsamic vinegar
- 1/8 tbspn ground ginger
- 1 tbspn soy sauce
- 1 garlic clove
- Pepper
- Salt

Glorious Coconut Pork Chops

Prep Time	Time to cook	Serv
10 min	15 min	2

Directions:
1. Preheat the AirFryer to 350 F.
2. In a small bowl, mix together coconut butter, coconut oil, garlic, parsley, pepper, and salt.
3. Rub coconut butter mixture over pork chops and place in the refrigerator for 1 hour.
4. Place grill pan in the AirFryer.
5. Place marinated chops into the AirFryer and cook for 7 min.
6. Turn pork chops to another side and cook for 8 min.
7. Enjoy.

Ingredients:
- 4 pork chops
- 1 tbspn coconut oil
- 1 tbspn coconut butter
- 1 tbspn fresh parsley, minced
- 3 garlic cloves, grated
- Pepper
- Salt

Calories	Fat	Sugar	Protein	Carbohydrates	Cholesterol
629	50 g	0.4 g	35 g	3 g	140 mg

Enjoyable Pork Chops

Prep Time	Time to cook	Serv
10 min	20 min	4

Directions:
1. Coat pork chops with Mr. dash seasoning, pepper, and salt.
2. Place pork chops in the AirFryer and cook at 360 F for 10 min.
3. Turn pork chops to another side and cook for 10 min more.
4. Enjoy.

Ingredients:
- 4 pork chops, boneless
- 1 1/2 tbspn Mr. Dash seasoning
- Pepper
- Salt

Calories	Fat	Sugar	Protein	Carbohydrates	Cholesterol
255	20 g	0 g	20 g	0 g	70 mg

Fabulos Pork Loin

Prep Time	Time to cook	Serv
5 min	40 min	6

Directions:
1. Coat meat with olive oil, pepper, garlic salt, and herb de Provence.
2. Place in the AirFryer and cook at 360 F for 25 min.
3. Turn to another side and cook for 15 min more.
4. Enjoy.

Ingredients:
- 3 lbs pork loin cut in half
- 1/2 tbspn garlic salt
- 1/4 tbspn pepper
- 1 1/2 tbspn herbs de Provence
- 1 tbspn olive oil

Calories	Fat	Sugar	Protein	Carbohydrates	Cholesterol
569	34 g	0.5 g	60 g	0.5 g	180 mg

Appetizing Mustard Pork Tenderloin

Prep Time: 10 min
Time to cook: 15 min
Serv: 2

Directions:
1. Preheat the AirFryer to 390 F.
2. In a bowl, mix together bell pepper strips, herb de Provence, onion, pepper, and salt.
3. Add 1/2 tbspn oil and mix well.
4. Season pork tenderloin with mustard, pepper, and salt.
5. Coat pork tenderloin with remaining oil.
6. Place pork tenderloin pieces into the AirFryer pan and top with bell pepper mixture.
7. Place pan in the AirFryer and cook for 15 min. Stir halfway through.
8. Enjoy.

Ingredients:
- 1 pork tenderloin, cut into pieces
- 1/2 tbspn mustard
- 1 onion, sliced
- 1 bell pepper, cut into strips
- 1 tbspn oil
- 2 tbspn herb de Provence
- Pepper
- Salt

Calories	Fat	Sugar	Protein	Carbohydrates	Cholesterol
275	12 g	4 g	31 g	10 g	83 mg

Charming McCornick Pork Chops

Prep Time: 10 min
Time to cook: 15 min
Serv: 2

Directions:
1. Season pork chops with pepper and salt.
2. Drizzle milk over the pork chops.
3. Place pork chops in a zip-lock bag with flour and shake well to coat. Marinate pork chops for 30 min.
4. Place marinated pork chops into the AirFryer basket and cook at 380 F for 15 min. Turn halfway through.
5. Enjoy.

Ingredients:
- 2 pork chops
- 1/2 tbspn McCormick Montreal chicken seasoning
- 2 tbspn arrowroot flour
- 1 1/2 tbspn coconut milk
- Salt

Calories	Fat	Sugar	Protein	Carbohydrates	Cholesterol
290	19 g	0.5 g	20 g	7 g	70 mg

Delish Mustard Pork Chops

Prep Time: 10 min
Time to cook: 12 min
Serv: 2

Directions:
1. In a small bowl, mix together steak seasoning, swerve, and mustard.
2. Rub steak seasoning mixture over pork chops and place into the AirFryer basket.
3. Cook at 350 F for 12 min. Turn halfway through.
4. Enjoy.

Ingredients:
- 1/2 lb pork chops, boneless
- 1 tbspn Swerve
- 1/2 tbspn steak seasoning blend
- 1/2 tbspn mustard

Calories	Fat	Sugar	Protein	Carbohydrates	Cholesterol
395	27 g	8 g	24 g	9 g	95 mg

Thoothsome Vietnamese Pork Chop

Prep Time	Time to cook	Serv
10 min	15 min	2

Directions:
1. Add all ingredients into the bowl and coat well. Place in refrigerator for 2 hours.
2. Preheat the AirFryer to 400 F.
3. Place marinated pork chops into the AirFryer and cook for 7 min.
4. Turn pork chops to another side and cook for 5 min more.
5. Enjoy.

Ingredients:
- 2 pork chops
- 1 tbspn olive oil
- 1 tbspn soy sauce
- 1 tbspn pepper
- 2 1/2 tbspn lemongrass, minced
- 1 tbspn onion, minced
- 3 garlic cloves, minced

Calories	Fat	Sugar	Protein	Carbohydrates	Cholesterol
340	28 g	0.5 g	20 g	6 g	70 mg

Tasty Veggie Pork Tenderloin

Prep Time	Time to cook	Serv
10 min	15 min	2

Directions:
1. Preheat the AirFryer to 390 F.
2. In AirFryer baking dish mix together 1/2 tbspnn olive oil, herb de Provence, bell pepper, onion, garlic powder, onion powder, and salt.
3. Season meat with pepper, mustard, and salt. Drizzle with remaining oil and place in the dish on top of onion and pepper mixture.
4. Place the dish in the AirFryer and cook for 8 min.
5. Stir everything well and cook for 7 min more.
6. Enjoy.

Ingredients:
- 10 ounces pork tenderloin, cut into small pieces
- 1/2 tbspn mustard
- 1 onion, sliced
- 1/2 red bell pepper, cut into strips
- 1/2 yellow bell pepper, cut into strips
- 1/4 tbspn garlic powder
- 1/4 tbspn onion powder
- 1/4 tbspn pepper
- 1 tbspn olive oil
- 2 tbspn herb de Provence

Calories	Fat	Sugar	Protein	Carbohydrates	Cholesterol
325	14 g	6 g	41 g	11 g	110 mg

Wonderful Asian Pork

Prep Time	Time to cook	Serv
10 min	15 min	4

Directions:
1. Add all ingredients into the bowl and mix well and place in the refrigerator for 1 hour.
2. Place marinated meat and onion slices into the AirFryer.
3. Cook at 400 F for 15 min. Toss halfway through.
4. Enjoy.

Ingredients:
- 1 lb pork shoulder, boneless and cut into
- 1/2 inch sliced
- 3 tbspn green onions, sliced
- 3 garlic cloves, diced
- 1 tbspn ginger, diced
- 2 tbspn red pepper paste
- 1 onion, sliced
- 1 tbspn sesame seeds
- 3/4 tbspn cayenne pepper
- 1 tbspn sesame oil
- 1 tbspn rice wine

Calories	Fat	Sugar	Protein	Carbohydrates	Cholesterol
405	30 g	3 g	30 g	8 g	105 mg

Delightful Classic Pork

Prep Time	Time to cook	Serv
10 min	10 min	4

Directions:
1. In a bowl, whisk together onion, pepper, lemongrass paste, fish sauce, garlic, sweetener, and oil.
2. Add meat slices into the bowl and coat well. Place in the fridge for 1 hour.
3. Place marinated meat in the AirFryer basket and cook at 400 F for 10 min. Turn halfway through.
4. Enjoy.

Ingredients:
- 1 lb pork shoulder, thinly sliced
- 1 tbspn fish sauce
- 3 garlic cloves, diced
- 1 tbspn Swerve
- 2 tbspn olive oil
- 1/4 cup onion, diced
- 1/2 tbspn pepper
- 1 tbspn lemongrass paste

Calories	Fat	Sugar	Protein	Carbohydrates	Cholesterol
415	32 g	4 g	27 g	5 g	105 mg

Simple Pork Chops

Prep Time	Time to cook	Serv
5 min	10 min	4

Directions:
1. Preheat the AirFryer to 400 F.
2. In a small bowl, mix together paprika, garlic salt, sage, pepper, cayenne pepper, and cumin.
3. Rub pork chops with spice mixture and place into the AirFryer and cook for 10 min. Turn halfway through.
4. Enjoy.

Ingredients:
- 4 pork chops
- 2 tbspn olive oil
- 1/2 tbspn dried sage
- 1/2 tbspn cayenne pepper
- 1/4 tbspn pepper
- 1 tbspn ground cumin
- 1 tbspn paprika
- 1/2 tbspn garlic salt

Calories	Fat	Sugar	Protein	Carbohydrates	Cholesterol
275	20 g	0.4 g	20 g	1 g	153 mg

Scrummy Garlic Pork Chops

Prep Time	Time to cook	Serv
5 min	20 min	5

Directions:
1. In a small bowl, mix together garlic, parsley, oil, and lemon juice.
2. Season pork chops with pepper and salt.
3. Rub garlic mixture over the pork chops and allow to marinate for 30 min.
4. Add marinated pork chops into the AirFryer and cook at 400 F for 10 min.
5. Turn pork chops to another side and cook for 10 min more.
6. Enjoy.

Ingredients:
- 2 lbs pork chops
- 2 tbspn garlic, diced
- 1 tbspn fresh parsley
- 2 tbspn olive oil
- 2 tbspn fresh lemon juice
- Pepper
- Salt

Calories	Fat	Sugar	Protein	Carbohydrates	Cholesterol
625	50 g	0.5 g	40 g	2 g	124 mg

Perfect Cheese Herb Pork Chops

Prep Time	Time to cook	Serv
5 min	9 min	2

Directions:
1. Preheat the AirFryer to 350 F.
2. Mix together almond flour, Cajun seasoning, herb de Provence, paprika, and cheese.
3. Spray pork chops with cooking spray and coat pork chops with almond flour mixture and place into the AirFryer basket.
4. Cook for 9 min.
5. Enjoy.

Ingredients:
- 2 pork chops, boneless
- 1 tbspn herb de Provence
- 1 tbspn paprika
- 4 tbspn parmesan cheese, grated
- 1/3 cup almond flour
- 1/2 tbspn Cajun seasoning

Calories	Fat	Sugar	Protein	Carbohydrates	Cholesterol
340	26 g	0.5 g	24 g	2 g	124 mg

Luscious Creole Pork Chops

Prep Time	Time to cook	Serv
10 min	12 min	6

Directions:
1. Preheat the AirFryer to 360 F.
2. Add all ingredients except pork chops into the zip-lock bag. Mix well.
3. Add pork chops into the bag. Seal bag and shake until well coated.
4. Spray AirFryer basket with cooking spray.
5. Place pork chops into the AirFryer basket and cook for 12 min.
6. Enjoy.

Ingredients:
- 1 1/2 lbs pork chops, boneless
- 1 tbspn garlic powder
- 5 tbspn parmesan cheese, grated
- 1/3 cup almond flour
- 1 1/2 tbspn paprika
- 1 tbspn Creole seasoning

Calories	Fat	Sugar	Protein	Carbohydrates	Cholesterol
400	31 g	0.4 g	28 g	1 g	243 mg

Fantastic Pork

Prep Time	Time to cook	Serv
10 min	20 min	6

Directions:
1. Add meat and jerk paste into the bowl and coat well. Place in the fridge for overnight.
2. Spray AirFryer basket with cooking spray.
3. Preheat the AirFryer to 390 F.
4. Add marinated meat into the AirFryer and cook for 20 min.
5. Turn halfway through.
6. Enjoy.

Ingredients:
- 1 1/2 lbs pork butt, minced into pieces
- 3 tbspn jerk paste

Calories	Fat	Sugar	Protein	Carbohydrates	Cholesterol
325	12 g	0 g	52 g	0.5 g	124 mg

Lamb

Flavourful Herbed Lamb Chops

Prep Time	Time to cook	Serv
1 hour 10 min	13 min	6

Directions:
1. Prepare the marinade and for this, place all its Ingredients in a bowl and whisk until combined.
2. Pour the marinade in a large plastic bag, add lamb chops in it, seal the bag, then turn it upside down to coat lamb chops with the marinade and let it marinate in the refrigerator for a minimum of 1 hour.
3. Then switch on the AirFryer, insert fryer basket, grease it with olive oil, then shut with its lid, set the fryer at 390 degrees f, and preheat for 5 min.
4. Meanwhile, Open the fryer, add marinated lamb chops in it, close with its lid and cook for 8 min until nicely golden and toasted, turning the lamb chops halfway through the frying.
5. When AirFryer beeps, open its lid, transfer lamb chops onto a serving plate.

Ingredients:
- 1-pound lamb chops, pastured
- For the marinade:
- 2 tbspn lemon juice
- 1 tspn dried rosemary
- 1 tspn salt
- 1 tspn dried thyme
- 1 tspn coriander
- 1 tspn dried oregano
- 2 tbspn olive oil

Calories	Fat	Fiber	Protein	Carbs
177.4	8 g	0.5 g	23.4 g	1.7 g

Savory Lamb Sirloin Steak

Prep Time	Time to cook	Serv
40 min	20 min	4

Directions:
1. Make cuts in the lamb chops by using a knife, then place them in a large bowl and add prepared marinade in it.
2. Mix well until lamb chops are coated with the marinade and let them marinate in the refrigerator for a minimum of 30 min.
3. Then switch on the AirFryer, insert fryer basket, grease it with olive oil, then shut with its lid, set the fryer at 330 degrees f, and preheat for 5 min.
4. Open the fryer, add lamb chops in it, close with its lid and cook for 15 min until nicely golden and toasted, flipping the steaks halfway through the frying.
5. When AirFryer beeps, open its lid, transfer lamb steaks onto a serving plate and serve.

Ingredients:
- 1-pound lamb sirloin steaks, pastured, boneless
- For the marinade:
- ½ of white onion, peeled
- 1 tspn ground fennel
- Five cloves of garlic, peeled
- 4 slices of ginger
- 1 tspn salt
- 1/2 tspn ground cardamom
- 1 tspn garam masala
- 1 tspn ground cinnamon
- 1 tspn cayenne pepper

Calories	Fat	Fiber	Protein	Carbs
182	7 g	1 g	24 g	3 g

Charming Garlic Rosemary Lamb Chops

Prep Time	Time to cook	Serv
1 hour 10 min	12 min	4

Directions:
1. Take the fryer pan, place lamb chops in it, season the top with ½ tspn black pepper and ¾ tspn salt, then drizzle evenly with oil and spread with 1 tspn dicedgarlic.
2. Add garlic cloves and rosemary and then let the lamb chops marinate in the pan into the refrigerator for a minimum of 1 hour.
3. Then switch on the AirFryer, insert fryer pan, then shut with its lid, set the fryer at 360 degrees f, and cook for 6 min.
4. Flip the lamb chops, season them with remaining salt and black pepper, add remaining dicedgarlic, and continue cooking for 6 min or until lamb chops are cooked.
5. When AirFryer beeps, open its lid, transfer lamb chops onto a serving plate and serve.

Calories	Fat	Fiber	Protein	Carbs
616	28 g	0.3 g	83 g	1 g

Ingredients:
- 4 lamb chops, pastured
- 1 tspn ground black pepper
- 2 tspns dicedgarlic
- 1 ½ tspn salt
- 2 tspns olive oil
- 4 cloves of garlic, peeled
- 4 rosemary sprigs

Dreamy Lamb Curry

Prep Time	Time to cook	Serv
10 min	35 min	4

Directions:
1. Add oil into the AirFryer and set the pot on sauté mode.
2. Add bay leaves and onion to the pot and sauté until softened.
3. Add ginger-garlic paste, meat, and all spices and Stir.
4. Add remaining ingredients and Stir.
5. Seal fryer with lid and cook on manual high pressure for 5 min.
6. Once d1, then allow to extrication pressure naturally then open the lid.
7. Stir and serve.

Calories	Fat	Sugar	Protein	Carbohydrates	Cholesterol
436	207 g	4.9 g	47 g	10.7 g	148 mg

Ingredients:
- 1 1/2 lbs lamb chunks
- 1 1/2 tbspn ginger garlic paste
- 1 1/4 cups can tomato, minced
- 1/4 tbspn fennel powder
- 1/2 tbspn coriander powder
- 2 bay leaves
- 2 onion, minced
- 1 tbspn olive oil
- 1 tbspn garam masala
- 1 tbspn chili powder
- 1/2 tbspn cumin powder
- Salt

Fabulous Herb Seasoned Lamb

Prep Time	Time to cook	Serv
10 min	40 min	4

Directions:
1. Season meat with pepper and salt.
2. Add oil into the AirFryer and set the container on sauté mode.
3. Add meat to the pot and sauté until browned.
4. Add garlic and sauté for 30 seconds.
5. Add wine and Stir.
6. Add remaining ingredients and Stir.
7. Seal fryer with lid and cook on manual high pressure for 15 min.
8. Once d1, then allow to extrication pressure naturally then open the lid.
9. Enjoy.

Ingredients:
- 2 lbs. lamb, boneless and cut into chunks
- 1 tbspn rosemary, minced
- 2 carrots, minced
- 1 large onion, minced
- 1 cup red wine
- 2 garlic cloves, sliced
- 1 tbspn olive oil
- 2 tbspn tomato paste
- 1/2 cup chicken stock
- 1/2 tbspn oregano, minced
- 2 tbspn thyme, minced
- Pepper
- Salt

Delightful Lamb Korma

Prep Time	Time to cook	Serv
10 min	20 min	4

Directions:
1. Put some oil into the AirFryer and set the container on sauté mode.
2. Add ginger-garlic paste and cook for a min.
3. Add 1/4 cup water, tomato paste, and all spices. Stir.
4. Add coconut milk, remaining water, and meat. Stir.
5. Seal fryer with lid and cook on manual high pressure for 15 min.
6. Once d1, then allow to extrication pressure naturally then open the lid.
7. Stir in lime juice.
8. Garnish with cilantro and serve.

Calories	Fat	Sugar	Protein	Cholesterol
423	35.98 g	3.3 g	20.6 g	80 mg

Ingredients:
- 1 lb lamb leg, cut into pieces
- 1/2 tbspn fresh lime juice
- 2 tbspn cilantro, minced
- 1/4 tbspn cardamom powder
- 1 tbspn paprika
- 1/2 tbspn cayenne pepper
- 1/2 tbspn turmeric
- 1 1/2 tbspn garam masala
- 3/4 cup water
- 1/2 cup coconut milk
- 2 tbspn tomato paste
- 2 tbspn ginger garlic paste
- 1 onion, minced
- 1 tbspn olive oil
- 1 tbspn salt

Tasty & Spicy Lamb

Prep Time	Time to cook	Serv
10 min	35 min	4

Directions:
1. Set AirFryer on sauté mode.
2. Season meat with pepper and salt and place into the pot.
3. Cook meat for 5 min.
4. Add remaining ingredients and Stir.
5. Seal fryer with lid and cook on manual high pressure for 15 min.
6. Once d1, then allow to extrication pressure naturally for 10 min then extrication using the quick-extrication method. Open the lid.

Calories	Fat	Sugar	Protein	Cholesterol
487	32.8 g	7.3 g	35.5 g	125 mg

Ingredients:
- 1 lb. lamb, cut into pieces
- 2 tbspn lemon juice
- 1/2 cup fresh cilantro, minced
- 2 onions, minced
- 2 cups chicken stock
- 1 cup of coconut milk
- 3 tbspn butter
- 1 cup grape tomatoes, minced
- 1/2 tbspn cumin powder
- 1 1/2 tbspn turmeric
- 2 tbspn garam masala
- 2 1/2 tbspn chili powder
- 2 tbspn apple cider
- 1 tbspn salt

Adorable Lamb Stew

Prep Time	Time to cook	Serv
10 min	30 min	3

Directions:
1. Add oil into the AirFryer and set the container on sauté mode.
2. Add garlic and meat and sauté for a min.
3. Season with thyme, oregano, chili powder, and salt.
4. Stir everything well and cook for 5 min.
5. Add zucchini and cook for 3-4 min.
6. Add cabbage, chili pepper, and stock. Stir.
7. Seal fryer with lid and cook on manual high pressure for 12 min.
8. Once d1, then allow to extrication pressure naturally for 10 min then extrication using the quick-extrication method. Open the lid.
9. Stir and serve.

Ingredients:
- 1 lb. lamb loin, cut into pieces
- 2 cups chicken stock
- 1 chili pepper, minced
- 1 cup cabbage, shredded
- 1 zucchini, sliced
- 1/2 tbspn dried thyme
- 1 tbspn oregano
- ½ tbspn chili powder
- 3 tbspn olive oil
- 2 garlic cloves, crushed
- 1 tbspn salt

Exquisite Lamb Shanks

Prep Time	Time to cook	Serv
10 min	35 min	4

Directions:
1. Put all ingredients into the instant fryer and Stir.
2. Seal fryer with lid and cook on manual high pressure for 25 min.
3. Once d1, then allow to extrication pressure naturally for 10 min then extrication using the quick-extrication method. Open the lid.
4. Enjoy.

Calories	Fat	Sugar	Protein	Carbohydrates	Cholesterol
309	18 g	2.9 g	29.7 g	6.6 g	77 mg

Ingredients:
- 4 lamb shanks
- 3 garlic cloves
- 1 small onion, minced
- 1/4 cup apple cider vinegar
- 3 tbspn olive oil
- 3 cups chicken broth
- 7 ounces mushrooms, sliced
- 1/2 tbspn dried rosemary
- 1 tomato, minced
- 1/4 cup leeks, minced
- 2 celery stalks, minced
- 2 tbspn sea salt

Marvelous Asian Lamb Curry

Prep Time	Time to cook	Serv
10 min	30 min	4

Directions:
1. Add oil into the AirFryer and set the container on sauté mode.
2. Add bay leaves and onion to the pot and cook for 5 min.
3. Add ginger-garlic paste, meat, and all spices and Stir.
4. Put together the remaining ingredients and Stir to combine.
5. Cook on manual high pressure for 5 min seal pot with a lid and.
6. Once d1, then allow to extrication pressure naturally for 10 min then extrication using the quick-extrication method. Open the lid.
7. Stir and serve.

Calories	Fat	Sugar	Protein	Cholesterol
433	20.8 g	5.4 g	47.4 g	148 mg

Ingredients:
- 1 1/2 lbs. lamb chunks
- 2 tbspn ginger garlic paste
- 1 1/2 cups can tomato, minced
- 1/2 tbspn fennel powder
- 1/2 tbspn coriander powder
- 1/2 tbspn garam masala
- 1 tbspn chili powder
- 2 bay leaves
- 2 onion, minced
- 1 tbspn oil
- 3/4 tbspn cumin powder
- Salt

Soulful Indian Lamb Curry

Prep Time	Time to cook	Serv
10 min	20 min	6

Directions:
1. Season meat with pepper and salt.
2. Add oil into the AirFryer and set the container on sauté mode.
3. Add garlic and onion to the pot and sauté for 3-4 min.
4. Add curry paste and coconut cream and cook for 4-5 min.
5. Add meat, fish sauce, soy sauce, broth, and coconut milk. Stir.
6. Cook on manual high pressure for 8 min on the fryer.
7. Once d1, then extrication pressure using the quick-extrication method than open the lid.
8. Add lime juice and green beans and cook on sauté mode for 4 min.
9. Garnish with cilantro and serve.

Calories	Fat	Sugar	Protein	Cholesterol
413	28.6 g	1.8 g	29.9 g	107 mg

Ingredients:
- 2 lbs lamb meat, b1-in
- 2 1/2 tbspn green curry paste
- 1/2 cup coconut cream
- 1/4 cup cilantro, minced
- 1/2 tbspn lime juice
- 6 ounces green beans, minced
- 1/2 tbspn soy sauce
- 1/2 tbspn fish sauce
- 2 garlic cloves, crushed
- 1/2 cup chicken broth
- 4.5 ounces coconut milk
- 1 small onion, diced
- 1 tbspn olive oil
- Pepper
- Salt

Simple Rogan Josh

Prep Time	Time to cook	Serv
10 min	35 min	4

Direction`s:
1. Add all ingredients into the bowl and Stir.
2. Place bowl in the refrigerator for 2 hours.
3. Add marinated meat with marinade into the AirFryer.
4. Seal fryer with lid and cook on manual high pressure for 20 min.
5. Once d1, then allow to extrication pressure naturally for 10 min then extrication using the quick-extrication method. Open the lid.
6. Enjoy.

Calories	Fat	Sugar	Protein	Cholesterol
620	42.9 g	2.7 g	44.8 g	161 mg

Ingredients:
- 1 lb. leg of lamb, cut into cubes
- 2 garlic cloves, diced
- 1/4 tbspn ground cinnamon
- 1 small onion, diced
- 1 tbspn tomato paste
- 1/2 cup yogurt
- 1/4 cup water
- 1/2 tbspn turmeric
- 1 tbspn paprika
- 2 tbspn garam masala
- 1/4 cup cilantro, minced
- 1/2 tbspn cayenne pepper
- 2 tbspn ginger, diced
- 1 tbspn salt

Delish Cheesy Lamb Chops

Prep Time	Time to cook	Serv
10 min	18 min	3

Directions:
1. Season lamb chops with chili, garlic powder, and salt.
2. Place lamb chops into the AirFryer and cook for 4 min on each side.
3. Remove lamb chops from pot and place on a plate.
4. Pour water to the pot then place a trivet in the bowl.
5. Place lamb chops on the trivet.
6. Seal fryer with lid and cook on manual high pressure for 10 min.
7. Once d1, then extrication pressure using the quick-extrication method than open the lid.
8. Enjoy.

Calories	Fat	Sugar	Protein	Cholesterol
530	19.3 g	2.7 g	44.8 g	161 mg

Ingredients:
- 3 lamb chops
- 1/2 tbspn garlic powder
- 1 tbspn olive oil
- 3/4 cup parmesan cheese
- 1/4 tbspn dried basil, crushed
- 1 cup of water
- 1/4 tbspn dried oregano, crushed
- Pepper
- Salt

Thoothsome Garlicky Lamb

Prep Time	Time to cook	Serv
10 min	17 min	6

Directions:
1. Add oil into the AirFryer and set the container on sauté mode.
2. Add meat to the pot and cook for 5 min.
3. Put the ginger and garlic and cook for 1-2 min.
4. Add remaining ingredients and Stir.
5. Seal fryer with lid and cook on manual high for 12 min.
6. Once d1, then extrication pressure using the quick-extrication method than open the lid.
7. Enjoy.

Calories	Fat	Sugar	Protein	Cholesterol
319	13.5 g	0.5 g	44.1 g	136 mg

Ingredients:
- 2 lbs. lamb steak, cut into strips
- 1 tbspn olive oil
- 2 1/2 scallions, minced
- 3 tbspn water
- 2 tbspn arrowroot
- 1/2 cup soy sauce, low-sodium
- 1/2 cup water
- 4 garlic cloves, diced

Spectacular Mustard Lamb Loin Chops

Prep Time	Time to cook	Serv
15 min	30 min	4

Directions:
1. Preheat the AirFryer to 390 o F and grease an AirFryer basket.
2. Mix the mustard, lemon juice, oil, tarragon, salt, and black pepper in a large bowl.
3. Coat the chops generously with the mustard mixture and arrange in the AirFryer basket.
4. Cook for about 15 min, flipping once in between and dish out to serve hot.

Ingredients:
- 4-ounces lamb loin chops
- 2 tbspns Dijon mustard
- 1 tbspn fresh lemon juice
- ½ tspn olive oil
- 1 tspn dried tarragon
- Salt and black pepper, to taste

Calories	Fat	Sugar	Protein	Carbohydrates	Sodium
433	17.6 g	0.2 g	64.1 g	0.6 g	201 mg

Cute Pesto Coated Rack of Lamb

Prep Time	Time to cook	Serv
15 min	15 min	4

Directions:
1. Preheat the AirFryer to 200 o F and grease an AirFryer basket.
2. Put the mint, garlic, oil, honey, salt, and black pepper in a blender and pulse until smooth to make pesto.
3. Coat the rack of lamb with this pesto on both sides and arrange in the AirFryer basket.
4. Cook for about 15 min and cut the rack into individual chops to serve.

Ingredients:
- ½ bunch fresh mint
- 1½-pound sack of lamb
- 1 garlic clove
- ¼ cup extra-virgin olive oil
- ½ tbspn honey
- Salt and black pepper, to taste

Calories	Fat	Sugar	Protein	Carbohydrates	Sodium
406	27.7 g	2.2 g	34.9 g	2.9 g	161 mg

Unbelievable Spiced Lamb Steaks

Prep Time	Time to cook	Serv
15 min	15 min	3

Directions:
1. Preheat the AirFryer to 330 F and grease an AirFryer basket.
2. Put the onion, garlic, ginger, and spices in a blender and pulse until smooth.
3. Coat the lamb steaks with this mixture on both sides and refrigerate to marinate for about 24 hours.
4. Arrange the lamb steaks in the AirFryer basket and cook for about 15 min, flipping once in between.
5. Dish out the steaks in a platter and serve warm.

Ingredients:
- ½ onion, roughly minced
- 1½ pounds boneless lamb sirloin steaks
- Five garlic cloves, peeled
- 1 tbspn fresh ginger, peeled
- 1 tspn garam masala
- 1 tspn ground fennel
- ½ tspn ground cumin
- ½ tspn ground cinnamon
- ½ tspn cayenne pepper
- Salt and black pepper, to taste

Calories	Fat	Sugar	Protein	Carbohydrates	Sodium
252	16.7 g	0.7 g	21.7 g	4.2 g	42 mg

Pretty Leg of Lamb

Prep Time	Time to cook	Serv
20 min	30 min	6

Directions:
1. Preheat the AirFryer to 300 F and grease an AirFryer basket.
2. Make slits in the leg of lamb with a sharp knife.
3. Mix 2 tbspns of oil, herbs, garlic, salt, and black pepper in a bowl.
4. Coat the leg of lamb with oil mixture generously and arrange it in the AirFryer basket.
5. Cook for about 75 min and set the AirFryer to 390 o F.
6. Coat the Brussels sprout evenly with the remaining oil and honey and arrange them in the AirFryer basket with the leg of lamb.
7. Cook for about 15 min and dish out to serve warm.

Calories	Fat	Sugar	Protein	Carbohydrates	Sodium
449	19.9 g	8.2 g	51.7 g	16.6 g	185 mg

Ingredients:
- 2¼ pounds leg of lamb
- 1 tbspn fresh rosemary, diced
- 1 tbspn fresh lemon thyme
- 1½ pounds Brussels sprouts, trimmed
- 3 tbspns olive oil, divided
- 1 garlic clove, diced
- Salt and ground black pepper, as required
- 2 tbspns honey

Gorgeous Lamb Kebabs

Prep Time	Time to cook	Serv
20 min	8 min	6

Directions:
1. Preheat the AirFryer to 355 F and grease an AirFryer basket.
2. Mix lamb, pistachios, eggs, juice, chili flakes, flour, cumin seeds, fennel seeds, coriander seeds, mint, parsley, salt, and black pepper in an exceedingly large bowl.
3. Thread the lamb mixture onto metal skewers to form sausages and coat with olive oil.
4. Place the skewers in the AirFryer basket and cook for about 8 min.
5. Dish out in a platter and serve hot.

Calories	Fat	Sugar	Protein	Carbohydrates	Sodium
284	15.8 g	1.1 g	27.9 g	8.4 g	932 mg

Ingredients:
- 4 eggs, beaten
- 1 cup pistachios, minced
- 1 pound ground lamb
- 4 tbspns plain flour
- 4 tbspns flat-leaf parsley, minced
- 2 tspns chili flakes
- 4 garlic cloves, diced
- 2 tbspns fresh lemon juice
- 2 tspns cumin seeds
- 1 tspn fennel seeds
- 2 tspns dried mint
- 2 tspns salt
- Olive oil
- 1 tspn coriander seeds
- 1 tspn freshly ground black pepper

Nourishing Lamb with Potatoes

Prep Time	Time to cook	Serv
20 min	15 min	2

Directions:
1. Preheat the AirFryer to 355 F and arrange a divider in the AirFryer.
2. Rub the lamb evenly with garlic and rosemary and place on 1 side of AirFryer divider.
3. Cook for about 20 min and meanwhile, microwave the potatoes for about 4 min.
4. Dish out the potatoes in a large bowl and stir in the olive oil and onions.
5. Transfer into the AirFryer divider and change the side of the lamb rump.
6. Cook for about 15 min, flipping once in between and dish out in a bowl.

Ingredients:
- ½ pound lamb meat
- 2 small potatoes, peeled and halved
- ½ small onion, peeled and halved
- ¼ cup frouncesen sweet potato fries
- 1 garlic clove, crushed
- ½ tbspn dried rosemary, crushed
- 1 tspn olive oil

Wonderful Garlic-Rosemary Lamb BBQ

Prep Time	Time to cook	Serv
15 min	12 min	2

Directions:
1. In a shallow dish, mix well all ingredients and marinate for 3 hours.
2. Thread lamb pieces in skewers. Place on skewer rack in the AirFryer.
3. For 12 min, cook on 390F. Halfway through Time to cook, turnover skewers. If needed, cook in batches.
4. Enjoy.

Ingredients:
- 1-lb cubed lamb leg
- juice of 1 lemon
- fresh rosemary
- 3 smashed garlic cloves
- salt and pepper
- 1/2 cup olive oil

Calories	Fat	Carbs	Protein
560	39.1 g	5.4 g	46.5 g

Appetizing Lamb Patties

Prep Time	Time to cook	Serv
10 min	20 min	4

Directions:
1. Preheat the AirFryer to 375 F.
2. Add all ingredients into the bowl and mix until well combined.
3. Spray AirFryer basket with cooking spray.
4. Make the equal shape of patties from meat mixture and place into the AirFryer basket.
5. Cook lamb patties for 10 min then turn to another side and cook for 10 min more.
6. Enjoy.

Ingredients:
- 1 1/2 lbs ground lamb
- 1/3 cup feta cheese, crumbled
- 1 tbspn oregano
- 1/4 tbspn pepper
- 1/2 tbspn salt

Calories	Fat	Sugar	Protein	Cholesterol
351	15.2 g	0.5 g	49.6 g	164 mg

Enjoyable Lemon Mustard Lamb Chops

Prep Time	Time to cook	Serv
10 min	15 min	4

Directions:
1. Preheat the AirFryer to 390 F.
2. In a small bowl, mix together mustard, lemon juice, tarragon, and olive oil.
3. Brush mustard mixture over lamb chops.
4. Place lamb chops in AirFryer basket and cook for 15 min. Turn halfway through.
5. Enjoy.

Ingredients:
- 8 lamb chops
- 1 tbspn lemon juice
- 1 tbspn tarragon
- 1/2 tbspn olive oil
- 2 tbspn Dijon mustard
- Pepper
- Salt

Calories	Fat	Sugar	Protein	Cholesterol
328	13.4 g	0.2 g	48.1 g	163 mg

Lovely Lamb Meatballs

Prep Time	Time to cook	Serv
10 min	14 min	8

Directions:
1. Preheat the AirFryer to 400 F.
2. Spray AirFryer basket with cooking spray.
3. Add all ingredients into the large bowl and mix until well combined.
4. Make small balls from meat mixture and place into the AirFryer basket and cook for 14 min. Shake basket twice while cooking.
5. Enjoy.

Calories	Fat	Sugar	Protein	Carbohydrates	Cholesterol
121	4 g	0.5 g	16 g	2 g	70 mg

Ingredients:
- 1 egg, lightly beaten
- 1 lb ground lamb
- ¼ tbspn bay leaf, crushed
- 1 tbspn ground coriander
- ¼ tbspn cayenne pepper
- ¼ tbspn turmeric
- 1 onion, minced
- 2 garlic cloves, diced
- ¼ tbspn pepper
- 1 tbspn salt

Delectable Spicy Lamb Chops

Prep Time	Time to cook	Serv
10 min	10 min	6

Directions:
1. In a large bowl, mix together oil, butter, lime zest, chili pepper, chili flakes, onion powder, garlic powder, and cayenne pepper.
2. Add lamb chops to the bowl and coat well with marinade and place in the refrigerator for 30 min.
3. Spray AirFryer basket with cooking spray.
4. Place marinated pork chops into the AirFryer basket and cook for 10 min.
5. Turn pork chops halfway through.
6. Enjoy.

Calories	Fat	Sugar	Protein	Carbohydrates	Cholesterol
253	12 g	0.4 g	32 g	1 g	105 mg

Ingredients:
- 1 ½ lbs lamb chops
- 1 tbspn butter, melted
- 1 tbspn olive oil
- 1 ½ tbspn cayenne pepper
- 1 tbspn garlic powder
- 1 tbspn onion powder
- ½ tbspn red chili flakes
- 1 tbspn chili pepper
- ½ tbspn lime zest

Scrumptious Lamb Roast

Prep Time	Time to cook	Serv
5 min	1 hour 30 min	6

Directions:
1. Make small cuts on meat using a sharp knife.
2. Poke garlic slices into the cuts. Season meat with pepper and salt.
3. Mix together oil and rosemary and rub over the meat.
4. Place meat into the AirFryer and cook at 400 F for 15 min.
5. Turn temperature to 320 F for 1 hour 15 min.
6. Enjoy.

Calories	Fat	Sugar	Protein	Carbohydrates	Cholesterol
595	25 g	0 g	85 g	2 g	423 mg

Ingredients:
- 2 1/2 lbs lamb leg roast
- 1 tbspn dried rosemary
- 3 garlic cloves, sliced
- 1 tbspn olive oil
- Pepper
- Salt

Glorious Dried Herbs Lamb Chops

Prep Time	Time to cook	Serv
10 min	20 min	4

Directions:
1. Add all ingredients except lamb chops into the zip-lock bag.
2. Add lamb chops to the bag. Seal bag and shake well and place in the fridge for overnight.
3. Place marinated lamb chops into the AirFryer.
4. Cook at 390 F for 3 min.
5. Turn lamb chops to another side and cook for 4 min more.
6. Enjoy.

Calories	Fat	Sugar	Protein	Carbohydrates	Cholesterol
275	16 g	0.5 g	30 g	1 g	124 mg

Ingredients:
- 1 lb lamb chops
- 1 tbspn oregano
- 1 tbspn thyme
- 1 tbspn rosemary
- 2 tbspn fresh lemon juice
- 2 tbspn olive oil
- 1 tbspn coriander
- 1/4 tbspn pepper
- 1 tbspn salt

Magical Lemon Herb Lamb Chops

Prep Time	Time to cook	Serv
5 min	7 min	4

Directions:
1. Preheat the AirFryer to 390 F.
2. Add all ingredients except lamb chops in a zip-lock bag and shake well to mix.
3. Add lamb chops and coat well with herb mixture and place in the refrigerator for 1 hour.
4. Place marinated lamb chops into the AirFryer and cook for 3 min.
5. Turn lamb chops to another side and cook for 4 min more.
6. Enjoy.

Calories	Fat	Sugar	Protein	Carbohydrates	Cholesterol
275	15 g	0.5 g	33 g	1 g	105 mg

Ingredients:
- 1 lb lamb chops
- 1 tbspn oregano
- 1 tbspn thyme
- 1 tbspn rosemary
- 2 tbspn lemon juice
- 2 tbspn olive oil
- 1/4 tbspn basil
- 1/4 tbspn tarragon
- 1 tbspn coriander
- 1 tbspn salt

Luscious Lamb Rack

Prep Time	Time to cook	Serv
10 min	30 min	6

Directions:
1. Mix together oil and garlic.
2. Brush oil and garlic mixture over the rack of lamb. Season with pepper and salt.
3. Preheat the AirFryer to 210 F.
4. Mix together thyme and rosemary.
5. Coat lamb with egg then with herb mixture.
6. Place lamb rack in the AirFryer basket and cook for 25 min.
7. Turn temperature to 390 F and cook for 5 min more.
8. Enjoy.

Calories	Fat	Sugar	Protein	Carbohydrates	Cholesterol
255	15 g	0.3 g	29 g	1 g	114 mg

Ingredients:
- 1 egg, lightly beaten
- 1 tbspn fresh thyme, minced
- 1 3/4 lbs rack of lamb
- 1 tbspn fresh rosemary, minced
- 1 tbspn olive oil
- 2 garlic cloves, minced
- Pepper
- Salt

Savory Cayenne Cumin Lamb

Prep Time	Time to cook	Serv
10 min	10 min	4

Directions:
1. In a bowl, mix together ground cumin, chili peppers, garlic, olive oil, cayenne, and salt.
2. Add meat to the bowl and coat well. Place in refrigerator for 1 hour.
3. Place marinated meat into the AirFryer and cook at 360 F for 10 min.
4. Enjoy.

Calories	Fat	Sugar	Protein	Carbohydrates	Cholesterol
285	15 g	0.5 g	33 g	2 g	105 mg

Ingredients:
- 1 lb lamb, cut into 1-inch pieces
- 2 tbspn olive oil
- 1 tbspn cayenne
- 2 tbspn ground cumin
- 2 chili peppers, minced
- 1 tbspn garlic, diced
- 1 tbspn salt

Seductive Thyme Garlic Lamb Chops

Prep Time	Time to cook	Serv
5 min	12 min	4

Directions:
1. Preheat the AirFryer to 390 F.
2. Season lamb chops with pepper and salt.
3. In a small bowl, mix together thyme, oil, and garlic and rub over lamb chops.
4. Place lamb chops into the AirFryer and cook for 12 min. Turn halfway through.
5. Enjoy.

Calories	Fat	Sugar	Protein	Carbohydrates	Cholesterol
415	35 g	0.5 g	20 g	1 g	124 mg

Ingredients:
- 4 lamb chops
- 4 garlic cloves, diced
- 3 tbspn olive oil
- 1 tbspn dried thyme
- Pepper
- Salt

Magnificent Cumin Lamb

Prep Time	Time to cook	Serv
10 min	10 min	4

Directions:
1. In a small bowl, mix together cumin and cayenne.
2. Rub meat with cumin mixture and place in a large bowl.
3. Add oil, soy sauce, garlic, chili peppers, stevia, and salt over the meat. Coat well and place in the refrigerator for overnight.
4. Add marinated meat to the AirFryer and cook at 360 F for 10 min.
5. Enjoy.

Calories	Fat	Sugar	Protein	Carbohydrates	Cholesterol
285	16 g	0.5 g	33 g	2 g	123 mg

Ingredients:
- 1 lb lamb, cut into 2-inch pieces
- 1/4 tbspn liquid stevia
- 2 tbspn olive oil
- 1/2 tbspn cayenne
- 2 tbspn ground cumin
- 2 red chili peppers, minced
- 1 tbspn garlic, diced
- 1 tbspn soy sauce
- 1 tbspn salt

Seafood Recipes

Delicious Crab Cakes

Prep Time	Time to cook	Serv
10 min	10 min	4

Directions:
1. Add all ingredients except butter in a mixing bowl and mix until well combined.
2. Make 4 equal shapes of patties from mixture and place on parchment lined plate.
3. Place plate in the fridge for 30 min.
4. Spray AirFryer basket with cooking spray.
5. Brush melted butter on both sides of crab patties.
6. Place crab patties in AirFryer basket and cook for 10 min at 350 F.
7. Turn patties halfway through.
8. Enjoy.

Calories	Fat	Sugar	Protein	Cholesterol
136	12.6 g	0.5 g	10.3 g	88 mg

Ingredients:
- 8 ounces crab meat
- 2 tbspn butter, melted
- 2 tbspn Dijon mustard
- 1 tbspn mayonnaise
- 1 egg, lightly beaten
- 1/2 tbspn old bay seasoning
- 1 green onion, sliced
- 2 tbspn parsley, minced
- 1/4 cup almond flour
- 1/4 tbspn pepper
- 1/2 tbspn salt

Tasty Tuna Patties

Prep Time	Time to cook	Serv
10 min	10 min	2

Directions:
1. Preheat the AirFryer to 400 F.
2. Add all ingredients in a mixing bowl and mix until well combined.
3. Spray AirFryer basket with cooking spray.
4. Make 4 patties from mixture and place in the AirFryer basket.
5. Cook patties for 10 min at 400 F if you want crispier patties then cook for 3 min more.
6. Enjoy.

Calories	Fat	Sugar	Protein	Cholesterol
414	20.6 g	1.3 g	48.8 g	58 mg

Ingredients:
- 2 cans tuna
- 1/2 lemon juice
- 1/2 tbspn onion powder
- 1 tbspn garlic powder
- 1/2 tbspn dried dill
- 1 1/2 tbspn mayonnaise
- 1 1/2 tbspn almond flour
- 1/4 tbspn pepper
- 1/4 tbspn salt

Adorable Salmon

Prep Time	Time to cook	Serv
5 min	10 min	2

Directions:
1. Coat salmon fillets with olive oil and season with pepper and salt.
2. Place salmon fillets in AirFryer basket and cook at 360 F for 8-10 min.
3. Enjoy.

Calories	Fat	Sugar	Protein	Cholesterol
256	13.3 g	0 g	34.5 g	78 mg

Ingredients:
- 2 salmon fillets, skinless and boneless
- 1 tbspn olive oil
- Pepper
- Salt

Enjoyable White Fish

Prep Time	Time to cook	Serv
10 min	10 min	2

Directions:
1. Spray AirFryer basket with cooking spray.
2. Preheat the AirFryer to 360 F.
3. Coat fish fillets with olive oil and season with onion powder, lemon pepper seasoning, garlic powder, pepper, and salt.
4. Place fish fillets in AirFryer basket and cook for 10-12 min.
5. Enjoy.

Calories	Fat	Sugar	Protein	Cholesterol
358	19.8 g	0.4 g	41.9 g	131 mg

Ingredients:
- 12 ounces white fish fillets
- 1/2 tbspn onion powder
- 1/2 tbspn lemon pepper seasoning
- 1/2 tbspn garlic powder
- 1 tbspn olive oil
- Pepper
- Salt

Exquisite Shrimp with Veggie

Prep Time	Time to cook	Serv
10 min	20 min	4

Directions:
1. Line AirFryer basket with aluminum foil.
2. Add all ingredients into the large mixing bowl and toss well.
3. Transfer shrimp and vegetable mixture into the AirFryer basket and cook at 350 F for 10 min.
4. Toss well and cook for 10 min more.
5. Enjoy.

Calories	Fat	Sugar	Protein	Carbohydrates	Cholesterol
101	4 g	1 g	2 g	14 g	3 mg

Ingredients:
- 50 small shrimp
- 1 tbspn Cajun seasoning
- 1 bag of frouncesen mix vegetables
- 1 tbspn olive oil

Savory Salmon Patties

Prep Time	Time to cook	Serv
10 min	7 min	2

Directions:
1. Add all ingredients except lemon slices into the bowl and mix until well combined.
2. Spray AirFryer basket with cooking spray.
3. Place lemon slice into the AirFryer basket.
4. Make the equal shape of patties from salmon mixture and place on top of lemon slices into the AirFryer basket.
5. Cook at 390 F for 7 min.
6. Enjoy.

Calories	Fat	Sugar	Protein	Carbohydrates	Cholesterol
184	9.2 g	0.4 g	24.9 g	1 g	132 mg

Ingredients:
- 8 ounces salmon fillet, diced
- 1 lemon, sliced
- 1/2 tbspn garlic powder
- 1 egg, lightly beaten
- 1/8 tbspn salt

Fabulous Salmon

Prep Time	Time to cook	Serv
10 min	10 min	2

Directions:
1. Preheat the AirFryer to 350 F.
2. Coat salmon fillets with olive oil and season with paprika, cardamom, and salt and place into the AirFryer basket.
3. Cook salmon for 10-12 min. Turn halfway through.
4. Enjoy.

Ingredients:
- 2 salmon fillets
- 1 tbspn olive oil
- 1/4 tbspn ground cardamom
- 1/2 tbspn paprika
- Salt

Calories	Fat	Sugar	Protein	Carbohydrates	Cholesterol
160	1 g	0.5 g	22 g	1 g	60 mg

Fantastic Shrimp Scampi

Prep Time	Time to cook	Serv
10 min	10 min	4

Directions:
1. Preheat the AirFryer to 370 F.
2. Mix together shrimp, lemon wedges, olive oil, and garlic cloves in a bowl.
3. Pour shrimp mixture into the AirFryer pan and place into the AirFryer and cook for 10 min.
4. Drizzle with melted butter and sprinkle with parmesan cheese.
5. Enjoy.

Ingredients:
- 1 lb shrimp, peeled and deveined
- 10 garlic cloves, peeled
- 2 tbspn olive oil
- 1 fresh lemon, cut into wedges
- 1/4 cup parmesan cheese, grated
- 2 tbspn butter, melted

Calories	Fat	Sugar	Protein	Carbohydrates	Cholesterol
295	17 g	0.1 g	29 g	4 g	260 mg

Wonderful Parmesan Walnut Salmon

Prep Time	Time to cook	Serv
10 min	12 min	4

Directions:
1. Preheat the AirFryer to 370 F.
2. Spray an AirFryer baking dish with cooking spray.
3. Place salmon on a baking dish.
4. Add walnuts into the food processor and process until finely ground.
5. Mix ground walnuts with parmesan cheese, oil, and lemon rind. Stir.
6. Spoon walnut mixture over the salmon and press gently.
7. Place in the AirFryer and cook for 12 min.
8. Enjoy.

Ingredients:
- 4 salmon fillets
- 1/4 cup parmesan cheese, grated
- 1/2 cup walnuts
- 1 tbspn olive oil
- 1 tbspn lemon rind

Calories	Fat	Sugar	Protein	Cholesterol
420	27.4 g	0.3 g	46.3 g	98 mg

Scrumpitious Cajun Shrimp

Prep Time	Time to cook	Serv
10 min	8 min	4

Directions:
1. Add all ingredients into the large bowl and toss well to coat. Place in the fridge for 1 hour. Spray AirFryer basket with cooking spray.
2. Add marinated shrimp into the AirFryer basket and cook at 400 F for 8 min.
3. Enjoy.

Calories	Fat	Sugar	Protein	Carbohydrates	Cholesterol
201	9.1 g	0.3 g	26.1 g	3.6 g	239 mg

Ingredients:
- 1 lb shrimp, peeled and deveined
- 1 lime, cut into wedges
- 1/2 tbspn chipotle chili in adobo, diced
- 1 tbspn Cajun seasoning
- 2 tbspn olive oil
- Pepper
- Salt

Delish Miso Fish

Prep Time	Time to cook	Serv
10 min	10 min	2

Directions:
1. Add all ingredients to the zip-lock bag. Shake well place in the refrigerator for overnight.
2. Place marinated fish fillets into the AirFryer basket and cook at 350 F for 10 min.
3. Enjoy.

Calories	Fat	Sugar	Protein	Carbohydrates	Cholesterol
229	2.6 g	6.1 g	43.4 g	10.9 g	99 mg

Ingredients:
- 2 cod fish fillets
- 1 tbspn garlic, minced
- 2 tbspn swerve
- 2 tbspn miso

Admirable Tilapia Fish Fillets

Prep Time	Time to cook	Serv
10 min	7 min	2

Directions:
1. Spray AirFryer basket with cooking spray.
2. Place fish fillets into the AirFryer basket and season with lemon pepper, old bay seasoning, pepper, and salt.
3. Spray fish fillets with cooking spray and cook at 400 F for 7 min.
4. Enjoy.

Calories	Fat	Sugar	Protein	Carbohydrates	Cholesterol
80	2 g	0 g	15 g	0.2 g	45 mg

Ingredients:
- 2 tilapia fillets
- 1 tbspn old bay seasoning
- 1/2 tbspn butter
- 1/4 tbspn lemon pepper
- Pepper
- Salt

Delectable Garlic Mayo Shrimp

Prep Time	Time to cook	Serv
10 min	8 min	2

Directions:
1. In a bowl, mix together mayonnaise, paprika, sriracha, garlic, ketchup, and salt.
2. Add shrimp into the bowl and coat well.
3. Spray AirFryer basket with cooking spray. Transfer shrimp into the AirFryer basket and cook at 325 F for 8 min. Shake halfway through.
4. Enjoy.

Ingredients:
- 1/2 lb shrimp, peeled
- 1/2 tbspn ketchup
- 1 1/2 tbspn mayonnaise
- 1/4 tbspn paprika
- 1/2 tbspn sriracha
- 1/2 tbspn garlic, diced
- 1/4 tbspn salt

Charming Spicy Prawns

Prep Time	Time to cook	Serv
10 min	8 min	2

Directions:
1. Preheat the AirFryer to 350 F.
2. In a bowl, mix together spices add prawns. Spray AirFryer basket with cooking spray.
3. Transfer prawns into the AirFryer basket and cook for 8 min.
4. Enjoy.

Ingredients:
- 6 prawns
- 1/4 tbspn pepper
- 1/2 tbspn chili powder
- 1 tbspn chili flakes
- 1/4 tbspn salt

Calories	Fat	Sugar	Protein	Carbohydrates	Cholesterol
80	1.2 g	0.1 g	15.2 g	1 g	140 mg

Enchanting Salmon Fillets

Prep Time	Time to cook	Serv
10 min	7 min	2

Directions:
1. Rub salmon fillet with oil, paprika, pepper, and salt.
2. Place salmon fillets in the AirFryer basket and cook at 390 F for 7 min.
3. Enjoy.

Ingredients:
- 2 salmon fillets
- 2 tbspn olive oil
- 2 tbspn paprika
- Pepper
- Salt

Calories	Fat	Sugar	Protein	Carbohydrates	Cholesterol
280	15 g	0.2 g	35 g	1.2 g	75 mg

Scrummy Shrimp

Prep Time	Time to cook	Serv
10 min	6 min	2

Directions:
1. Preheat the AirFryer to 390 F.
2. Add all ingredients into the bowl and toss well.
3. Transfer shrimp into the AirFryer basket and cook for 6 min.
4. Enjoy.

Ingredients:
- 1/2 lb shrimp, peeled and deveined
- 1/2 tbspn old bay seasoning
- 1 tbspn cayenne pepper
- 1 tbspn olive oil
- 1/4 tbspn paprika
- 1/8 tbspn salt

Calories	Fat	Sugar	Protein	Carbohydrates	Cholesterol
195	9 g	0.1 g	26 g	2 g	0 mg

Appetizing Catfish

Prep Time	Time to cook	Serv
10 min	20 min	4

Directions:
1. Preheat the AirFryer to 400 F.
2. Spray AirFryer basket with cooking spray.
3. Seasoned fish with seasoning and place into the AirFryer basket.
4. Drizzle fish fillets with oil and cook for 10 min.
5. Turn fish to another side and cook for 10 min more.
6. Garnish with parsley and serve.

Ingredients:
- 4 catfish fillets
- 1 tbspn olive oil
- 1/4 cup fish seasoning
- 1 tbspn fresh parsley, minced

Calories	Fat	Sugar	Protein	Cholesterol
245	15 g	0 g	24 g	0 mg

Simple Bacon Shrimp

Prep Time	Time to cook	Serv
10 min	7 min	4

Directions:
1. Preheat the AirFryer to 390 F.
2. Spray AirFryer basket with cooking spray.
3. Wrap shrimp with bacon slice and place into the AirFryer basket and cook for 5 min.
4. Turn shrimp to another side and cook for 2 min more. Season shrimp with pepper.
5. Enjoy.

Ingredients:
- 16 shrimp, deveined
- 1/4 tbspn pepper
- 16 bacon slices

Calories	Fat	Sugar	Protein	Carbohydrates	Cholesterol
515	33 g	0 g	45 g	2 g	0 mg

Seductive Almond Coconut Shrimp

Prep Time	Time to cook	Serv
10 min	5 min	4

Directions:
1. Preheat the AirFryer to 400 F.
2. Spray AirFryer basket with cooking spray.
3. Whisk egg whites in a shallow dish.
4. In a bowl, mix together the shredded coconut, almond flour, and cayenne pepper.
5. Dip shrimp into the egg mixture then coat with coconut mixture.
6. Place coated shrimp into the AirFryer basket and cook for 5 min.
7. Enjoy.

Ingredients:
- 16 ounces shrimp, peeled
- 1/2 cup almond flour
- 2 egg whites
- 1/4 tbspn cayenne pepper
- 1/2 cup unsweetened shredded coconut
- 1/2 tbspn salt

Calories	Fat	Sugar	Protein	Carbohydrates	Cholesterol
200	7 g	1 g	28 g	4 g	0 mg

Magnificent Cajun Cheese Shrimp

Prep Time	Time to cook	Serv
10 min	5 min	4

Directions:
1. Add all ingredients into the bowl and toss well.
2. Spray AirFryer basket with cooking spray.
3. Transfer shrimp mixture into the AirFryer basket and cook at 390 F for 5 min. Shake halfway through.
4. Enjoy.

Ingredients:
- 1 lb shrimp
- 1/2 cup almond flour
- 1 tbspn olive oil
- 1 tbspn Cajun seasoning
- 2 tbspn parmesan cheese
- 2 garlic cloves, diced

Calories	Fat	Sugar	Protein	Carbohydrates	Cholesterol
175	5 g	0.2 g	27 g	3 g	0 mg

Delightful Creamy Shrimp

Prep Time: 10 min
Time to cook: 8 min
Serv: 4

Directions:
1. In a bowl, mix together mayonnaise, paprika, sriracha, garlic, ketchup, and salt. Add shrimp and Stir.
2. Add shrimp mixture into the AirFryer baking dish and place in the AirFryer.
3. Cook at 325 F for 8 min. Stir halfway through.
4. Enjoy.

Ingredients:
- 1 lb shrimp, peeled
- 1 tbspn garlic, diced
- 1 tbspn tomato ketchup
- 3 tbspn mayonnaise
- 1/2 tbspn paprika
- 1 tbspn sriracha
- 1/2 tbspn salt

Calories	Fat	Sugar	Protein	Carbohydrates	Cholesterol
185	5 g	1 g	25 g	6 g	0 mg

Luscious Chili Garlic Shrimp

Prep Time: 10 min
Time to cook: 7 min
Serv: 4

Directions:
1. Preheat the AirFryer to 400 F.
2. Spray AirFryer basket with cooking spray.
3. Add all ingredients into the bowl and toss well.
4. Add shrimp into the AirFryer basket and cook for 5 min. Shake basket twice.
5. Enjoy.

Ingredients:
- 1 lb shrimp, peeled and deveined
- 1 tbspn olive oil
- 1 lemon, sliced
- 1 red chili pepper, sliced
- 1/2 tbspn garlic powder
- Pepper
- Salt

Calories	Fat	Sugar	Protein	Carbohydrates	Cholesterol
170	5 g	0.5 g	25 g	3 g	0 mg

Easy Salmon Patties

Prep Time: 10 min
Time to cook: 10 min
Serv: 2

Directions:
1. Spray AirFryer basket with cooking spray.
2. Add all ingredients into the bowl and mix until well combined.
3. Spray AirFryer basket with cooking spray.
4. Make patties from salmon mixture and place into the AirFryer basket.
5. Cook at 370 F for 5 min.
6. Turn patties to another side and cook for 5 min more.
7. Enjoy.

Ingredients:
- 14 ounces salmon
- 1/2 onion, diced
- 1 egg, lightly beaten
- 1 tbspn dill
- 1/2 cup almond flour

Calories	Fat	Sugar	Protein	Carbohydrates	Cholesterol
350	15 g	1 g	44 g	3 g	0 mg

Pretty Lemon Garlic Shrimps

Prep Time	Time to cook	Serv
15 min	8 min	2

Directions:
1. Preheat the AirFryer to 400F and grease an AirFryer basket.
2. Mix lemon juice, olive oil, lemon pepper, paprika, and garlic powder in a large bowl.
3. Stir in the shrimp and toss until well combined.
4. Arrange shrimp into the AirFryer basket in a single layer and cook for about 8 min.
5. Dish out the shrimp in serving plates and serve warm.

Calories	Fat	Sugar	Protein	Carbohydrates	Sodium
260	12.4 g	0.1 g	35.6 g	0.3 g	619 mg

Ingredients:
- ¾ pound medium shrimp, peeled and deveined
- 1½ tbspns fresh lemon juice
- 1 tbspn olive oil
- 1 tspn lemon pepper
- ¼ tspn paprika
- ¼ tspn garlic powder

Unbelievable Creamy Breaded Shrimp

Prep Time	Time to cook	Serv
15 min	20 min	3

Directions:
1. Preheat the AirFryer to 400F and grease an AirFryer basket.
2. Place flour in a shallow bowl and mix the mayonnaise, chili sauce, and Sriracha sauce in another bowl.
3. Place the breadcrumbs in a third bowl.
4. Coat each shrimp with the flour, dip into mayonnaise mixture and finally, dredge in the breadcrumbs.
5. Arrange half of the coated shrimps into the AirFryer basket and cook for about 10 min.
6. Dish out the coated shrimps onto serving plates and repeat with the remaining mixture.

Calories	Fat	Sugar	Protein	Carbohydrates	Sodium
540	18.2 g	10.6 g	36.8 g	33.1 g	813 mg

Ingredients:
- ¼ cup all-purpose flour
- 1 cup panko breadcrumbs
- 1 pound shrimp, peeled and deveined
- ½ cup mayonnaise
- ¼ cup sweet chili sauce
- 1 tbspn Sriracha sauce

Fabulous Coconut Crusted Shrimp

Prep Time	Time to cook	Serv
15 min	40 min	3

Directions:
1. Preheat the AirFryer to 350 o F and grease an AirFryer basket.
2. Place the coconut milk in a shallow bowl.
3. Mix coconut, breadcrumbs, salt, and black pepper in another bowl.
4. Dip each shrimp into coconut milk and, finally, dredge in the coconut mixture.
5. Arrange half of the shrimps into the AirFryer basket and cook for about 20 min.
6. Dish out the shrimps onto serving plates and repeat with the remaining mixture to help.

Calories	Fat	Sugar	Protein	Carbohydrates	Sodium
408	23.7 g	3.4 g	31 g	11.7 g	253 mg

Ingredients:
- 8 ounces of coconut milk
- ½ cup sweetened coconut, shredded
- ½ cup panko breadcrumbs
- 1 pound large shrimp, peeled and deveined
- Salt and black pepper, to taste

Lovely Rice Flour Coated Shrimp

Prep Time	Time to cook	Serv
20 min	20 min	3

Directions:
1. Preheat the AirFryer to 325 F and grease an AirFryer basket.
2. Mix rice flour, olive oil, sugar, salt, and black pepper in a bowl.
3. Stir in the shrimp and transfer half of the shrimp to the AirFryer basket.
4. Cook for about 10 min, flipping once in between.
5. Dish out the mixture onto serving plates and repeat with the remaining dough.

Calories	Fat	Sugar	Protein	Carbohydrates	Sodium
299	12 g	0.8 g	35 g	11.1 g	419 mg

Ingredients:
- 3 tbspns rice flour
- 1 pound shrimp, peeled and deveined
- 2 tbspns olive oil
- 1 tspn powdered sugar
- Salt and black pepper, as required

Magical Buttered Scallops

Prep Time	Time to cook	Serv
15 min	4 min	2

Directions:
1. Preheat the AirFryer to 390 F and grease an AirFryer basket.
2. Mix scallops, butter, thyme, salt, and black pepper in a bowl.
3. Arrange scallops in the AirFryer basket and cook for about 4 min.
4. Dish out the scallops in a platter and serve hot.

Calories	Fat	Sugar	Protein	Carbohydrates	Sodium
202	7.1 g	0 g	28.7 g	4.4 g	393 mg

Ingredients:
- ¾ pound sea scallops, cleaned and patted very dry
- 1 tbspn butter, melted
- ½ tbspn fresh thyme, diced
- Salt and black pepper, as required

Thoothsome Honey Glazed Salmon

Prep Time	Time to cook	Serv
10 min	8 min	2

Directions:
1. Sprinkle the salmon fillets with salt and then coat with syrup.
2. Press "Power Button" of Air Fry Oven and turn the dial to select the "Air Fry" mode.
3. Press the Time button and again turn the dial to set the Time to cook to 8 min.
4. Now push the Temp button and rotate the dial to set the temperature at 355 degrees F.
5. Press the "Start/Pause" button to start.
6. When the unit beeps to show that it is preheated, open the lid.
7. Arrange the salmon fillets in greased "Air Fry Basket" and insert them in the oven.
8. Serve hot.

Ingredients:
- 2 (6-ounces.) salmon fillets
- Salt, as required
- 2 tbspns honey

Glorious Sweet & Sour Glazed Salmon

Prep Time Time to cook Serv
12 min 20 min 2

Ingredients:
- 1/3 cup soy sauce
- 1/3 cup honey
- 3 tspns rice wine vinegar
- 1 tspn water
- 4 (3½-ounces.) salmon fillets

Directions:
1. In a small shallow container, mix the soy sauce, honey, vinegar, and water.
2. In another small bowl, reserve about half of the mixture.
3. Add salmon fillets in the remaining mixture and coat well.
4. Cover the bowl and refrigerate to marinate for about 2 hours.
5. Press "Power Button" of Air Fry Oven and turn the dial to select the "Air Fry" mode.
6. Press the Time button and again turn the dial to set the Time to cook to 12 min.
7. Now push the Temp button and rotate the dial to set the temperature at 355 degrees F.
8. Press the "Start/Pause" button to start.
9. When the unit beeps to show that it is preheated, open the lid.
10. Arrange the salmon fillets in greased "Air Fry Basket" and insert them in the oven.
11. Flip the salmon fillets once halfway through and coat with the reserved marinade after every 3 min.
12. Serve hot.

Calories	Fat	Carbs	Protein	Sugar	Cholesterol
462	12.3 g	49.8 g	41.3 g	47.1 g	88 mg

Dreamy Salmon Parcel

Prep Time Time to cook Serv
15 min 23 min 2

Ingredients:
- 2 (4-ounces.) salmon fillets
- Six asparagus stalks
- ¼ cup white sauce
- 1 tspn oil
- ¼ cup champagne
- Salt and ground black pepper, as required

Directions:
1. In a shallow container, mix all the ingredients.
2. Divide the salmon mixture over 2 pieces of foil evenly.
3. Seal the foil around the salmon mixture to form the packet.
4. Press "Power Button" of Air Fry Oven and turn the dial to select the "Air Fry" mode.
5. Press the Time button and again turn the dial to set the Time to cook to 13 min.
6. Now push the Temp button and rotate the dial to set the temperature at 355 degrees F.
7. Press the "Start/Pause" button to start.
8. When the unit beeps to show that it is preheated, open the lid.
9. Arrange the salmon parcels in "Air Fry Basket" and insert them in the oven.
10. Serve hot.

Calories	Fat	Carbs	Protein	Sugar	Cholesterol
243	12.7 g	9.4 g	25 g	6.2 g	52 mg

Exciting Ranch Tilapia

Prep Time: 15 min
Time to cook: 13 min
Serv: 4

Directions:
1. In a shallow bowl, beat the eggs.
2. In another bowl, add the cornflakes, ranch dressing, and oil and mix until a crumbly mixture forms.
3. Dip the fish fillets into the egg and then coat with the breadcrumbs mixture.
4. Press "Power Button" of Air Fry Oven and turn the dial to select the "Air Fry" mode.
5. Press the Time button and again turn the dial to set the Time to cook to 13 min.
6. Now push the Temp button and rotate the dial to set the temperature at 356 degrees F.
7. Press the "Start/Pause" button to start.
8. When the unit beeps to show that it is preheated, open the lid.
9. Arrange the tilapia fillets in greased "Air Fry Basket" and insert it in the oven.
10. Serve hot.

Ingredients:
- ¾ cup cornflakes, crushed
- 1 (1-ounces.) packet dry ranch-style dressing mix
- 2½ tbspns vegetable oil
- 2 eggs
- 4 (6-ounces.) tilapia fillets

Calories	Fat	Carbs	Protein	Sugar	Cholesterol
267	12.2 g	5.1 g	34.9 g	0.9 g	1685 mg

Nourishing Spicy Catfish

Prep Time: 15 min
Time to cook: 13 min
Serv: 2

Directions
1. Get a bowl and mix the flour, paprika, garlic powder, and salt.
2. Add the catfish fillets and coat with the mixture evenly.
3. Now, coat each fillet with oil.
4. Press "Power Button" of Air Fry Oven and turn the dial to select the "Air Fry" mode.
5. Press the Time button and again turn the dial to set the Time to cook to 13 min.
6. Now push the Temp button and rotate the dial to set the temperature at 400 degrees F.
7. Press the "Start/Pause" button to start.
8. When the unit beeps to show that it is preheated, open the lid.
9. Arrange the fish fillets in greased "Air Fry Basket" and insert it in the oven.
10. Flip the fish fillets once halfway through.
11. Serve hot.

Ingredients:
- 2 tbspns almond flour
- 1 tspn red chili powder
- ½ tspn paprika
- ½ tspn garlic powder
- Salt, as required
- 2 (6-ounces.) catfish fillets
- 1 tbspn olive oil

Calories	Fat	Carbs	Protein	Sugar	Cholesterol
340	23.5 g	3 g	28.3 g	0.3 g	80 mg

Savory Fish Sticks

Prep Time	Time to cook	Serv
10 min	10 min	4

Directions:
1. Spray AirFryer basket with cooking spray.
2. In a small bowl, whisk together mayonnaise, water, and mustard.
3. In a shallow bowl, mix together pork rind, pepper, Cajun seasoning, and salt.
4. Dip fish pieces in mayo mixture and coat with pork rind mixture and place in the AirFryer basket.
5. Cook at 400 F for 5 min. Turn fish sticks to another side and cook for 5 min more.
6. Enjoy.

Calories	Fat	Protein	Sugar	Cholesterol
397	36.4 g	14.7 g	1 g	4 mg

Ingredients:
- 1 lb white fish, cut into pieces
- 3/4 tbspn Cajun seasoning
- 1 1/2 cups pork rind, crushed
- 2 tbspn water
- 2 tbspn Dijon mustard
- 1/4 cup mayonnaise
- Pepper
- Salt

Flavorful Parmesan Shrimp

Prep Time	Time to cook	Serv
10 min	10 min	6

Directions:
1. In a large mixing bowl, combine together garlic, oil, onion powder, oregano, pepper, and cheese.
2. Add shrimp in a bowl and toss until well coated.
3. Spray AirFryer basket with cooking spray.
4. Add shrimp into the AirFryer basket and cook at 350 F for 8-10 min.
5. Enjoy.

Calories	Fat	Protein	Sugar	Cholesterol
233	7.9 g	35.6 g	0.1 g	32 mg

Ingredients:
- 2 lbs cooked shrimp, peeled and deveined
- 2 tbspn olive oil
- 1/2 tbspn onion powder
- 1 tbspn basil
- 1/2 tbspn oregano
- 2/3 cup parmesan cheese, grated
- 3 garlic cloves, diced
- 1/4 tbspn pepper

Cute Salmon Fillets

Prep Time	Time to cook	Serv
10 min	15 min	2

Directions:
1. Place lemon slices into the AirFryer basket.
2. Season salmon with pepper and salt and place on top of lemon slices into the AirFryer basket.
3. Cook salmon at 330 F for 15 min.
4. Meanwhile, in a bowl, mix together yogurt, garlic powder, lemon juice, dill, pepper, and salt.
5. Place salmon on serving plate and top with yogurt mixture.
6. Enjoy.

Calories	Fat	Protein	Sugar	Cholesterol
195	7 g	24 g	2 g	65 mg

Ingredients:
- 2 salmon fillets
- 1/2 tbspn garlic powder
- 1/4 cup plain yogurt
- 1 tbspn fresh lemon juice
- 1 tbspn fresh dill, minced
- 1 lemon, sliced
- Pepper
- Salt

Delicious Lemon Chili Salmon

Prep Time	Time to cook	Serv
10 min	17 min	4

Directions:
1. Preheat the AirFryer to 325 F.
2. Place salmon fillets in AirFryer baking pan and drizzle with olive oil, lemon juice, and orange juice.
3. Sprinkle chili slices over salmon and season with pepper and salt.
4. Place pan in the AirFryer and cook for 15-17 min.
5. Garnish with dill and serve.

Calories	Fat	Protein	Sugar	Cholesterol
339	17.5 g	44 g	2 g	100 mg

Ingredients:
- 2 lbs salmon fillet, skinless and boneless
- 2 lemon juice
- 1 orange juice
- 1 tbspn olive oil
- 1 bunch fresh dill
- 1 chili, sliced
- Pepper
- Salt

Amazingly Pesto Salmon

Prep Time	Time to cook	Serv
10 min	16 min	4

Directions:
1. Preheat the AirFryer to 370 F.
2. Spray AirFryer basket with cooking spray.
3. Season salmon fillet with pepper and salt and place into the AirFryer basket.
4. In a bowl, mix together mayonnaise, parmesan cheese, and pesto and spread over the salmon fillet.
5. Cook salmon for 14-16 min.
6. Meanwhile, in a pan sauté spinach with olive oil until spinach is wilted, about 2-3 min. Season with pepper and salt.
7. Transfer spinach in serving plate and top with cooked salmon.
8. Enjoy.

Calories	Fat	Protein	Sugar	Cholesterol
545	39.6 g	43 g	3.1 g	110 mg

Ingredients:
- 25 ounces salmon fillet
- 1 tbspn green pesto
- 1 cup mayonnaise
- 1/2 ounces olive oil
- 1 lb fresh spinach
- 2 ounces parmesan cheese, grated
- Pepper
- Salt

Tasty Lemon Shrimp

Prep Time	Time to cook	Serv
10 min	8 min	2

Directions:
1. In a bowl, mix together oil, lemon juice, garlic powder, paprika, and lemon pepper.
2. Add shrimp to the bowl and toss well to coat.
3. Spray AirFryer basket with cooking spray.
4. Transfer shrimp into the AirFryer basket and cook at 400 F for 8 min.
5. Garnish with lemon slices and serve.

Calories	Fat	Protein	Sugar	Cholesterol
381	17.1 g	50.6 g	0.6 g	358 mg

Ingredients:
- 12 ounces shrimp, peeled and deveined
- 1 lemon sliced
- 1/4 tbspn garlic powder
- 1/4 tbspn paprika
- 1 tbspn lemon pepper
- 1 lemon juice
- 1 tbspn olive oil

Adorable Creamy Crab Dip

Prep Time	Time to cook	Serv
10 min	7 min	2

Directions:
1. In an AirFryer baking dish, mix together crabmeat, hot sauce, scallions, cheese, mayonnaise, pepper, and salt.
2. Place dish into the AirFryer basket and cook at 400 F for 7 min.
3. Add parsley and lemon juice. Stir.
4. Enjoy.

Calories	Fat	Protein	Sugar	Cholesterol
295	21 g	20 g	1.3 g	90 mg

Ingredients:
- 1/2 cup crabmeat, cooked
- 1/2 tbspn pepper
- 1 tbspn hot sauce
- 1/4 cup scallions
- 1 cup cheese, grated
- 1 tbspn mayonnaise
- 1 tbspn parsley, minced
- 1 tbspn lemon juice
- 1/4 tbspn salt

Enjoyable Fish Packets

Prep Time	Time to cook	Serv
10 min	15 min	2

Directions:
1. In a bowl, mix together butter, lemon juice, tarragon, and salt. Add vegetables and toss well. Set aside.
2. Take 2 parchments paper pieces to fold vegetables and fish.
3. Spray fish with cooking spray and season with pepper and salt.
4. Place a fish fillet on each parchment paper piece and top with vegetables.
5. Fold parchment paper around the fish and vegetables.
6. Place veggie fish packets into the AirFryer basket and cook at 350 F for 15 min.
7. Enjoy.

Calories	Fat	Protein	Sugar	Cholesterol
281	8 g	41 g	3 g	100 mg

Ingredients:
- 2 cod fish fillets
- 1/2 tbspn dried tarragon
- 1/2 cup bell peppers, sliced
- 1/4 cup celery, cut into julienne
- 1/2 cup carrots, cut into julienne
- 1 tbspn olive oil 1 tbspn lemon juice
- 2 pats butter, melted
- Pepper
- Salt

Fantastic Scallops

Prep Time	Time to cook	Serv
10 min	10 min	2

Directions:
1. Spray AirFryer baking pan with cooking spray.
2. Add spinach in the pan.
3. Spray scallops with cooking spray and season with pepper and salt.
4. Place scallops on top of spinach.
5. In a small bowl, mix together garlic, basil, tomato paste, whipping cream, pepper, and salt and pour over scallops and spinach.
6. Place pan into the AirFryer and cook at 350 F for 10 min.
7. Enjoy.

Calories	Fat	Protein	Sugar	Cholesterol
311	18.3 g	26 g	1 g	100 mg

Ingredients:
- 8 sea scallops
- 1 tbspn tomato paste
- 3/4 cup heavy whipping cream
- 12 ounces frouncesen spinach, thawed and drained
- 1 tbspn garlic, diced
- 1 tbspn fresh basil, minced
- 1/2 tbspn pepper
- 1/2 tbspn salt

Delish King Prawns

Prep Time: 10 min
Time to cook: 6 min
Serv: 4

Directions:
1. Preheat the AirFryer to 350 F.
2. Spray AirFryer basket with cooking spray.
3. Add prawns, chili flakes, chili powder, pepper, and salt to the bowl and toss well.
4. Transfer shrimp to the AirFryer basket and cook for 6 min.
5. In a small bowl, mix together mayonnaise, ketchup, and vinegar.
6. Serve with mayo mixture and enjoy.

Ingredients:
- 12 king prawns
- 1 tbspn vinegar
- 1 tbspn ketchup
- 3 tbspn mayonnaise
- 1/2 tbspn pepper
- 1 tbspn chili powder
- 1 tbspn red chili flakes
- 1/2 tbspn sea salt

Calories	Fat	Protein	Sugar	Cholesterol
130	5 g	15 g	1 g	0 mg

Admirable Lemon Butter Salmon

Prep Time: 10 min
Time to cook: 11 min
Serv: 2

Directions:
1. Preheat the AirFryer to 350 F.
2. Spray AirFryer basket with cooking spray.
3. Season salmon with pepper and salt and place into the AirFryer basket and cook for 6 min.
4. Meanwhile, in a saucepan, add remaining ingredients and heat over low heat for 4-5 min.
5. Place cooked salmon on serving dish then pour prepared sauce over salmon.
6. Enjoy.

Ingredients:
- 2 salmon fillets
- 1/2 tbspn olive oil
- 2 tbspn garlic, diced
- 2 tbspn butter
- 2 tbspn fresh lemon juice
- 1/4 cup white wine
- Pepper
- Salt

Calories	Fat	Protein	Sugar	Cholesterol
379	23 g	35 g	0.5 g	0 mg

Savory Cheese Crust Salmon

Prep Time: 10 min
Time to cook: 10 min
Serv: 5

Directions:
1. Preheat the AirFryer to 425 F.
2. Add salmon, seasoning, and olive oil to the bowl and mix well.
3. Place salmon fillet into the AirFryer basket.
4. In another bowl, mix together cheese, garlic, and parsley.
5. Sprinkle cheese mixture on top of salmon and cook for 10 min.
6. Enjoy.

Ingredients:
- 5 salmon fillets
- 1 tbspn Italian seasoning
- 2 garlic cloves, diced
- 1 cup parmesan cheese, shredded
- 1 tbspn paprika
- 1 tbspn olive oil
- 1/4 cup fresh parsley, minced
- Pepper
- Salt

Calories	Fat	Protein	Sugar	Cholesterol
333	18 g	40 g	0.4 g	0 mg

Delightful Lemon Crab Patties

Prep Time	Time to cook	Serv
10 min	10 min	4

Directions:
1. Preheat the AirFryer to 400 F.
2. Spray AirFryer basket with cooking spray.
3. Add 1/2 almond flour into the mixing bowl.
4. Add remaining ingredients and mix until well combined.
5. Make patties from mixture and coat with remaining almond flour and place into the AirFryer basket.
6. Cook patties for 5 min then turn to another side and cook for 5 min more.
7. Enjoy.

Calories	Fat	Protein	Sugar	Cholesterol
184	11 g	12 g	1 g	0 mg

Ingredients:
- 1 egg
- 12 ounces crabmeat
- 2 green onion, minced
- 1/4 cup mayonnaise
- 1 cup almond flour
- 1 tbspn old bay seasoning
- 1 tbspn red pepper flakes
- 1 tbspn fresh lemon juice

Wonderful Basil Parmesan Shrimp

Prep Time	Time to cook	Serv
10 min	10 min	6

Directions:
1. Add all ingredients into the bowl and toss well.
2. Spray AirFryer basket with cooking spray.
3. Transfer shrimp into the AirFryer basket and cook at 350 F for 10 min.
4. Enjoy.

Calories	Fat	Protein	Sugar	Cholesterol
290	10 g	40 g	0.3 g	0 mg

Ingredients:
- 2 lbs shrimp, peeled and deveined
- 1 tbspn basil
- 1/2 tbspn oregano
- 1 tbspn pepper
- 2/3 cup parmesan cheese, grated
- 2 garlic cloves, diced
- 2 tbspn olive oil
- 1 tbspn onion powder

Perfect Cheesy Crab Dip

Prep Time	Time to cook	Serv
10 min	7 min	4

Directions:
1. Add all ingredients except parsley and lemon juice in AirFryer baking dish and Stir.
2. Place dish in the AirFryer basket and cook at 400 F for 7 min.
3. Add parsley and lemon juice. Mix well.
4. Enjoy.

Calories	Fat	Protein	Sugar	Cholesterol
305	22 g	20 g	1 g	0 mg

Ingredients:
- 1 cup crabmeat, cooked
- 2 tbspn fresh parsley, minced
- 2 tbspn fresh lemon juice
- 2 cups Jalapeno jack cheese, grated
- 2 tbspn hot sauce
- 1/2 cup green onions, sliced
- 1/4 cup mayonnaise
- 1 tbspn pepper
- 1/2 tbspn salt

Charming Thai Shrimp

Prep Time	Time to cook	Serv
10 min	10 min	4

Directions:
1. Spray AirFryer basket with cooking spray.
2. Toss shrimp with arrowroot powder and place into the AirFryer basket.
3. Cook shrimp at 350 F for 5 min. Shake basket well and cook for 5 min more.
4. Meanwhile, in a bowl, mix together soy sauce, ginger, garlic, and chili sauce.
5. Add shrimp to the bowl and toss well.
6. Garnish with green onions and sesame seeds.
7. Enjoy.

Ingredients:
- 1 lb shrimp, peeled and deveined
- 1 tbspn sesame seeds, toasted
- 2 garlic cloves, diced
- 2 tbspn soy sauce
- 2 tbspn Thai chili sauce
- 1 tbspn arrowroot powder
- 1 tbspn green onion, sliced
- 1/8 tbspn ginger, diced

Great Salmon Quiche

Prep Time	Time to cook	Serv
5 min	12 min	4

Directions:
1. Preparing the Ingredients. Clean and cut the salmon into small cubes.
2. Heat the Instant Crisp AirFryer to 375 degrees
3. Pour the lemon juice over the salmon cubes and allow them to marinate for an hour.
4. Combine a tbspnn of water with the butter, flour, and yolk in a large bowl.
5. On a clean surface, use a rolling pin to form a circle of dough. Place this into the quiche pan, using your fingers to adhere the pastry to the edges
6. Whisk the cream, mustard, and eggs together. Season with salt and pepper. Add the marinated salmon into the bowl and combine.
7. Pour the content of the bowl into the dough-lined quiche pan
8. Air Frying. Put the pan in the Instant Crisp AirFryer tray, close AirFryer lid, and cook for 25 min until browned and crispy.

Ingredients:
- 5 ounces. salmon fillet
- 1/2 tbspn lemon juice
- 1/2 cup flour
- 1/4 cup butter, melted
- 2 eggs and 1 egg yolk
- 3 tbspn. whipped cream
- Tbps. mustard
- Black Pepper to taste
- Salt and Pepper
- Quiche Pan

Tasty Salmon Patties

Prep Time	Time to cook	Serv
8 min	7 min	4

Directions:
1. Preparing the Ingredients. Drain can of salmon into a bowl and keep liquid. Discard skin and b1s.
2. Add salt, pepper, and egg to salmon, mixing well with hands to incorporate. Make patties.
3. Dredge in flour and remaining egg. If it seems dry, spoon reserved salmon liquid from the can onto patties.
4. Air Frying. Add patties to the Instant Crisp AirFryer. Close AirFryer lid and cook 7 min at 378 degrees till golden, making sure to flip once during the cooking process.

Ingredients:
- 1 tbspn. olive oil
- 1 tbspn. ghee
- ¼ tbspn. salt
- 1/8 tbspn. pepper
- 1 egg
- 1 C. almond flour
- 1 can wild Alaskan pink salmon

Enjoyable Beer-Battered Fish and Chips

Prep Time	Time to cook	Serv
5 min	30 min	4

Directions:
1. Preparing the Ingredients. Beat the eggs with a beer in a medium bowl. In another medium bowl, combine the flour and cornstarch and season with the garlic powder and salt and pepper to taste.
2. Spray the Instant Crisp AirFryer basket with cooking oil.
3. Dip each cod fillet in the flour and cornstarch mixture and then in the egg and beer mixture. Dip the cod in the flour and cornstarch a second time.
4. Air Frying. Place the cod in the Instant Crisp AirFryer. Do not stack. Cook in batches.
5. Spray with cooking oil. Close AirFryer lid and cook for 8 min.
6. Open the Instant Crisp AirFryer and flip the cod. Cook for an additional 7 min.
7. Remove the cooked cod from the Instant Crisp AirFryer, then repeat steps 4 and 5 for the remaining fillets.
8. Serve with prepared air-fried frouncesen fries. Frouncesen fries will need to be cooked for 18 to 20 min at 400°F.
9. Cool before serving.

Calories	Fat	Protein	Fiber	Carbs
325	4 g	26 g	1 g	41

Ingredients:
- 2 eggs
- 1 cup malty beer, such as Pabst Blue Ribbon
- 1 cup all-purpose flour
- ½ cup cornstarch
- 1 tspn garlic powder
- Salt
- Pepper
- Cooking oil
- (4-ounce) cod fillets

Soulful Tuna Stuffed Potatoes

Prep Time	Time to cook	Serv
5 min	30 min	4

Directions:
1. Preparing the Ingredients. In a large bowl of water, soak the potatoes for about 30 min. Drain well and pat dry with a paper towel.
2. Preheat the Instant Crisp AirFryer to 355 degrees F. Place the potatoes in a fryer basket.
3. Air Frying. Close AirFryer lid and cook for about 30 min.
4. Meanwhile, in a bowl, add tuna, yogurt, red chili powder, salt, black pepper, and half of the scallion and with a potato masher, mash the mixture thoroughly.
5. Remove the potatoes from the Instant Crisp AirFryer and place it onto a smooth surface.
6. Carefully cut each potato from the top side lengthwise.
7. With your fingers, press the open side of potato halves slightly. Stuff the free potato portion with tuna mixture evenly.
8. Sprinkle with the capers and remaining scallion. Serve immediately.

Calories	Fat	Protein	Sugar	Carbs
211	6 g	21 g	1 g	55

Ingredients:
- 4 starchy potatoes
- ½ tbspn olive oil
- 1 (6-ounce) can tuna, drained
- 2 tbspns plain Greek yogurt
- 1 tspn red chili powder
- Ground black pepper, salt
- 1 scallion, minced and divided
- 1 tbspn capers

Delish Prawn Burgers

Prep Time	Time to cook	Serv
20 min	6 min	2

Directions:
1. Preheat the AirFryer to 390 F and grease an AirFryer basket.
2. Mix the prawns, breadcrumbs, onion, ginger, garlic, and spices in a bowl.
3. Make small-sized patties from the mixture and transfer to the AirFryer basket.
4. Cook for about 6 min and dish out in a platter.
5. Serve immediately warm alongside the baby greens.

Calories	Fat	Protein	Sugar
240	2.7 g	18 g	4 g

Ingredients:
- ½ cup prawns, peeled, deveined and finely minced
- ½ cup breadcrumbs
- 2-3 tbspns onion, finely minced
- 3 cups fresh baby greens
- ½ tspn ginger, diced
- ½ tspn garlic, diced
- ½ tspn red chili powder
- ½ tspn ground cumin
- ¼ tspn ground turmeric
- Salt and ground black pepper, as required

Glorious Fish & Chips

Prep Time	Time to cook	Serv
10 min	10 min	4

Directions:
1. Put the whisk eggs in a shallow bowl, and the bread crumbs in a second shallow bowl.
2. Sprinkle the fish with flour and season with salt and pepper. Dredge the fillets in the egg, remove, and coat with the bread crumbs. Spritz the coated fillets with cooking spray. In a large bowl, toss the potato planks with the olive oil. Place the potatoes in your AirFryer's basket and top with the breaded fish. Fry at 375°F for 15 min, turning halfway through the Time to cook until the fish is cooked (cut into the thickest part, it will be opaque and flake easily with a fork).
3. In a small size of the bowl, mix the coleslaw mix, olive oil, lime juice, radishes, shallot, and cilantro. Mix well. Season to taste with salt and pepper. Set aside until serving. Repurtose tip: This citrusy slaw is a great way to add crunch to a Slow Cooker Pulled Pork sandwich.

Calories	Fat	Protein	Carbs
366	13 g	29 g	30 g

Ingredients:
- 2 large eggs, lightly beaten
- ½ cup plain bread crumbs
- 4 (4-ounce) tilapia or haddock fillets
- All-purpose flour
- Celtic sea salt or kosher salt
- Freshly ground black pepper
- Olive oil cooking spray
- 2 russet potatoes, cut into ¼-inch planks
- 1 tbspn extra-virgin olive oil
- 2 cups coleslaw mix
- 1 tbspn extra-virgin olive oil
- Juice of 1 lime
- 4 radishes, thinly sliced
- 1 shallot, thinly sliced
- 2 tbspns minced fresh cilantro
- Celtic sea salt or kosher salt
- Freshly ground black pepper

Dreamy Shrimp & Sausage Paella

Prep Time	Time to cook	Serv
5 min	35 min	4

Directions:
1. In a large huge frover medium heat, heat the olive oil.
2. If the oil is medium hot, add the onion and red bell pepper. Sauté for 3 to 5 min to soften.
3. Add the chorizo. Cook for 5 min to brown.
4. Stir in the rice, chicken stock, and saffron threads. Cook for 20 min, or until most of the stock is absorbed and the rice is soft.
5. Add the shrimp and peas. Wait for 5 min or until the shrimp are opaque and cooked through.
6. Stir in the parsley and lemon juice. Season to taste with salt.

Calories	Fat	Protein	Carbs
605	9 g	41 g	88 g

Ingredients:
- 1 tbspn extra-virgin olive oil
- 1 onion, minced
- 1 red bell pepper, minced
- 4 ounces chicken chorizo, diced
- 2 cups long-grain white rice
- 5 cups Chicken Stock, or low-sodium store-bought chicken stock
- Generous pinch saffron threads
- 1 pound fresh shrimp, peeled and deveined
- 1 cup peas, fresh or frouncesen
- ¼ cup fresh parsley
- Juice of 1 lemon
- Celtic sea salt or kosher salt

Simple Pressure Cooker Shrimp Boil

Prep Time	Time to cook	Serv
5 min	16 min	4

Directions:
1. In your pressure cooker, combine the potatoes, sausage, chicken stock, corn, seasoning, hot sauce, and shrimp. Place and locked up cooker to High pressure for 1 min.
2. When the Time to cook ends, let the pressure extrication naturally for 10 min; manually extrication any remaining pressure.
3. Stir butter and parsley carefully. Serve with the lemon wedges for squeezing.
4. Ingredient tip: Using frouncesen shrimp in this recipe makes it easy, but the longer Time to cook also means they won't overcook.

Calories	Fat	Protein	Carbs
401	11 g	40 g	35 g

Ingredients:
- 1 pound baby red potatoes, halved
- 2 andouille links, sliced
- 1 cup Chicken Stock, or low-sodium store-bought chicken stock
- 4 ears fresh corn, shucked and halved crosswise
- 1 tbspn reduced-sodium Old Bay seasoning
- 1 tbspn hot sauce
- 1 pound has frouncesen (jumbo) peel-and-eat shrimp
- 1 tbspn unsalted butter
- ¼ cup fresh parsley leaves
- 1 lemon, cut into wedges

Scrumptious Oven-Blackened Tilapia

Prep Time	Time to cook	Serv
10 min	15 min	4

Directions:
1. Preheat the oven to 400°F.
2. In a bowl, whisk together the paprika, salt, onion powder, garlic powder, parsley, and cayenne. Place the tilapia fillets on 1 side of a sheet pan. Coat them with cooking spray and rub each with the blackening rub.
3. Spread the zucchini noodles on the other side of the pan. Drizzle with the olive oil.
4. Baking the tilapia for almost 15 min, or until the tilapia is cooked. Season the zucchini noodles to taste with salt and pepper. Serve the tilapia on top of the zucchini, with the lemon wedges on the side for squeezing.

Calories	Fat	Protein	Carbs
158	5 g	23 g	7 g

Ingredients:
- 2 tbspns paprika
- 1 tspn Celtic sea salt or kosher salt, plus more for seasoning
- 1 tspn onion powder
- 1 tspn garlic powder
- 1 tspn dried parsley
- ¼ tspn cayenne pepper
- 4 (4-ounce) tilapia fillets
- Olive oil cooking spray, for preparing the fish
- 1 pound zucchini noodles
- 1 tbspn extra-virgin olive oil
- Freshly ground black pepper
- 1 lemon, cut into wedges

Encharting Crab Herb Croquettes

Prep Time	Time to cook	Serv
10 min	18 min	6

Directions:
1. Preheat your AirFryer to 355°F. Add breadcrumbs with salt and pepper in a bowl. In another small bowl, add the egg whites. Add all the remaining ingredients into another bowl and mix well. Make croquettes from crab mixture and dip into egg whites, and then into breadcrumbs. Place into an AirFryer and cook for 18-min.

Calories	Fat	Protein	Carbs
295	9.3 g	15.3 g	8.6 g

Ingredients:
- 1 lb. crab meat
- 1 cup breadcrumbs
- 2 egg whites
- Salt and black pepper to taste
- ½ tspn parsley, minced
- ¼ tspn chives
- ¼ tspn tarragon
- 2 tbspn celeries, minced
- 4 tbspnn mayonnaise
- 4 tbspns light sour cream
- 1 tspn olive oil
- ½ tspn lime juice
- ½ cup red pepper, minced
- ¼ cup onion, minced

Scrummy Herb Salmon Fillet

Prep Time	Time to cook	Serv
2 min	8 min	2

Directions:
1. Rub the seasoning all over the salmon. Preheat your AirFryer to 350°F. Place the seasoned salmon fillet into an AirFryer basket and cook for 8-min.

Calories	Fat	Protein	Carbs
298	9.3 g	10.2 g	8.6 g

Ingredients:
- ½ lb. salmon fillet
- ¼ tspn thyme
- 1 tspn garlic powder
- ½ tspn cayenne pepper
- ½ tspn paprika
- ¼ tspn sage
- ¼ tspn oregano
- Salt and pepper to taste

Luscious Crunchy Fish Taco

Prep Time	Time to cook	Serv
5 min	18 min	4

Directions:
1. Cut the cod fillets lengthwise into 2-inch pieces and season with salt and pepper. Dip each cod strip into tempura butter then into breadcrumbs. Preheat your AirFryer to 340°F and cook cod for 13-min. Spread guacamole on each tortilla. Place cod stick on tortilla and top with minced cilantro and salsa. Squeeze lemon juice on top, then fold and serve.

Calories	Fat	Protein	Carbs
300	10.3 g	14.8 g	8.9 g

Ingredients:
- 12-ounce cod fillet
- Salt and black pepper to taste
- 1 cup tempura batter
- 1 cup breadcrumbs
- ½ cup guacamole
- 6-flour tortillas
- 2 tbspns cilantro, freshly minced
- ½ cup of salsa
- 1 lemon, juiced

Fabulous Potato Fish Cake

Prep Time	Time to cook	Serv
10 min	15 min	2

Directions:
1. Add ingredients to a mixing bowl and combine well. Make round patties and place them in the fridge for 1 hour. Place the patties into the AirFryer at 375°F for 15-min.

Calories	Fat	Protein	Carbs
167	9 g	5 g	14 g

Ingredients:
- 1 ½ cups white fish, cooked
- Pepper and salt to taste
- 1 ½ tbspn of milk
- ½ cup of mashed potatoes
- 1 tbspn butter
- 2 tspns gluten-free flour
- 1 tspn parsley
- ½ tspn sage

Exquisite Garlic Salmon Patties

Prep Time	Time to cook	Serv
6 min	15 min	3

Directions:
1. Add drained salmon into a bowl and with a fork flake the salmon. Add garlic powder, mayonnaise, flour, cornmeal, onion, egg, pepper, and salt. Mix well. Make round patties with mix and place them in the AirFryer. Air fry at 300°F for 15-min.

Calories	Fat	Protein	Carbs
244	11 g	22 g	14 g

Ingredients:
- 1 egg
- 14-ounce can of salmon, drained
- Salt and pepper to taste
- 2 tbspns mayonnaise
- ½ tspn garlic powder
- 4 tbspns onion, diced
- 4 tbspns gluten-free flour
- 4 tbspns cornmeal

Admirable Cod Parcel

Prep Time	Time to cook	Serv
20 min	15 min	2

Directions
1. In a large bowl, mix the butter, lemon juice, tarragon, salt, and black pepper.
2. Add the bell pepper, carrot, and fennel bulb and generously coat with the mixture.
3. Arrange 2 large parchment squares onto a smooth surface.
4. Coat the cod fillets with oil and then sprinkle evenly with salt and black pepper.
5. Arrange 1 cod fillet onto each parchment square and top each evenly with the vegetables.
6. Top with any remaining sauce from the bowl.
7. Fold the parchment paper and crimp the sides to secure fish and vegetables.
8. Press "Power Button" of Air Fry Oven and turn the dial to select the "Air Fry" mode.
9. Press the Time button and again turn the dial to set the Time to cook to 15 min.
10. Now push the Temp button and rotate the dial to set the temperature at 350 degrees F.
11. Press the "Start/Pause" button to start.
12. When the unit beeps to show that it is preheated, open the lid.
13. Arrange the cod parcels in "Air Fry Basket" and insert it in the oven.

Ingredients:
- 2 tbspns butter, melted
- 1 tbspn fresh lemon juice
- ½ tspn dried tarragon
- Salt and ground black pepper, as required
- ½ cup red bell peppers, seeded and thinly sliced
- ½ cup carrots, peeled and julienned
- ½ cup fennel bulbs, julienned
- 2 (5-ounces.) frouncesen cod fillets, thawed
- 1 tbspn olive oil

Appetizing Salmon with Prawns & Pasta

Prep Time	Time to cook	Serv
20 min	18 min	4

Directions:
1. In a considerable size pan of salted boiling water, add the pasta and cook for about 8-10 min or until desired doneness.
2. Meanwhile, at the bottom of a baking pan, spread 1 tbspn of pesto.
3. Place salmon steaks and tomatoes over pesto in a single layer and drizzle with the oil.
4. Arrange the prawns on top in a single layer.
5. Drizzle with lemon juice and sprinkle with thyme.
6. Press "Power Button" of Air Fry Oven and turn the dial to select the "Air Fry" mode.
7. Press the Time button and again turn the dial to set the Time to cook to 8 min.
8. Now push the Temp button and rotate the dial to set the temperature at 390 degrees F.
9. Press the "Start/Pause" button to start.
10. When the unit beeps to show that it is preheated, open the lid.
11. Arrange the baking pan in "Air Fry Basket" and insert it in the oven.
12. Draining the pasta and transfer into a large bowl.
13. Adding the remaining pesto and toss to coat thoroughly.
14. Divide the pasta onto serving plate and top with salmon mixture.

Ingredients:
- 14 ounces. pasta (of your choice)
- 4 tbspns pesto, divided
- 4 (4-ounces.) salmon steaks
- 2 tbspns olive oil
- ½ lb. cherry tomatoes, minced
- Eight large prawns, peeled and deveined
- 2 tbspns fresh lemon juice
- 2 tbspns fresh thyme, minced

Hearty Salmon Burgers

Prep Time	Time to cook	Serv
20 min	22 min	6

Directions:
1. In a pan of the boiling water, cook the potatoes for about 10 min.
2. Drain the potatoes well.
3. Transfer the potatoes into a bowl and mash with a potato masher.
4. Set aside to cool completely.
5. In another bowl, add the salmon and flake with a fork.
6. Add the cooked potatoes, egg, parboiled vegetables, parsley, dill, salt, and black pepper and mix until well combined.
7. Make six equal-sized patties from the mixture.
8. Coat patties with breadcrumb evenly and then drizzle with the oil evenly.
9. Press "Power Button" of Air Fry Oven and turn the dial to select the "Air Fry" mode.
10. Press the Time button and again turn the dial to set the Time to cook to 12 min.
11. Now push the Temp button and rotate the dial to set the temperature at 355 degrees F.
12. Press the "Start/Pause" button to start.
13. When the unit beeps to show that it is preheated, open the lid.
14. Arrange the patties in greased "Air Fry Basket" and insert it in the oven.
15. Flip the patties once halfway through.
16. Serve hot.

Ingredients:
- 3 large russet potatoes, peeled and cubed
- 1 (6-ounces.) cooked salmon fillet
- 1 egg
- ¾ cup frouncesen vegetables (of your choice), parboiled and drained
- 2 tbspns fresh parsley, minced
- 1 tspn fresh dill, minced
- Salt and ground black pepper, as required
- 1 cup breadcrumbs
- ¼ cup olive oil

Seductive Cod Burgers

Prep Time	Time to cook	Serv
15 min	7 min	6

Directions
1. In a food processor, add cod filets, lime zest, egg, chili paste, salt, and lime juice and pulse until smooth.
2. Transfer the cod mixture into a bowl.
3. Add 1½ tbspns coconut, scallion, and parsley and mix until well combined.
4. Make six equal-sized patties from the mixture.
5. In a shallow dish, place the remaining coconut.
6. Coat the patties in coconut evenly.
7. Press "Power Button" of Air Fry Oven and turn the dial to select the "Air Fry" mode.
8. Press the Time button and again turn the dial to set the Time to cook to 7 min.
9. Now push the Temp button and rotate the dial to set the temperature at 375 degrees F.
10. Press the "Start/Pause" button to start.
11. When the unit beeps to show that it is preheated, open the lid.
12. Arrange the patties in greased "Air Fry Basket" and insert it in the oven.
13. Serve hot.

Ingredients:
- ½ lb. cod fillets
- ½ tspn fresh lime zest, grated finely
- ½ egg
- ½ tspn red chili paste
- Salt, to taste
- ½ tbspnn fresh lime juice
- 3 tbspns coconut, grated and divided
- 1 small scallion, minced finely
- 1 tbspn fresh parsley, minced

Magnificent Chinese Cod

Prep Time	Time to cook	Serv
15 min	15 min	2

Directions:
1. Season each cod fillet evenly with salt and black pepper and drizzle with sesame oil.
2. Set aside at room temperature for about 15-20 min. D
3. ip the fish fillets into the egg and then coat with the breadcrumbs mixture.
4. Press "Power Button" of Air Fry Oven and turn the dial to select the "Air Fry" mode.
5. Press the Time button and again turn the dial to set the Time to cook to 12 min.
6. Now push the Temp button and rotate the dial to set the temperature at 355 degrees F.
7. Press the "Start/Pause" button to start.
8. When the unit beeps to show that it is preheated, open the lid.
9. Arrange the cod fillets in greased "Air Fry Basket" and insert it in the oven.
10. Meanwhile, in a small pan, add the water and bring it to a boil.
11. Add the rock sugar and both soy sauces and cook until sugar is dissolved, stirring continuously.
12. Remove from the heat and set aside.
13. Remove the cod fillets from the oven and transfer onto serving plates.
14. Top each fillet with scallion and cilantro.
15. In a shallow fryer, heat the olive oil over medium heat and sauté the ginger slices for about 2-3 min.
16. Remove the frying pan from heat and discard the ginger slices.
17. Carefully, pour the hot oil evenly over cod fillets.
18. Top with the sauce mixture and serve.

Ingredients:
- 2 (7-ounces.) cod fillets
- Salt and ground black pepper, as required
- ¼ tspn sesame oil
- 1 cup of water
- Five little squares rock sugar
- Five tbspns light soy sauce
- 1 tspn dark soy sauce
- 2 scallions (green part), sliced
- ¼ cup fresh cilantro, minced
- 3 tbspns olive oil
- Five ginger slices

Yummy Salmon with Broccoli

Prep Time	Time to cook	Serv
15 min	12 min	2

Direction:
1. In a bowl, mix the broccoli, 1 tbspnn of oil, salt, and black pepper. In another bowl, mix well the ginger, soy sauce, vinegar, sugar, and cornstarch.
2. Coat the salmon fillets with remaining oil and then with the ginger mixture.
3. Press "Power Button" of Air Fry Oven and turn the dial to select the "Air Fry" mode.
4. Press the Time button and again turn the dial to set the Time to cook to 12 min.
5. Now push the Temp button and rotate the dial to set the temperature at 375 degrees F.
6. Press the "Start/Pause" button to start.
7. When the unit beeps to show that it is preheated, open the lid.
8. Arrange the broccoli florets in greased "Air Fry Basket" and top with the salmon fillets.
9. Insert the basket in the oven.

Ingredients:
- 1½ cups small broccoli florets
- 2 tbspns vegetable oil, divided
- Salt and ground black pepper, as required
- 1 (½-inch) piece fresh ginger, grated
- 1 tbspn soy sauce
- 1 tspn rice vinegar
- 1 tspn light brown sugar
- ¼ tspn cornstarch
- 2 (6-ounces.) skin-on salmon fillets
- 1 scallion, thinly sliced

Desserts

Peanut Butter Cookies

Prep Time	Time to cook	Serv
15 min	10 min	4

Direction:
1. Consistency is achieved, and the mixture has begun to thicken.
2. Take eight equal-sized amounts of the mixture and mold each 1 into a ball. Flatten them with your palm to form cookies about 2 inches thick.
3. Cover the bottom of your fryer with a sheet of parchment paper and lay the cookies inside.
4. Fry at 320°F for six min before turning the cookies over. Leave to cook an additional 2 min.
5. Remove the cookies from the fryer and allow to cool before serving.

Ingredients:
- 1 cup no-sugar-added smooth peanut butter
- 1 egg
- 1 tbspn. vanilla extract
- 1/3 cup granular erythritol

Calories	Fat	Protein	Sugar
74	4 g	3 g	1 g

Chocolate-Covered Maple Bacon

Prep Time	Time to cook	Serv
10 min	5 min	3

Direction:
1. Place the bacon in the fryer's basket and add the erythritol on top. Cook for six min at 350°F and turn the bacon over. Leave to cook another six min or until the bacon is sufficiently crispy.
2. Take the bacon out of the fryer and leave it to cool.
3. Microwave the chocolate chips and coconut oil together for half a min. Remove from the microwave and mix it before stirring in the maple extract.
4. Set the bacon flat on a piece of parchment paper and pour the mixture over. Allow hardening in the refrigerator for roughly five min before serving.

Ingredients:
- Eight slices sugar-free bacon
- 1 tbspn. granular erythritol
- 1/3 cup low-carb, sugar-free chocolate chips
- 1 tbspn. coconut oil
- ½ tbspn. maple extract

Calories	Fat	Protein	Sugar
80	6 g	7 g	10 g

Pumpkin Spice Pecans

Prep Time	Time to cook	Serv
10 min	5 min	3

Direction:
1. In a bowl, stir together the egg white, pumpkin pie spice, vanilla extract, and granular erythritol. Toss with the pecans to coat, before transferring the pecans to the fryer.
2. Cook at 300°F for six min, occasionally giving the basket a good shake.
3. Allow the pecans to cool completely before serving. Keep them in an airtight container and consume within 3 days.

Ingredients:
- 1 egg white
- ½ tbspn. pumpkin pie spice
- ½ tbspn. vanilla extract
- ¼ cup granular erythritol
- 1 cup whole pecans

Cinnamon Sugar Pork Rinds

Prep Time	Time to cook	Serv
10 min	5 min	3

Direction:
1. Coat the peels with the melted butter.
2. Cinnamon and pour over the pork rinds, ensuring the skins are covered entirely and evenly.
3. Transfer the pork rinds into the fryer and cook at 400°F for five min.

Calories	Fat	Protein	Sugar
40	4 g	32 g	13 g

Ingredients:
- 2 ounces. pork rinds
- 2 tbspn. unsalted butter, melted
- ¼ cup powdered erythritol
- ½ tbspn. ground cinnamon

Toasted Coconut Flakes

Prep Time	Time to cook	Serv
10 min	5 min	3

Direction:
1. oil, granular erythritol, and a pinch of salt, ensuring that the chips are coated completely.
2. Place the coconut flakes in your fryer and cook at 300°F for 3 min, giving the basket a good shake a few times throughout the Time to cook. Fry until golden and serve.

Calories	Fat	Protein	Sugar
20	2 g	3 g	15 g

Ingredients:
- 1 cup unsweetened coconut flakes
- 2 tbspn. coconut oil, melted
- ¼ cup granular erythritol
- Salt

Blackberry Crisp

Prep Time	Time to cook	Serv
15 min	12 min	3

Direction:
1. In a bowl, combine the lemon juice, erythritol, xanthan gum, and blackberries.
2. Transfer to a round baking dish about six inches in diameter and seal with aluminum foil.
3. Put the dish in the fryer and leave to cook for twelve min at 350°F.
4. Take care when removing the dish from the fryer. Give the blackberries another stir and top with the granola.
5. Return the dish to the fryer and cook for an additional 3 min, this time at 320°F. Serve once the granola has turned brown and enjoy.

Calories	Fat	Protein	Sugar
54	6 g	7 g	9 g

Ingredients:
- 2 tbspn. lemon juice
- 1/3 cup powdered erythritol
- ¼ tbspn. xantham gum
- 2 cup blackberries
- 1 cup crunchy granola

Churros

Prep Time	Time to cook	Serv
15 min	10 min	6

Direction:
1. In a saucepan, bring the water and butter to a boil. Once it is bubbling, add the almond flour and mix to create a doughy consistency.
2. Transfer the dough into a piping bag.
3. Preheat the fryer at 380°F.
4. Pipe the dough into the fryer in several 3-inch-long segments. Cook for ten min before removing from the fryer and coating in the cinnamon sugar.
5. Serve with the low-carb chocolate sauce of your choice.

Calories	Fat	Protein	Sugar
34	23 g	3 g	10 g

Ingredients:
- ½ cup of water
- ¼ cup butter
- ½ cup almond flour
- 3 eggs
- 2 ½ tbspn. cinnamon sugar

Peanut Butter Cookies

Prep Time	Time to cook	Serv
15 min	11 min	2

Direction:
1. Combine the salt, erythritol, and peanut butter in a bowl, incorporating everything well. Break the egg over the mixture and mix to create a dough.
2. Flatten the dough using a rolling pin and cut into shapes with a knife or cookie cutter. Make a crisscross on the top of each cookie with a fork.
3. Preheat your fryer at 360°F.
4. Once the fryer has warmed up, put the cookies inside, and leave to cool for ten min. Take care when taking them out and allow them to cool before enjoying.

Calories	Fat	Protein	Sugar
34	5 g	13 g	14 g

Ingredients:
- ¼ tbspn. salt
- 4 tbspn. erythritol
- ½ cup peanut butter
- 1 egg

Avocado Pudding

Prep Time	Time to cook	Serv
20 min	13 min	4

Direction:
1. Preheat your fryer at 360°F.
2. Halve the avocado, twist to open, and scoop out the pit.
3. Throw in the Stevia, cocoa powder, almond milk, and vanilla extract and combine everything with a hand mixer.
4. Transfer this mixture to the basket of your fryer and cook for 3 min.

Calories	Fat	Protein	Sugar
60	7 g	9 g	16 g

Ingredients:
- 1 avocado
- 3 tbspn. liquid Stevia
- 1 tbspn. cocoa powder
- 4 tbspn. unsweetened almond milk
- ¼ tbspn. vanilla extract

Chia Pudding

Prep Time	Time to cook	Serv
20 min	4 min	2

Direction:
1. Preheat the fryer at 360°F.
2. In a bowl, gently combine the chia seeds with the milk and Stevia, before mixing the coconut oil and butter. Spoon seven equal-sized portions into seven ramekins and set these inside the fryer.
3. Cook for 4 min. Take care when removing the ramekins from the fryer and allow it to cool for 4 min before serving.

Calories	Fat	Protein	Sugar
12	6 g	4 g	4 g

Ingredients:
- 1 cup chia seeds
- 1 cup unsweetened coconut milk
- 1 tbspn. liquid Stevia
- 1 tbspn. coconut oil
- 1 tbspn. butter

Bacon Cookies

Prep Time	Time to cook	Serv
15 min	7 min	3

Direction:
1. In a bowl, mix the ginger, baking soda, peanut butter, and Swerve together, making sure to combine everything well.
2. Stir in the minced bacon.
3. Preheat your fryer at 350°F.
4. When the fryer is warm, put the cookies inside and cook for seven min. Take care when taking them out of the fryer and allow to cool before serving.

Calories	Fat	Protein	Sugar
50	14 g	12 g	13 g

Ingredients:
- ¼ tbspn. ginger
- 1/5 tbspn. baking soda
- 2/3 cup peanut butter
- 2 tbspn. Swerve
- 3 slices bacon, cooked and minced

Sweet and Cinnamon Donut Holes

Prep Time	Time to cook	Serv
15 min	10 min	16

Directions:
1. On a clean work surface, separate the jumbo biscuit dough into 16 equal-sized balls, about 1½ inches thick.
2. Spritz the AirFryer basket with cooking spray. Arrange the balls in the basket, making sure they are not stacked. Spray them with cooking spray.
3. Put the AirFryer lid on and cook in batches in the preheated AirFryer at 375°F for 8 min. Shake the basket when the lid screen indicates 'TURN FOOD' during Time to cook.
4. Remove the balls (donut holes) from the basket to a bowl. Serve alongside the cinnamon mixture.

Ingredients:
- 1 can (8-ounce) jumbo biscuit dough
- 2 tbspns cinnamon
- 1 tbspn stevia
- Cooking spray

Calories	Fat	Protein	Fiber	Carbohydrates	Sodium
24	3 g	1 g	1 g	1g	158 mg

Chocolate Peanut Butter and Jelly S'mores

Prep Time	Time to cook	Serv
5 min	5 min	1

Directions:
1. Start the S' mores by putting the peanut butter cup on 1 graham cracker square. Spread the raspberry jam and marshmallow on top.
2. Then spritz with cooking spray. Gently arrange the S' mores into the AirFryer basket.
3. Put the AirFryer lid on and cook in the preheated AirFryer at 400°F for about 1 min or until the marshmallow is softened.
4. Remove from the basket and top with remaining graham cracker square to serve.

Calories	Fat	Protein	Carbohydrates	Sodium
249	8.2 g	3.9 g	41.8g	281 mg

Ingredients:
- 2 chocolate graham cracker squares, divided
- 1 chocolate-covered peanut butter cup
- 1 tspn seedless raspberry jam
- 1 large marshmallow
- Cooking spray

Choco-Bana-Chips

Prep Time	Time to cook	Serv
10 min	10 min	2

Directions:
1. Coat the banana slices with agave syrup and lemon zest in a bowl.
2. Arrange the bananas in the AirFryer basket and spritz with cooking spray.
3. Put the AirFryer lid on and bake in the preheated AirFryer at 375°F for 12 min.
4. Flip the bananas over when the lid screen indicates 'TURN FOOD' during the cooking.
5. Meanwhile, combine the melted coconut oil with cocoa powder in a separate bowl and stir to mix well.
6. Transfer the banana chips to a plate and serve with chocolate glaze.

Calories	Fat	Protein	Sugar	Carbs
203	7.6 g	1.9 g	22.8g	37.2 g

Ingredients:
- 2 banana, cut into slices
- 1 tbspn agave syrup
- ¼ tspn lemon zest
- 1 tbspn coconut oil, melted
- 1 tbspn cocoa powder
- Cooking spray

Fiesta pastries

Prep Time	Time to cook	Serv
15 min	20 min	8

Directions:
1. Preheat the AirFryer to 390 of and grease an AirFryer basket.
2. Mix all ingredients in a bowl except puff pastry.
3. Arrange about 1 tspn of this mixture in the center of each square.
4. Fold each square into a triangle and slightly press the edges with a fork.
5. Arrange the pastries in the AirFryer basket and cook for about 10 min.
6. Dish out and serve immediately.

Ingredients:
- ½ of apple, peeled, cored and minced
- 1 tspn fresh orange zest, grated finely
- 7.05-ounce prepared frouncesen puff pastry, cut into 16 squares
- ½ tbspn white Sugar
- ½ tspn ground
- cinnamon

Crispy Fruit Tacos

Prep Time	Time to cook	Serv
5 min	5 min	2

Directions:
1. Preheat the AirFryer to 300 degrees f and grease an AirFryer basket.
2. Put 2 tbspns of strawberry jelly over each tortilla and top with blueberries and raspberries.
3. Sprinkle with powdered sugar and transfer into the AirFryer basket.
4. Cook for about 5 min until crispy and serve.

Calories	Fat	Protein	Carbohydrates	Sodium
202	0.8 g	1.7 g	49.2g	11 mg

Ingredients:
- 2 soft shell tortillas
- 4 tbspns strawberry jelly
- ¼ cup blueberries
- ¼ cup raspberries
- 2 tbspns powdered Sugar

Dark Chocolate Lava Cakes

Prep Time	Time to cook	Serv
10 min	10 min	4

Directions:
1. Grease 4 ramekins with butter. Preheat Cuisinart on Bake function to 375 F. Beats the eggs and sugar until frothy. Stir in butter and chocolate; gently fold in the flour. Divide the mixture between the ramekins and bake for 10 min. Let cool for 2 min before turning the cakes upside down onto serving plates.

Calories	Fat	Protein	Carbohydrates	Sodium
300	23.9 g	34.1 g	54.1g	445 mg

Ingredients:
- 3 ½ ounces butter, melted
- 3 ½ tbspn sugar
- 1 ½ tbspn self-rising flour
- 3 ½ ounces dark chocolate, melted
- 2 eggs

Perfect Chocolate Soufflé

Prep Time	Time to cook	Serv
15 min	10 min	2

Directions:
1. Beat the yolks along with the sugar and vanilla extract; stir in butter, chocolate, and flour. Preheat Cuisinart on Bake function to 330 F. Whisks the whites until a stiff peak forms. Working in batches, gently combine the egg whites with the chocolate mixture. Divide the batter between 2 greased ramekins. Cook for 14-18 min. Serve.

Ingredients:
- 2 eggs, whites, and yolks separated
- ¼ cup butter, melted
- 2 tbspn flour
- 3 tbspn sugar
- 3 ounces chocolate, melted
- ½ tbspn vanilla extract

Homemade Doughnuts

Prep Time	Time to cook	Serv
10 min	15 min	4

Directions:
1. Preheat Cuisinart on Bake function to 350 F. Beats the butter with the sugar until smooth. Whisk in the egg and milk. In a bowl, combine flour with baking powder. Fold in the butter mixture.
2. Form donut shapes and cut off the center with cookie cutters. Arrange on a lined baking sheet and cook in for 15 min. Serve with whipped cream or icing.

Ingredients:
- 8 ounces self-rising flour
- 1 tbspn baking powder
- ½ cup milk
- 2 ½ tbspn butter
- 1 egg
- 2 ounces brown sugar

Authentic Raisin Apple Treat

Prep Time	Time to cook	Serv
5 min	10 min	4

Directions:
1. Preheat Cuisinart on Bake function to 360 F. In a bowl, mix sugar, almonds, and raisins. Blend the mixture using a hand mixer. Fill cored apples with the almond mixture. Place the apples in a baking tray and cook for 10 min. Serve with a sprinkle of powdered sugar.

Calories	Fat	Protein	Carbohydrates	Sodium
595	65.9 g	12.1 g	64.1g	439 mg

Ingredients:
- 4 apples, cored
- 1 ½ ounces almonds
- ¾ ounces raisins
- 2 tbspn sugar

Crumble with Blackberries & Apricots

Prep Time	Time to cook	Serv
10 min	20 min	4

Directions:
1. Preheat Cuisinart on Bake function to 390 F. Add apricots to a bowl and mix with lemon juice, 2 tbspn sugar, and blackberries. Spread the mixture onto the greased AirFryer baking pan. In another bowl, mix flour and remaining sugar. Add 1 tbspn of cold water and butter and keep mixing until you have a crumbly mixture; top with crumb mixture. Cook for 20 min.

Calories	Fat	Protein	Carbohydrates	Sodium
193	25.9 g	16.1 g	64.1g	736 mg

Ingredients:
- 2 ½ cups fresh apricots, cubed
- 1 cup fresh blackberries
- ½ cup of sugar
- 2 tbspn lemon Juice
- 1 cup flour
- 5 tbspn butter

Healthy Bananas

Prep Time	Time to cook	Serv
3 min	12 min	8

Directions
1. Preheat Cuisinart on Toast function to 350 F. Combines the oil and breadcrumbs in a small bowl. Coat the bananas with the cornflour first, brush them with egg white, and dip them in the breadcrumb mixture. Arrange on a lined baking sheet and cook for 8-12 min. Serve.

Ingredients:
- Eight bananas
- 3 tbspn vegetable oil
- 3 tbspn cornflour
- 1 egg white
- ¾ cup breadcrumbs

Almond biscuit

Prep Time	Time to cook	Serv
15 min	30 min	4

Directions:
1. In a bowl, add egg whites and lemon juice. Beat using an electric mixer until foamy. Slowly add the sugar and continue beating until completely combined; stir in almond and vanilla extracts. Line the AirFryer pan with parchment paper. Fill a piping bag with the meringue mixture and pipe as many mounds on the baking pan as you can, leaving 2-inch spaces between each mound.
2. Cook at 350 F for 5 min on the Bake function. Reduce the temperature to 320 F and bake for 15 more min. Then, reduce the heat to 190 F and cook for 15 min. Let cool for 2 hours. Drizzle with dark chocolate and serve.

Ingredients:
- Eight egg whites
- ½ tbspn almond extract
- 1 ⅓ cups sugar
- 2 tbspn lemon juice
- 1 ½ tbspn vanilla extract
- Melted dark chocolate to drizzle

Triangle Toast

Prep Time	Time to cook	Serv
10 min	5 min	6

Directions:
1. Preparing the Ingredients. Melt coconut oil and mix with sweetener until dissolved. Mix in remaining ingredients minus bread till incorporated.
2. Spread mixture onto bread, covering all areas.
3. Air Frying. Place coated pieces of bread in your Instant Crisp AirFryer. Close AirFryer lid and cook 5 min at 400 degrees.
4. Remove and cut diagonally. Enjoy!

Calories	Fat	Protein	Sugar
124	2 g	0 g	4 g

Ingredients:
- 2 tbspn. pepper
- 1 ½ tbspn. vanilla extract
- 1 ½ tbspn. cinnamon
- ½ C. sweetener of choice
- 1 C. coconut oil
- 12 slices whole-wheat bread

Air sinker

Prep Time	Time to cook	Serv
10 min	5 min	8

Directions:
1. Preparing the ingredients. Preheat the unit by selecting Bake/Roast, setting the temperature to 300°F, and setting the time to 5 min. Press Start/Stop to begin. Mix allspice, sugar, sweetener, and cinnamon.
2. Take out biscuits from can and with a circle cookie cutter, cut holes from centers, and place into Instant Crisp AirFryer.
3. Air Frying the Dish. Close the AirFryer, Lid. Select Bake, set the temperature to 350°F, and set the time to 5 min. Select Start to begin. As batches are cooked, use a brush to coat with melted coconut oil and dip each into sugar mixture.
4. Serve warm!

Calories	Fat	Protein	Fiber
181	98 g	3 g	1 g

Ingredients:
- Pinch of allspice
- 4 tbspn. dark brown sugar
- ½ - 1 tbspn. cinnamon
- 1/3 C. granulated sweetener
- 3 tbspn. melted coconut oil
- 1 can of biscuits

Delicious cake

Prep Time	Time to cook	Serv
5 min	8 min	6

Directions:
1. Preparing the Ingredients. Layout pie crust and slice into equal-sized squares. Place 2 tbspn. Filling into each square and seal crust with a fork.
2. Air Frying. Place into the Instant Crisp AirFryer Instant Crisp AirFryer. Close the AirFryer, Lid. Select Bake, set the temperature to 390°F, and set the time to 8 min until golden in color. Select Start to begin.

Calories	Fat	Protein	Sugar
278	10 g	5 g	4 g

Ingredients:
- 15-ounces no-sugar-added apple pie filling
- 1 store-bought crust

Yummy Pud

Prep Time	Time to cook	Serv
25 min	20 min	6

Directions:
1. In a bowl, combine all the ingredients and Stir.
2. Divide into ramekins, put them in the fryer and cook at 340°f for 20 min
3. Serve the pudding cold.

Calories	Fat	Protein	Carbs
200	4 g	6 g	4 g

Ingredients:
- 1 cup red currants, blended
- 1 cup coconut cream
- 1 cup black currants, blended
- 3 tbspn. Stevia

Vanilla biscuit

Prep Time	Time to cook	Serv
17 min	12 min	12

Directions:
1. Whisk well and take a bowl and mix all the ingredients.
2. Spread this on a cookie sheet that fits the AirFryer lined with parchment paper, introduce in the fryer and cook at 350°f and bake for 12 min.
3. Cool down and serve

Calories	Fat	Protein	Carbs	Fiber
130	12 g	5 g	3 g	1 g

Ingredients:
- 1 cup almond butter, soft
- 1 egg
- 2 tbspn. Erythritol
- 1 tbspn. Vanilla extract

Ginger plums

Prep Time	Time to cook	Serv
25 min	20 min	6

Directions:
1. In a pan that fits the AirFryer, combine the plums with the rest of the ingredients, toss gently.
2. Cook at 360°f for 20 min and put the pan in the AirFryer
3. Serve cold

Calories	Fat	Protein	Carbs	Fiber
170	5 g	5 g	3 g	1 g

Ingredients:
- 6 plums; cut into wedges
- 10 drops stevia
- Zest of 1 lemon, grated
- 2 tbspn. Water
- 1 tbspn. Ginger, ground
- ½ tbspn. Cinnamon powder

Greek coconut

Prep Time	Time to cook	Serv
35 min	30 min	12

Directions:
1. Take a bowl and mix all the ingredients and whisk well.
2. Pour this into a cake pan that fits the AirFryer lined with parchment paper.
3. Cook at 330°F for 30 min and put the pan in the AirFryer

Calories	Fat	Protein	Carbs	Fiber
181	13 g	5 g	4 g	2 g

Ingredients:
- Six eggs whisked
- 8 ounces. Greek yogurt
- 9 ounces. Coconut flour
- 4 tbspn. Stevia
- 1 tbspn. Vanilla extract
- 1 tbspn. Baking powder

Coconut cheese

Prep Time	Time to cook	Serv
15 min	10 min	6

Directions:
1. Take a bowl and mix all the ingredients and whisk well.
2. Divide into small ramekins, put them in the fryer, and cook at 320°F and bake for 10 min.

Calories	Fat	Protein	Carbs	Fiber
164	4 g	5 g	5 g	2 g

Ingredients:
- 8 ounces. Cream cheese, soft
- 3 eggs
- 2 tbspn. Butter; melted
- 3 tbspn. Coconut, shredded and unsweetened
- 4 tbspn. Swerve

Fruit Cream

Prep Time	Time to cook	Serv
25 min	20 min	4

Directions:
1. Mix all the ingredients in an exceedingly bowl and whisk very well.
2. Divide this into 4 ramekins, put them within the AirFryer, and cook at 340°F for 20 min.

Calories	Fat	Protein	Carbs	Fiber
171	4 g	4 g	4 g	2 g

Ingredients:
- 1 lb. Plums pitted and minced.
- 1 ½ cups heavy cream
- ¼ cup swerve
- 1 tbspn. Lemon juice

Angel pie

Prep Time	Time to cook	Serv
5 min	35 min	4

Directions:
1. Preheat the AirFryer oven for 5 min.
2. Mix the egg whites and cream of tartar.
3. Use a hand mixer and whisk until white and fluffy.
4. Add the rest of the ingredients except for the butter and whisk for another min. Pour into a baking dish.
5. Place in the AirFryer basket and cook for 30 min at 400°F or if a toothpick inserted in the middle comes out clean.
6. Drizzle with melted butter once cooled.

Calories	Fat	Protein	Fiber
65	5 g	3.1 g	1 g

Ingredients:
- ¼ cup butter, melted
- 1 cup powdered erythritol
- 1 tspn strawberry extract
- 12 egg whites
- 2 tspns cream of tartar
- A pinch of salt

Yummy Dumplings

Prep Time	Time to cook	Serv
10 min	25 min	4

Directions:
1. Ensure your AirFryer oven is preheated to 356 degrees.
2. Core and peel apples and mix with raisins and sugar.
3. Place a bit of apple mixture into puff pastry sheets and brush sides with melted coconut oil.
4. Place into the AirFryer. Cook 25 min, turning halfway through. It will be golden when d1.

Calories	Fat	Protein	Sugar
367	7 g	2 g	5 g

Ingredients:
- 2 tbspn. melted coconut oil
- 2 puff pastry sheets
- 1 tbspn. brown sugar
- 2 tbspn. raisins
- 2 small apples of choice

Soft Donuts

Prep Time	Time to cook	Serv
5 min	10 min	9

Directions:
1. Separate the biscuit dough into eight biscuits and place them on a flat surface. Use any flat circle kitchen utensil or a biscuit cutter to chop a hole within the center of every cookie. You'll also cut the holes employing a knife.
2. Spray the AirFryer basket with vegetable oil.
3. Place 4 donuts within the AirFryer oven. Don't stack. Spray with vegetable oil. Set temperature to 350°F. Cook for 4 min.
4. Open the AirFryer and flip the donuts. Cook for an extra 4 min.
5. Remove the cooked donuts from the AirFryer oven, then repeat for the remaining 4 donuts.
6. Drizzle chocolate sauce over the donuts and enjoy while warm.

Ingredients:
- (8-ounce) can jumbo biscuits
- Cooking oil
- Chocolate sauce, such as Hershey's

Calories	Fat	Protein	Fiber
181	98 g	3 g	1 g

Wontons Sweet Cream

Prep Time	Time to cook	Serv
5 min	5 min	16

Directions:
1. Mix sweetener and cream cheese together.
2. Layout 4 wontons at a time and cover with a dish towel to prevent drying out.
3. Place ½ of a tspn of cream cheese mixture into each wrapper.
4. Dip finger into egg/water mixture and fold diagonally to form a triangle. Seal edges well.
5. Repeat with the remaining ingredients.
6. Place filled wontons into the AirFryer oven and cook 5 min at 400 degrees, shaking halfway through cooking.

Ingredients:
- 1 egg mixed with a bit of water
- Wonton wrappers
- ½ C. powdered erythritol
- 8 ounces softened cream cheese
- Olive oil

Calories	Fat	Protein	Sugar
303	3 g	0.5 g	4 g

Wonderful French Toast

Prep Time	Time to cook	Serv
5 min	15 min	8

Directions:
1. Preheat the AirFryer oven to 360 degrees.
2. Whisk eggs and thin out with almond milk.
3. Mix 1/3 cup of sweetener with lots of cinnamon.
4. Tear bread in half, ball up pieces, and press together to form a ball.
5. Soak bread balls in egg and then roll into cinnamon sugar, making sure to coat thoroughly.
6. Place coated bread balls into the AirFryer oven and bake 15 min.

Ingredients:
- Almond milk
- Cinnamon
- Sweetener
- 3 eggs
- 4 pieces of wheat bread

Calories	Fat	Protein	Sugar
289	11 g	0 g	4 g

Lovely Chickpeas

Prep Time	Time to cook	Serv
5 min	10 min	2

Directions:
1. Preheat AirFryer oven to 390 degrees.
2. Rinse and drain chickpeas.
3. Mix all ingredients and add them to the AirFryer.
4. Pour into the Oven rack/basket. On the middle-shelf of the AirFryer oven put on the rack. Set temperature to 390°F, and set time to 10 min.

Ingredients:
- 1 tbspn. sweetener
- 1 tbspn. cinnamon
- 1 C. chickpeas

Calories	Fat	Protein	Sugar
111	19 g	16 g	5 g

Amazing fried bananas

Prep Time	Time to cook	Serv
5 min	10 min	3

Directions:
1. Heat coconut oil and add breadcrumbs. Mix around 2-3 min until golden. Pour into a bowl.
2. Peel and cut bananas in half. Roll the half of each banana into flour, eggs, and crumb mixture.
3. Place into the AirFryer oven. Cook 10 min at 280 degrees.
4. A great addition to a healthy banana split!

Ingredients:
- 1 C. panko breadcrumbs
- 3 tbspn. cinnamon
- ½ C. almond flour
- 3 egg whites
- Eight ripe bananas
- 3 tbspn. vegan coconut oil

Calories	Fat	Protein	Sugar
219	10 g	3 g	5 g

Scrumptious Oreos

Prep Time	Time to cook	Serv
5 min	5 min	9

Directions:
1. Mix the ingredients all together with water.
2. Place a liner in the AirFryer basket with the parchment paper.
3. Spray some cooking oil over the parchment paper.
4. Dip each Oreo chocolate cookies in the pancake mixture and place it on the parchment paper without overlapping 1 another.
5. It is better to cook in batches if your AirFryer basket is small and cannot hold the entire cookies.
6. Set the temperature to 200 deg. Celsius and preheat the AirFryer.
7. Set the time into 8 min and flip half the way of cooking using a tong.
8. Drizzle the confecti1rs' sugar before serving.

Ingredients:
- Oreo chocolate cookies
- Pancake mix - ½ cup
- Confecti1rs' sugar – 1 tbspn
- Water - ⅓ cup
- Cooking spray – as required
- Parchment paper – for lining

Calories	Fiber	Protein	Sugar	Sodium
77	0.3 g	1.2 g	5 g	156 mg

Adorable banana break

Prep Time	Time to cook	Serv
10 min	15 min	4

Directions:
1. Take a medium-sized skillet or saucepan and melt your butter over medium heat
2. Add breadcrumbs into the melted butter and stir it for about 3-4 min
3. Once the breadcrumbs show a brown texture, remove them and keep them in a bowl
4. Take another bowl and crack in your egg
5. Take another bowl and add your flour
6. Peel your bananas carefully and slice it up
7. Mix up your sliced bananas, dredge it in your eggs and the breadcrumbs
8. redo the process until you have used up all the bananas
9. Dust the covered bananas with some cinnamon sugar
10. Cook the bananas in your AirFryer for about 10 min at 280 degrees F (137 °C)
11. Take your serving bowl and add a scoop of ice cream (vanilla, strawberry, and chocolate)
12. Add the bananas to the fryer and add them to the side of your Ice Cream
13. Put on the top some whipped cream and serve!

Ingredients:
- 3 tbspns of butter
- Bananas as required
- 3 Egg whites
- ½ a cup of cornflour
- 3 tbspns of Cinnamon Sugar
- 1 A cup of Panko Bread Crumbs

Calories	Fat	Protein
510	120 g	71 g

Advanced Chips

Prep Time	Time to cook	Serv
5 min	10 min	4

Direction:
1. Take your apples and wash them thoroughly
2. Finely chop them up into bite-sized portions
3. Take out the cooking basket of your AirFryer and add the apples to your cooking basket
4. Drizzle with some olive oil
5. Cook them for about 350 degrees F (176 °C) and let them cook for about 10 min
6. Get a substantial sized bowl and add the cooked apples
7. Toss with some cinnamon
8. Have fun!

Ingredients:
- Six pieces of Red Apples
- 1 tspn of Olive Oil
- 1 tspn of Ground Cinnamon

Calories	Fat	Protein	Carbohydrates
159	0 g	1 g	42 g

Banana muffin

Prep Time	Time to cook	Serv
5 min	8 min	5

Direction:
1. To preheat your AirFryer to a temperature of 340 F (171 °C)
2. Take a small-sized bowl and add flour, water, salt, and sesame seeds
3. Mix everything well until a smooth batter is formed
4. Take your bananas and coat them up in your flour
5. Take out your cooking basket and cook them for about 8 min
6. Serve!

Calories	Fat	Protein	Carbohydrates
242	9 g	5 g	38 g

Ingredients:
- 150g of Plain Flour
- Five peeled and sliced bananas
- 1 tspn of salt
- 30g of Sesame Seeds
- 1 cup of water

The Classical Cookies

Prep Time	Time to cook	Serv
18 min	8 min	8

Directions:
1. Take a small-sized bowl and beat your butter until it well and soft
2. Add sugar to the mix and keep hitting it until you have a very fluffy mixture
3. Stir in your flour, honey, milk, and chocolate
4. Mix everything well
5. Take out your AirFryer cooking basket and add the cookie shapes to your basket   Air Fry them for about 18 min at 356 degrees F (180 °C) until the center of your cookie is fully cooked
6. Serve!

Calories	Fat	Protein	Carbohydrates
192	10 g	2 g	25 g

Ingredients:
- 175g of Self-Rising Flour
- 100g of Butter
- 75g of Brown Sugar
- 60gof White Chocolate
- ¼ cup of Honey
- ¼ cup of Whole Milk

British Fingers

Prep Time	Time to cook	Serv
115 min	15 min	6

Directions:
1. Preheat your AirFryer to 356 degrees F (180 °C)
2. Take a bowl and add sugar, flour and mix well
3. Add butter and mix well until a smooth texture forms
4. Knead the mixture well
5. Cut up the dough into finger shapes and add some fork markings
6. Cook in your Fryer for about 12 min
7. Serve!

Calories	Fat	Protein	Carbohydrates
254	14 g	2 g	31 g

Ingredients:
- ¾ cup of butter
- ⅓ cup of caster sugar
- 1 and ¼ cup of plain flour

Airy clam

Prep Time	Time to cook	Serv
5 min	5 min	4

Directions:
1. Get a small-sized bowl and add your bread crumbs, parsley, garlic, oregano, lemon zest, and melted butter
2. Mix thoroughly to create the crumb mixture
3. Take a tbspnn of your crumb mix onto your exposed clam
4. Fill up a copper chef cake or similar pan with salt
5. Nestle your clam in the salt and let them cook for about 3 min at 400 degrees F (204 °C)
6. Put some garnish with some lemon wedges and fresh parsley
7. Serve!

Calories	Fat	Protein
119	2 g	6 g

Ingredients:
- 1 cup of unseasoned breadcrumbs
- ¼ cup of grated parmesan cheese
- ¼ cup of minced parsley
- 1 tspn of dried minced
- 3 cloves of dicedgarlic

Unusual Marshmallow

Prep Time	Time to cook	Serv
10 min	10 min	5

Directions:
1. Preheat your AirFryer to a temperature of 360 degrees F (182 °C)
2. Take 1 of your filo sheets and brush it up with butter
3. On top of your filo sheet, place another sheet and butter it up as well
4. Keep repeating until all leaves are used up
5. Cup the stalks into 3 pieces of 3x12 inch strips
6. Take about 1 tbspnn of peanut butter and marshmallow fluff and add them under your filo strips
7. Hold the sheet and fold it over your mixture, forming a triangle, and then keep folding it in a zigzag manner until all of the fillings has been wrapped up
8. Take some butter and tighten
9. Add the sheets to your cooking basket and cook for about 3-5 min
10. Serve with a sprinkle of salt

Ingredients:
- 4 sheets of defrosted filo pastry
- 4 tbspns of chunky peanut butter
- 4 tspns of marshmallow fluff
- 2 ounces of melted butter
- Just a pinch of sea salt

Divine apple pie

Prep Time	Time to cook	Serv
10 min	25 min	2

Directions:
1. Preheat your AirFryer to a temperature of 356 degrees F (180 0°C)
2. Peel your apples and core them up
3. Take a small bowl and add your sultanas and brown sugar
4. Add your apple on the puff pastry sheets and carefully fill the core with your sultana mix
5. Fold the pastry all around the dumplings
6. Add the dumpling to a small sheet of foil and brush it up with melted butter
7. Take out your cooking basket and transfer them to the tray
8. Let them cook for about 25 min till they show a nice and fancy brown color
9. Serve!

Ingredients:
- 2 tiny pieces of apples
- 2 tbspns of sultanas
- 1 tbspn of brown sugar
- 2 sheets of puff pastry
- 2 tbspns of melted butter

Flavorous sinker

Prep Time	Time to cook	Serv
15 min	6 min	8

Directions:
1. Line a baking sheet with parchment paper.
2. Set aside after mixing the sugar and cinnamon.
3. Remove the biscuits from the can and carefully separate them.
4. Place the biscuits onto the prepared baking sheet and, with a 1-inch round biscuit cutter, cut holes from the center of each cookie.
5. Place 4 donuts onto the lightly greased cooking pan in a single layer.
6. Arrange the drip pan at the bottom of the Instant Vortex Plus AirFryer Oven cooking chamber.
7. Pick "Air Fry" and then adjust the temperature to 350 degrees F.
8. Set the timer for 6 min and press the "Start."
9. When the display shows "Add Food" insert the cooking tray in the center position.
10. When the display shows "Turn Food," turn the donuts.
11. Remove the tray from Vortex when Time to cook is complete, r.
12. Brush warm donuts with melted butter and then coat with cinnamon sugar.
13. Repeat with the remaining donuts.
14. Serve warm.

Ingredients:
- ½ cup granulated sugar
- 1 tbspn ground cinnamon
- 1 (16.3-ounce) can make large flaky biscuits
- Olive oil cooking spray
- 4 tbspns unsalted butter, melted

Calories	Fiber	Protein	Sugar	Fat	Cholesterol
289	1.4 g	3.9 g	15.4 g	14.3 g	15 mg

Tender Tartlets

Prep Time	Time to cook	Serv
10 min	10 min	9

Directions:
1. Take a silicon mold cup and gently spray it with cooking spray
2. Take a skillet and melt some butter over medium heat
3. Add the butter to the silicon bowl
4. Add the spinach leaves alongside dicedup tomatoes
5. Drizzle them with the egg whites
6. Season the mix with some pepper and salt
7. Add the mixture to your Cooking basket and Air Fry them for about 10 min at a temperature of 356 degrees F (180 °C)
8. Serve hot and enjoy!

Ingredients:
- Bunch of Spinach leaves
- 1 Dicedtomatoes
- 1 Egg white
- Spray Oil/Melted Butter
- Salt
- Pepper

Calories	Fat	Protein
436	0 g	0 g

Selfmade Oreo

Prep Time	Time to cook	Serv
15 min	4 min	9

Directions:
1. Place the sheet of crescent roll dough onto a flat surface and unroll it.
2. With a knife, cut the dough into nine even squares.
3. Wrap each cookie in 1 dough square completely.
4. Arrange the Oreos onto a cooking tray.
5. Arrange the drip pan at the bottom of the Instant Vortex Plus AirFryer Oven cooking chamber.
6. Choose "Air Fry" and then adjust the temperature to 360 degrees F.
7. Set the timer for 4 min and press the "Start."
8. When the display shows "Add Food" insert the cooking tray in the center position.
9. When the display shows "Turn Food," turn the Oreos.
10. Remove the tray from Vortex when Time to cook is complete,
11. Serve warm.

Ingredients:
- 1 crescent sheet roll
- 9 Oreo cookies

Calories	Fiber	Protein	Sugar	Fat	Cholesterol
137	0.3 g	2.3 g	6.8 g	6.4 g	0 mg

Jamaica pie

Prep Time	Time to cook	Serv
15 min	25 min	6

Directions:
1. In a bowl, add all the ingredients and with an electric mixer, beat until well combined.
2. Arrange a parchment paper in the bottom of a greased 8-inch pan.
3. Now, arrange a foil piece around the cake pan.
4. Place the mixture into the prepared baking pan, and with the back of a spoon, smooth the top surface.
5. Arrange the drip pan at the bottom of the Instant Vortex Plus AirFryer Oven cooking chamber.
6. Select "Air Dry" and then adjust the temperature to 325 degrees F.
7. Set the timer for 25 min and press the "Start."
8. When the display shows "Add Food" place the baking pan over the drip pan.
9. When the display shows "Turn Food," do nothing.
10. When Time to cook is complete, remove the pan from Vortex and place onto a wire rack to cool for about 10 min.
11. Carefully, invert the cake onto a wire rack to cool completely before cutting.
12. Cut into desired-sized slices and serve.

Ingredients:
- ½ package yellow cake mix
- ½ (3.4-ounce) package Jell-O instant pudding
- 2 eggs
- ¼ cup of vegetable oil
- ¼ cup of water
- ¼ cup dark rum

Calories	Fiber	Protein	Sugar	Fat	Cholesterol
315	0.4 g	3.5 g	16.5 g	14.9 g	55 mg

Easy apple snack

Prep Time	Time to cook	Serv
10 min	8 min	6

Directions:
1. Rub apple slices with cinnamon and salt and place it into the AirFryer basket.
2. Cook at 390 F for 8 min. Turn halfway through.
3. Enjoy.

Calories	Protein	Sugar	Fat	Cholesterol	Carbohydrates
11	0.1 g	2.2 g	0 g	0 mg	3 g

Ingredients:
- 3 apples, wash, core and thinly slice
- 1 tbspn ground cinnamon
- Pinch of salt

Flavor apples

Prep Time	Time to cook	Serv
10 min	10 min	6

Directions:
1. Add apple slices in a mixing bowl and sprinkle sweetener, apple pie spice, and coconut oil over apple and toss to coat.
2. Transfer apple slices in the AirFryer dish.
3. Place dish in the AirFryer basket and cook at 350 F for 10 min.
4. Enjoy.

Calories	Protein	Sugar	Fat	Cholesterol	Carbohydrates
117	0.4 g	15.5 g	4.8 g	0 mg	20.7 g

Ingredients:
- 4 small apples, sliced
- 2 tbspn coconut oil, melted
- 1 tbspn apple pie spice
- 1/2 cup erythritol

Ricotta Pie

Prep Time	Time to cook	Serv
10 min	30 min	6

Directions:
1. Adding all ingredients into the bowl and mix until well combined.
2. Pour batter into the greased AirFryer baking dish.
3. Place dish into the AirFryer basket and cook at 350 F for 30 min.
4. Slice and serve.

Calories	Protein	Sugar	Fat	Cholesterol
259	8.7 g	0.7 g	23.8 g	104 mg

Ingredients:
- 3 eggs, lightly beaten
- 1 tbspn baking powder
- 1/2 cup ghee, melted
- 1 cup almond flour
- 1/3 cup Swerve
- 1 cup ricotta cheese, soft

Pineapple hunk

Prep Time	Time to cook	Serv
5 min	20 min	4

Directions:
1. Add pineapple slices, sweetener, and cinnamon into the zip-lock bag. Shake well and place into the fridge for 30 min.
2. Preheat the color AirFryer to 350 F.
3. Place pineapples slices into the AirFryer basket and cook for 20 min. Turn halfway through.

Ingredients:
- 4 pineapple slices
- 2 tbspn erythritol
- 1 tbspn cinnamon

Pleasant cream

Prep Time	Time to cook	Serv
10 min	20 min	2

Directions:
1. Add eggs in a bowl and beat using a hand mixer.
2. Add cream cheese, sweetener, vanilla, and almond milk and beat for 2 min. Spray 2 ramekins with cooking spray.
3. Pour batter into the prepared ramekins.
4. Preheat the color AirFryer to 350 F.
5. Place ramekins into the AirFryer basket and cook for 20 min.

Calories	Protein	Sugar	Fat	Cholesterol	Carbohydrates
381	18.5 g	1.2 g	32 g	473 mg	5.2 g

Ingredients:
- Five eggs
- 1/2 cup unsweetened almond milk
- 1/2 cup cream cheese
- 2 tbspn swerve
- 1 tbspn vanilla

Norwegian pint cake

Prep Time	Time to cook	Serv
5 min	10 min	1

Directions:
1. Add baking powder, protein powder, and cocoa powder in a heat-safe mug and mix well.
2. Add milk and Stir.
3. Place the mug in the AirFryer basket and cook at 390 F for 10 min.

Calories	Protein	Sugar	Fat	Cholesterol	Carbohydrates
79	11.2 g	1.1 g	2.4 g	20 mg	6.6 g

Ingredients:
- 1 scoop chocolate protein powder
- 1/2 tbspn baking powder
- 1/4 cup unsweetened almond milk
- 1 tbspn cocoa powder

Tasty ricotta pie

Prep Time	Time to cook	Serv
10 min	40 min	8

Directions:
1. Preheat the color AirFryer to 325 F.
2. With cooking spray AirFryer baking dish.
3. In a bowl, beat ricotta cheese until smooth. Whisk in the eggs 1 by 1.
4. Whisk in lemon juice and zest. Pour batter into the prepared baking dish.
5. Place dish into the AirFryer basket and cook for 40 min.

Calories	Protein	Sugar	Fat	Cholesterol	Carbohydrates
110	9.2 g	0.4 g	6.7 g	99 mg	3.1 g

Ingredients:
- 4 eggs
- 1 lemon juice
- 1 lb ricotta
- 1 lemon zest
- 1/4 cup Swerve

Swiss fondue

Prep Time	Time to cook	Serv
10 min	5 min	6

Directions:
1. Set the Instant Vortex on an AirFryer to 375 degrees F for 8 min. Combine white chocolate with fresh cream and sugar in a ramekin. Place the ramekin on the cooking tray. Insert the cooking tray in the Vortex when it displays "Add Food." Remove from the oven when Time to cook is complete. Stir in the candied orange peel and orange essence to serve in a fondue pot.

Ingredients:
- 250 g of Swiss white chocolate
- 2½ tspns of sugar
- 2½ tspns of orange essence
- 2½ tspns of candied orange peel, minced finely
- 250 g of fresh cream

Printed in Great Britain
by Amazon